MORAL CLAIMS IN WORLD AFFAIRS

MORAL CLAIMS IN WORLD AFFAIRS

EDITED BY RALPH PETTMAN

ST. MARTIN'S PRESS   NEW YORK

Copyright © 1979 Ralph Pettman

All rights reserved. For information write:
St. Martin's Press Inc., 175 Fifth Avenue, New York, N.Y. 10010
Printed in Great Britain
Library of Congress Catalog Card Number:
ISBN 0-312-547755-2
First published in the United States of America in 1979

Library of Congress Cataloging in Publication Data

Main entry under title:

Moral claims in world affairs.

   Includes index.
   1. International relations - Moral and religious aspects - Addresses, essays,
lectures. I. Pettman, Ralph.
JX1255.M58   1979   172'.4   78-11431
ISBN 0-312-54755-2

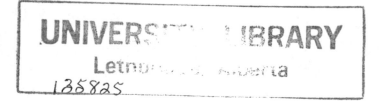

CONTENTS

PREFACE

Establishing national needs and the policies that flow from them as not only contingent or expedient (often, indeed, *despite* questions of contingency or expediency) but also 'right' and 'due', is meant to lend them a special and pervasive force. Statesmen alert their audiences in this way to the fact that whatever the claims being made, they pertain to more than reflex or merely reasoned matters, but moral ones as well. They signal an emphatic commitment, a state of enhanced resolve. Whatever is claimed merits close consideration, since it will carry more than its ordinary load of the values that any deed or decision affirms or denies.

For reasons like these practitioners of world affairs are tempted to invest even their most commonplace behaviour with a sense of moral sanctity. This tends over time to debase the currency, and negate any added significance the force of a moral as opposed to an incidental or instrumental demand might convey. The effect of a sense of righteousness or of unmet obligation comes to be lost; statesmen themselves are accused of cant or nationalistic self-justification. And yet the practice persists, and the charge of hypocrisy is vigorously denied.

The rise of the modern nation-state in a system that is 'ungoverned' in the more familiar sense is one obvious reason for the continued existence of these rather more fervent overtones to world affairs. Political sovereignty predisposes ethical sovereignty. The representatives of countries that compete for predominance or for privileged access to scarce resources will tend to buttress their behaviour in morally exclusivist as well as nationalistic terms. Individuals and groups within or without such countries, pressing rival claims to speak on behalf of some or all of the people, will likewise appeal to standards transcending those defined by ruling elites. Leaders of weaker states on the one hand, whether self-established or possessing some more general mandate, will declaim their moral superiority and thereby seek to compensate for the frustrations and insecurities inherent in their lack of tangible power. They will assert their 'due' share of global assets and reserves in the face of those who monopolise them, and lay 'rightful' claim to idiosyncratic objectives with a sense of conviction not apparent in their expressions of 'interest' alone. Stronger states on the other hand will reinforce their manifest power with declarations of moral intent, and resist any

contentions they find contrary on the implicit or explicit grounds that
such claims remain uninformed by the greater power's own superior
vision of the good world. This vision is never depicted as a purely
private one however. It is usually understood to possess public relevance to the global populace at large.

The following collection of essays is specifically addressed to this
question of partisan cosmopolitanism. Though not a novel ingress it is
a neglected one, and much might be done to elucidate parochial pan-
demics and their relevance for and impact upon the present-day world.
A preliminary attempt might also be made to pass behind the plethora
of competing value systems to delineate the general nature of moral
claims, and their consequences for global equity and order. Here we
perceive the possible emergence of a universal moral realm, based upon
the notion of distributive justice perhaps. To go beyond this would be
to offer some idea of what the substantive dictates of such a realm might
be; suggest the sort of area from which its logical justification might be
drawn; and examine the systemic level at which it is likely to be
achieved. The field is obviously a large and important one, and though
a comprehensive discussion would require more than a single volume,
an attempt has been made to confront some of these central issues in a
coherent and representative way.

Part One outlines a number of the conceptual areas in which contemporary debates proceed. Ralph Pettman attempts in an introductory
fashion to outline something of the scope of the subject and of the
various forays that have been made to rescue a single body of human
ideals from the multitude of possible systems that now prevail. The
tension between the 'statist' and 'class' paradigms of the world
system are indicated as analytically central in this regard. J.D.B. Miller
denies the applicability of ordinary moral considerations to world
affairs, citing group rather than universal ethics as the immediate source
of human behaviour, and 'reasons of state' rather than the brotherhood
of man as the operative principle in global politics. John Vincent
elaborates this basically 'realist' position, highlighting the whole
question of realism versus idealism, the value of equality, and the force
of the doctrine of human rights. He sketches clearly the nature of
dissent about the relevant 'levels' involved (that of the individual, the
state, and the 'society' of states as a whole), while opting for the
second of these levels as the one within which moral claims will be met.
Hedley Bull then addresses the issue of 'human rights' and attempts to
establish what they are, what special questions they raise in the contemporary political arena, and what, in general, we should do about them.

He argues that in terms of world politics the doctrine is a troubled one and that because *a priori* universal principles of an objective kind do not exist, ethical expectations derived from the Western experience will not necessarily find acceptance in the wider world. Hugh Smith endorses his verdict. The notion of levels is canvassed again, with a detailed discussion of the single issue of 'justice' (which he places prior to that of morality in the political realm), and the attempts that have been made to apply this issue beyond the realm of the nation-state. It is the state in the end, he argues, that is the most effective distributor of moral as well as material goods. Arthur Burns resurrects the dichotomy of 'good' and 'evil' as a necessary complement to the more familiar ethical distinction between 'justice' and 'injustice', and relates what he sees as a scriptural theme to the practice of armed collectives. 'Injustice', he says, 'has its place solely in the dimension of actions and institutions; but evil belongs also to the dimension of disposition, and indeed has its source there. . . . Injustice can sometimes be redressed by action, and free men are under constant obligation to do so. Evil can only be redeemed.' And to demonstrate the malignant or salutary nature of contemporary Western beliefs he concentrates upon one theme in particular: the 'balance of terror' and its contribution to global peace.

Part Two adopts a more concrete perspective. Here moral claims are considered *in situ*, as they emerge from specific situations that involve important moral conflicts, and as they are represented in the policies of two of the Powers. Jan Pettman reviews the complex values that contend in the African, and particularly the Southern African arena. The compromising presence of comprador elites, and the manifest failure of African countries to extricate themselves from external domination and exploitation, has been reflected in the shift, especially among radical liberation movements, from demands for 'black government' only to demands for social revolution throughout. The widespread ideological reperception required is unlikely to come about, however, and even more so for those who live under the influence of the monolithic racist regimes of the south. Claims by African leaders and their opponents for moral as well as political-economic autonomy can only be understood in this light. Michael Yahuda selects, in his discussion of China's foreign policy, from a broad range of ethical precepts lodged therein. The idea he elaborates is that of independence or 'self-renewal' — a concept, he maintains, which conveys a profound moral belief, which derives from extended historical experience, and represents a singular and germane aspect of the Chinese view of a

revised political-economic global order. Though not without its
ambiguities and ultimately subordinate, in the Maoist canon at least, to
the theory of permanent revolution, China's leaders have sought to
edify others, and in particular the inhabitants of the Third World, with
this widely disseminated creed. Vendulka Kubálková examines the
Soviet concept of morality. She looks, too, at its ideological character,
its Marxist heritage, and its fertile 'New Marxist' derivations. An
appreciation of the vagaries of ethical philosophy since the Russian
Revolution, an acquaintance with the working categories and concepts
that have provided the framework and many of the puzzles for Soviet
thinkers, the features of the 'moral code' of the party Programme of
1961, are all basic to our comprehension of Soviet belief and behaviour.
Contemporary notions like that of 'peaceful coexistence' take on added
significance as a result.

It hardly pre-empts what is to follow to say that moral claims are
made by diverse actors in global affairs, to multifarious purpose and
effect. The self-conscious sense of a supranational system that is said
to have characterised the European order of the nineteenth century,
or at least, that sense of a shared culture and values displayed by
European elites in their dealings with each other, is commonly held to
exist no more. Hence the premium often placed upon effective diplomacy. The most strident claims today, however, are those made by
representatives of the Third and Fourth Worlds, and these both reinforce
and compromise the picture of mankind as one of segmented 'states'.
They not only represent the voices of disadvantaged leaders who seek a
redistribution of global power, but they help identify an emergent
world system of 'horizontal' connections that arches over the considerable expanse of the globe where 'state' is a euphemism for whatever
regime is recognised as such by other 'states', irrespective of the social
and economic structures the geographic 'boundaries' contain. Reification
of the 'state' leads to a definition of the minimal content of a universal
morality in terms of common acceptance alone, and fails to accommodate the degree of supra-statal co-operation already necessary to
exploit more or less discrete populations, and to protect the living
standards of affluent countries and Third World elites. And though
claims upon the populations of rich states assume an answer in nation-
state form, one should ask by whom such answers are actually received?
Who makes 'Third World' claims? And ultimately on whose behalf? The
twentieth-century notion of a pluralistic world is one that, beyond a
certain as yet ill-defined point, loses its explanatory power. And a
complementary structuralist perception of world politics would be the

practical basis for a neo-universalist morality built out of a measure of rational utility and of human requirements, rather than the more familiar contemporary dictates of established access, dishonesty and greed.

PART ONE: THEORY

1 MORAL CLAIMS IN WORLD POLITICS

Ralph Pettman

Moral discourse is an integral aspect of any political conversation. The intrinsic character of the moral dimension makes it all the more surprising, then, when we find how little academic attention has been paid to moral claims in world affairs, and this particularly so given the post-behavioural plea for a return to matters of 'value' as well as 'fact',[1] the emergence of the issue of justice in the confrontation rhetoric between the global North and South, and the moves made by American President Carter into the realm of human rights. What *are* the claims, we may ask, made by key actors who dominate the scene, or made on behalf of those who lurk still half-regarded in the wings? Which claims seem justified, and how *are* they justified, and what general criteria for justification might there be? How do such claims conflict and how are they reconciled? What sanctions do they stand on? What lessons from the study of human societies in their diversity, and from the contemplation of the human condition in general, can be brought to bear? Is it really appropriate for statements about world politics to be couched in terms of 'morality' at all?

One can think of many reasons for the lack of attention noted above. There is the tendency, for example, to dismiss moral claims as moralism or as nothing but the rationalisation of interests and desires (a cynical and reductionist stance in this form). There is the problem of establishing standards by which to judge the applicability of a moral system in any particular case.[2] There are, furthermore, the serious meta-ethical problems one encounters in judging the content of a moral system itself, and in establishing what the status of 'right' or 'good' as opposed to 'wrong' or 'evil' propositions might entail.[3] Perhaps, too, there is an insidious sense of irrelevance at work, of man as 'trivial, arrogant, and a little mad'.[4] 'The great world,' Bertrand Russell argued, 'as far as we know it from the philosophy of nature, is neither good nor bad, and is not concerned to make us happy or unhappy. All such philosophies spring from self-importance and are best corrected by a little astronomy.'[5]

There is another more obvious explanation for such neglect. Moral expectations are continually disappointed in the confused realm of practical politics, partly because global dilemmas seem different and often incompatible with those we encounter on an individual plane. 'Power' and 'morality' tend to be dichotomised as a result, and the former is placed prior to the latter in understanding global affairs. And yet moral expectations persist, and continuous attempts are made to close the gap between the political levels of analysis and to discover in mankind one moral community — one ethic-bearing whole.

It would accommodate a transatlantic propensity still prevalent today for clarifying meanings and the complex loan of language, to begin by asking what the character of moral propositions in general might be, at least as represented by the debates that have been waged in the West since the Greeks developed the subject two and a half millennia ago.

The Greek legacy is obviously profound.[6] Socrates and the Sophists attempted in their own way to press important distinctions between a subjective and an objective realm, to discriminate between fact and value, between personal affirmation, social consensus and 'natural' decree. Prised apart in this way, meta-ethical discussion has been dominated ever since by attempts either to bridge the gaps these dichotomies represent or to resist such engineering and to drive the splintered bank-works further apart.

Greek philosophers sought reasons for moral claims other than those of tradition and use. Some seemed to say much more. Through thought alone, they argued, men might recover moral precepts satisfying the concerns of both the individual and the community at the same time. The definitive statement of a set of principles acceptable to all eluded them, though the idea of such a set has been held before theorists ever since, and before the 'practical' men that theorists held in thrall.

It was Plato who helped most to consolidate a lasting vision of a moral universe not only accessible to human reason but orderly, harmonious and pure.[7] Against Socratic critiques he erected an abstract intuition of Forms, of ideals inspired by the logic of mathematics that laid up eternal standards whereby human conduct might be assessed. In response, Aristotle arrived at a 'naturalistic' doctrine that was not only more pragmatic and more tolerant of human diversity, but also sought rather the satisfaction, albeit in a regular and rational way, of human desires — the happy fulfilment of such personal capacities as naturally obtain. Though contemporary assessments of what has become a perennial debate have seen among other things that attempt to disown it altogether, in one notable case as the unfortunate consequence of linguistic ambiguity,[8] it would seem that there is ample scope still for diverse perspectives, neither bound to personal predilections that prove irrelevant in the social sphere, nor predicated upon a public philosophy oblivious to private capacity or need.[9]

'Morals' are social products, held out of habit and self-interest to be sure, but motivated also by emphatic urges like love, and a sense of what is right and due. Human beings learn to prefer particular ways of relating to each other, and standards by which to assess their relationships and to endorse or censure what appear to be sociable or antisocial acts, as part of the general educative process whereby they assimilate expectations of how the world is meant to be. On the whole they seem to value the company and support of their more immediate fellows. Human survival depends upon reciprocal assistance, and a communitarian impulse is a (phylogenetically valuable, even perhaps by now a predetermined)[10] means to this end. Whatever the general motive, however, and whatever we may make of their fundamentals, the resultant behavioural preferences differ greatly in detail from group to group, and they change over time in response to changes in the 'culture' or its environment. In an important sense ordinary morality is largely inapplicable at the level of world affairs. Human identification is mostly quite immediate, and on the whole we donate our moral allegiancies to the group to which we feel we primarily belong. The moral codes that such groups practice and defend serve group interests, and moral conflicts are inevitably group conflicts as well.

One important problem in the study of world politics, then, is to determine how far the communitarian impulse does or should extend. What unit of analysis may be considered the most appropriate vehicle for moral claims — the individual, the group, the state (and those transnational institutions that possess at least some state-like characteristics), humankind as a whole, or classes of humankind defined in other than geo-political ways (by 'culture', for example, or by their relationship to the economic and productive forces that might underpin social forms)? 'Appropriate' with respect to what criteria? Given the constant threat of nuclear war or the emergent one of global ecological collapse, the contemporary moral constituency may now be one far removed from the cause of our immediate political concerns, including, it may be argued, the multitudes of those unborn. If a minority holds the power to preserve or destroy the human race as a whole, it may well be enjoined, in principle at least, with obligations to individuals quite remote from it in time and space. Sentiments like these commonly inspire the sort of rhetorical statements that affirm human solidarity.[11] They are rhetorical because global practice reflects competitive values and the radical historical process whereby European patterns have been firmly impressed upon the socio-political configuration of the world.

Are they relevant, however?

I would like to look more closely at what this configuration might be, and its possible consequence for moral claims. There is first, however, the more general question about the impact of present-day knowledge upon social structures, and the properties implicit in the concept of a 'modernised' man. Some brief discussion of these properties is warranted before turning to world affairs as such.

Most people are hard-pressed, it seems, to empathise with those not immediately associated with them. There are good reasons for this, partly to do with questions of scale. In the large societies that contemporary systems of industrial production can now support, we tend to think of ourselves as autonomous and isolate, with duties to carry out and entitlements to affirm.[12] In smaller ones, however, it becomes easier to appreciate the workings of 'effective mutuality'[13] and the reciprocal consequences in what people claim and do. If the criterion for assessing our acts is the 'sociality' of them, then the purely personal and selfish ones are more likely to be repressed in more intimate surroundings and less likely then to operate at cost to our confreres. 'The hunter and gatherer [for example] is lucky: he does not have the choice . . . what for us are virtues are, for him, necessities. We have the choice, and although we insist on intellectually maintaining those same virtues, the discrepancy between them and daily practice becomes increasingly great.'[14]

One key phenomenon here is that termed by Max Weber 'rationalisation'; implicit in present-day modes of managing economies and states is a profound preference for regularised means toward the attainment of preordained ends. 'Indeed, technique transforms ends into means',[15] seemingly independent of what we might otherwise intend. Thus, for example: 'Technical economic analysis is substituted for the older political economy included in which was a major concern with the moral structure of economic activity . . . Politics in turn becomes an arena for contention among rival techniques . . . Purposes drop out of sight and efficiency becomes the central concern.'[16]

Describing the process whereby human beings have become the victims of a technicised economy and a bureaucratic state, rendered, that is, progressively more alienated and anonymous, has become a sociological industry in its own right. These ideas, however, stem in the Westernised world from a deeper critique again. Built into modern science is a pitiless and impassive vision of fate that springs originally from the Greek tragedians and the Ionian world-view. Beside this heritage ran a naive revolt against the medieval scholastic divines that issued in a non-rational faith in the order of things, a faith science has 'never cared to justify or to explain' and one that has remained 'blandly indifferent to its refutation by Hume'.[17] This revolt presupposes as ultimate fact 'an irreducible . . . material, spread throughout space . . . senseless, valueless, purposeless . . . following a fixed routine imposed by external relations which do not spring from the nature of its being'.[18] All of which may have proved enormously productive in understanding physical, chemical and biological events but has had ambiguous consequences for society at large. Whatever instrumental advances now obtain, such a powerful presupposition has generated universalistic truths quite remote from ordinary human experience — a source of liberation and enrichment, but paradoxically one of impoverishment as well. It has sought explicit parallels between social and material affairs, and applied like methodological precepts to both.

Many analysts have now drawn attention to the repressive effects of technological civilisation, and severely qualified the equation intrinsic to the spirit of the age that 'science = reason = all good things'.[19] 'To what lengths will public faith in the wisdom and prowess of the technocracy extend?' Roszak enquires. He answers his own question in very pessimistic terms. 'That faith has already demonstrated itself to be without limit or qualification. How else is one to interpret public compliance . . . with the policy of thermonuclear deterrence? Here is a technological system . . . on which we allow our very survival as a species to depend. It is a reckless commitment, predicated upon a willingness to do genocide which is the moral scandal of the age. Yet we take both the hazard and the ethical obscenity of the matter in our stride . . .'[20]

One may question this diagnosis in whole or in part. It is too pitiless, we reply, in its conception of science as a life-denying force. While closing down some options, technocratic and bureaucratised states may open up others; they are not only the constrained and homogenising agents they might on first glance appear. The pernicious effects of a preference for regularity and expediency is counter-balanced by the fact that many new demands are made upon our sense of responsibility and of judgement, and one should not overlook the sheer number of people such systems can sustain. The balance-of-terror, the cataclysm so graphically poised before contemporary consciousness, presents extreme danger indeed, *and* a range of solemn opportunities as well. The ethical debate about nuclear weapons testifies to this. Scientifically induced eco-crises may well condemn a global host to poverty and despair, but many more are also given the chance to ask what their lives signify, and in their answers and foreign policies to define what it means to be humane.

This can be only the most summary of conclusions, but allowing for the fact that general questions about science and society are very diffuse indeed, they do provide a much needed perspective upon particular problems about contemporary political forms and the moral claims these predispose. While such questions can be pursued no further here, they permeate all else.

The most common conceptual paradigm in the discipline places primary stress upon 'states' and 'nation-states'. This has led theorists to discriminate between political and personal ethics, between the moral burdens of *states*men and those of their less strategically situated fellows who do not have to secure the welfare of the political whole. It is not far from a focus on the 'state' to doctrines that positively exalt its global status, to *realpolitik*, for example, and the notion that the most moral claims are those that preserve the national interest, however and by whom this is defined. Such a notion does not necessarily deny the effect of moral inhibitions upon what statesmen do. Many examples may be cited of national leaders exercising restraint when 'necessity' could have justified a round sweep with the flat of the blade. Enlightened self-interest is usually sufficient warning against crude power politics alone since a completely amoral set of state leaders who disregard all the claims of others might find themselves less powerful overall as the challenges they face grow apace. *Realpolitik* simply asserts that successful governments will treat most ethical imperatives as invalid, and acknowledge no obligation other than that of the national estate.

Statesmen are nonetheless products of the communities they represent and might be expected to carry into policy at least some of the moral injunctions they have been encouraged to observe in domestic spheres. We might logically suggest a compromise to cover the ground between personal predilections and the expedients of *raison d'état*. This compromise, Martin Wight has argued, seems 'peculiarly related to Western values'[21] (though he arrives at this conclusion without a single reference to a non-Western system of values). It assumes (1) 'that moral standards can be upheld without the heavens falling'; (2) 'that the fabric of social and political life will be maintained, without accepting the doctrine that to preserve it any measures are permissible'; and (3) 'that the upholding of moral standards will in itself tend to strengthen the fabric of political life'.[22] On the whole, global practice retreats from such moderation. From the 'statist' perspective powerful leaders have often been tempted to present their political claims as uniquely valid and universal decrees. Value habits that depict 'communism' as diabolical and morally contemptible, for example, or 'capitalism' as wholly carnivorous and the soul of human greed, make for a lack of moral restraint. Once antagonists have been cast, cynically or sincerely, as not just different or inferior politically or ideologically, but as the incarnations of the anti-Christ, then 'we' are relieved of the responsibility of moral choice and 'their' assertions can be safely despised.[23] Following Wight, the usual reply under these conditions has been the counsel of prudence, the pointing out that moral principles are not the only guide to those charged with the task of choosing particular policies and that they are not enough when it comes to assessing the outcomes of such policies and their various and often conflicting value costs and consequences.[24]

Much of this debate turns upon the central problem of the 'means-ends' process. The fact that immoral means may be justified in pursuit of some greater good, such as the preservation of the state, was clearly expressed by Niccolo Machiavelli, and he has been used to document the cynics' position ever since. 'A prince', he argued, 'cannot observe all those things which are considered good in men; being often obliged, in order to maintain the state, to act against faith, against charity, against humanity, and against religion . . . he must . . . not deviate from what is good, if possible, but be able to do evil if constrained . . .'[25]

One can point to something much more important in Machiavelli's stance. Implicit in it is a direct attack on one enduring assumption of Western political thought, that of the existence of 'natural law'.[26] Machiavelli himself evaded this tradition, and his neglect was malignant not benign because the morality of the Christian world he saw as simply incompatible for a prince with the sort of secular morality that was necessary to build a secure state. As Isaiah Berlin has argued: 'The notion of Raison d'état entails a conflict of values – those of private and public morality . . . For Machiavelli there is no conflict. Public life has its own rules: to which Christian ethics is a gratuitous obstacle.'[27] There is more to this than the argument that love and goodness cannot be realised in public life, and that generous motives may well be foolish and dangerous when pursued in the context of interstate competition. It goes further than the separation of politics from ethics; 'it is the uncovering of the possibility of more than one ethical system with no criterion common to the systems, whereby a rational choice can be made between them',[28] and not only for princes, perhaps, but as a root condition of human life: 'Why should justice and mercy, humility and *virtu,* happiness and knowledge, glory and liberty, magnificence and sanctity, coincide or indeed be compatible at all?'[29] Why indeed? But deny the notion of an objective and generalised set of human ideals, and a cornerstone of the Western philosophical tradition falls to the ground.

One may see all this as the necessary preface to a desirable alternative, which, given a preference for scepticism and toleration, is the notion of liberal compromise. Monistic certainties breed political extremes but unbridled diversity leads to moderation and away from the definitive resolution of human affairs.

Others have not been content with such anaemic good sense and have sought to rescue something of the original, fundamentalist doctrine and its activist resolve. H.L.A. Hart, for example, posits a modest minimum to 'natural law' based upon the observation that 'most men most of the time' wish to survive, and that '[I]n the absence of this content men, as they are, would have no reason for obeying voluntarily any rules', and using the obedient to coerce the rest would not work.[30] Man's bodily vulnerability, approximate equality, limited altruistic capabilities, restricted access to resources, and qualified understanding and strength of will, enjoin, Hart argues, a 'natural' sanction against intra-specific slaughter, plus a fundamental respect for 'mutual forbearance and compromise' and the *necessity* of a system informed by precepts of this kind. To this he adds 'some minimal form of the institution of property (. . . not necessarily individual . . .) and the distinctive kind of rule which requires respect for it', rules for the transfer, exchange and sale of the products of the division of human labour, 'recognition of promises as a source of obligation', and finally, *'voluntary* cooperation in a *coercive* system' as a protective guarantee against those who join but then seek to subvert the welfare of the whole.[31]

Except for personal sanctity and the propertarian ones the prescriptions given above are *procedural* only. One may seek for more substantive standards of a social or economic kind — minimal levels of health and nutritional wellbeing for example, without which life is not possible let alone enjoyed; and civil and political ones without which the means of material sustenance may never be secured. Thus Barrington Moore adopts as a 'working premise the moral position that human society ought to be organised in such a way as to eliminate useless suffering. . .'[32] There are problems with the notion of 'useless' suffering, since the fact of global 'development' may ultimately depend upon the human costs considered 'useful' or 'necessary' in the pursuit of economic strength or self-reliance. Measures of utility are closely related to those of political interest, and they change over time. Furthermore, though there *are* absolute needs that must be fulfilled for humans to survive, they do not always issue in self-evident standards that generally obtain. We need, in fact, not only a minimalist notion of human sustenance and how it might be obtained, but a maximalist concept of social justice as well.

The minimalist impulse lies behind documents codifying 'natural' or 'human' rights, which like 'natural law' have often been dismissed as value judgements masquerading in absolute metaphysical terms. To mark the twentieth anniversary of the Universal Declaration of Human Rights, UNESCO solicited from member states and others any text with a relationship to or a sense of 'human rights'. The compilers were no doubt predisposed to find common ground, but a significant body of related themes, despite the historical and anthropological diversity, did seem to emerge.[33] It is on the basis of some such empirical demonstration of uniformity that minimalist doctrines of human rights are usually maintained. These rest in turn on a Kantian conviction that man is an end in himself, and does not merit treatment as a means alone.

'Human' or 'natural' rights are a sub-category of moral rights in general, which are moral claims of a particularly important kind. They are considered, at least by their protagonists, to be *justified*. Rights get their peculiar force from the reasons that are advanced to back them up. In particular: 'A human right is a morally justifiable claim made on behalf of all men to the enjoyment and exercise of those basic freedoms, goods, and services which are considered necessary to achieve the human estate . . . Morally justifiable claims, are *proposals* to treat human beings in certain ways.'[34] They are justified in an abstract way by notions of what it means to be a human being; they are argued much more directly by detailing the consequences of meeting them or failing to do so; by describing what can flow from their subversion or disavowal. This way, too, they may issue in policies marginally less arbitrary than would otherwise prevail.

Again, what moral community are we talking about in world politics when we consider rights and the justification of moral claims? In the 'statist' perspective there is no viable world community, no supra-state society that constitutes a separate realm of experience that can offer its own definitions of the global good. 'Power' is vested in national leaders, and though moral stature is a part of this power, power as such generates its own expedient support and determines in considerable part the moral claims that emerge. In support of this position 'statist' theorists

cite the lack of a felt obligation on the part of rich countries to redistribute wealth and to meet the needs of the global poor.[35]

What, however, of those paradigms that do not affirm the 'finality'
of the state, but describe global structures that run across them? What,
for instance, of the neo-Marxist notion of 'class'?[36] Rather than states
competing for 'power', contemporary theories of imperialism, for
example, describe the world in terms of its modes of production,
distribution and exchange, and the social continuities these predispose.
'States' are seen as the conduits of rather deeper currents at work
among human beings, and in particular, as the products of contemporary 'capitalism' and the way this distinctive creature of the 'industrial revolution' has been manifest in world affairs. Though the doctrines
differ in many essential ways, it is generally argued that one effect of
European expansion over 300 years was to secure the exploitative
persistence of merchant capitalism in the colonised areas, at the
expense of the development of autonomous industries and self-sufficient
agricultures. Even after such domains were granted their formal independence, the liaison elites that manned the alluvial political machines
were more committed in their own interests to advancing diverse
metropolitan connections than the life chances of their mass clientele.
European states themselves bear many marks of the historic need for
large protected domestic markets and for political co-operation between
a residual nobility and a dynamic bourgeoisie. It is scarcely surprising,
then, that 'new' states should so profoundly reflect the growing divide
between rich and poor, a divide that has grown more significant in this
century when the costs of a process of globalisation carried on by
Western manufacturers, bankers, traders and armies have been more
clear. Global inequalities have been erected into global socio-economic
structures which are now skewed in fundamental ways. Whatever one
decides about the ultimate benefits to Western Europe of the inflow of
capital from plunder, tribute or unequal exchange, European expansion
obviously wreaked havoc upon the cultural infrastructures of the
societies they contacted or co-opted.[37] The advent of 'classes' on a
world scale has worked to the relative advantage of industrialised
'states', with particular transnationalising consequences for those created
later. In each 'state' case intermediary enclave elites share a world
community (a community in extent though not in the mass; in *breadth*
rather than *depth*) with the populations of the dynamic centres – comm
values, agreed rules of concourse, a globally integrated 'bourgeoisie'.

The cultural dimension of such an analysis is critical. The trans-
cultural psychology of profit maximisation[38] has deeply conditioned the

patterns of social interaction apparent today. And peripheral elites are quick to learn that their 'Northern' mentors love to teach: 'For in accepting cultural transmission the Periphery also implicitly validates for the Centre the culture developed in the centre' and creates a 'lasting demand for the latest innovations'.[39] The process is most evident when we consider global patterns of education — the critical part played by the preservation of metropolitan languages and by the installation of a sense of cultural inferiority and alienation in marginalised peoples around the world. Only 'Northern' ways, it is implied, can recreate themselves in a progressive fashion, and these ways the 'South' shall gratefully receive.[40] Moral claims made under circumstances like these are hard pressed to escape terms pre-defined by the 'North', since the 'North' is a powerful publicist in its own cause and 'comprador' elites are committed on the whole to keeping those without most ignorant and afraid.[41] Those who bear the burdens have little voice. They must come to a critical appraisal of the extended cause of their condition before they can speak; but to do that is to become conscious of circumstances specifically designed to assassinate, assimilate, or deceive.

If moral claims do not on the whole issue from the human masses on the periphery and are unlikely to do so, there are certainly more now of those articulate on their behalf. What empirical evidence is there that any of such second-order claims for material wellbeing, or politico-economic liberation, for 'pay-back' or for 'getting out from under', are justified? Here we reach one of the thorniest sections of the 'class' based view. If, for example, we could demonstrate that a transfer of resources had occurred historically from the colonies to the developing 'Northern' world, and continues today, then we could argue that Third World claims for economic redress and the opportunity to attempt something approaching self-reliance service a long-established debt and are justified; we establish a right which has been *earned,* not out of respect for creditors, but out of a justifiable claim for the payment of debts[42] or for self-determination.[43] Proposals for integrated commodity pro-grammes, price indexation, and the democratisation of international financial institutions to improve terms of trade, would be strengthened thereby. If, furthermore, as the 'dependencia' theorists assert, the process of overdevelopment in the global 'North' actually *creates* under-development elsewhere (defined in terms of failing nutritional standards, the loss of a sense of personal competence, and like indices) then the denial of claims for nourishment and autonomy are part of an unde-clared assault on the wellbeing of most of the world. The benefits of

economic growth are co-opted by the rich, and illusory offers of a
share, or outright repression and violence, are used to control the poor
and unemployed. This leads to the conventional Marxist stance that
moral claims are an act of class war, and rather than labour with
bourgeois precepts we must, in this view, condemn the exploiters and
call upon new values that will hasten their demise.

Demonstrating the empirical status of 'dependence' and 'exploitation'
is not a simple task however. 'Exploitation' in particular presents
problems because there is considerable debate about what we should
measure, and because it contains qualitative judgements that are not
easily expressed in quantitative terms. We are asked, primarily, to assess
the degree to which an exchange process is 'unfair'.[44] Empirical details
about terms of trade, tariff discrimination and capital flows are
obviously important. But the question of 'fairness' turns upon competing moral claims for a 'just' world economy, and there is therefore the
prior question of what 'justice' involves in the global context, and what
'justice as fairness' might mean.

We may readily distinguish general and particular, formal and substantive, arithmetical and proportionate, commutative and distributive
forms of 'justice', and there is no reason to take issue with these well
worn categories here. Such forms may be seen to reside in the individual,
state, or cosmopolitan domain.[45] But what, again, of the *class*? If we
accept the objective presence, as historical and contemporary evidence
suggests we should do, of a relatively standardised, urban, global elite
sharing similar values and interests and technocratic assumptions, and
we counterpose the poor and underemployed dwellers on the rural and
city fringes, then a 'political' economy of 'justice' can be given specific
shape and its claims made more clear.[46] In practice, the 'justice-constituency'[47] of the global hinterland cuts across that of the territorial society
or state. To talk as many do in terms of autonomous state regimes
arbitrating domestic disputes is to underrate, and drastically so, the
place of those regimes in a much wider system of social relationships,
and the way such arbitration does not proceed by *in*trinsic criteria alone.
To place present-day state regimes in sole control of 'development' and
'distribution' is to abdicate to the particular and usually self-regarding
interests of global and more particularly 'Third World' elites. To call
for *sacrifices* on the part of affluent states is to confuse a humid
euphemism with the debt-bound obligations that really prevail.[48]

If there is any strength to a claim by or on behalf of a submerged
global proletariat and peasantry we have to assess its formal standing
against that of the more 'satisfied' elites. Here the notion advanced by

John Rawls, which he specifically extends to any human collectivity, might be applied. To be just, Rawls says, is at least to be fair. When confronted by inequalities we should enquire whether they assume general precepts which any social group would have endorsed before it knew just where in the ensuing process of discrimination it would emerge — on the top or on the bottom or somewhere between.[49] How would we structure an ongoing global political economy if antagonists were to allot us our place therein? Contemporary global inequalities, we may safely assume, would rapidly recede (though not disappear) if they were to be measured by such contractual criteria as contribution to the common good, merit, and need. They are not on the whole so measured, except by those in the weakest position to enforce any radical conclusions. But the criteria exist, and they extend a promise of their own. The rejoinder that such promise may never be realised reminds us how difficult it is to sustain truly universalist values in the face of group interests and conflict.

Is 'justice' what we really want in the world anyway? Could we not cause more problems than we solve by our constant appeal to justifiable moral claims? Do we create happiness by alleviating suffering alone? May the tenacious pursuit of developmental self-reliance not jeopardise social freedoms or economic growth already extant? Is there not a need for *order* in world affairs regardless and perhaps even because of the gross discrepancies between global classes and the political discontent explicit or implicit therein? Is justice only to be achieved in a stable and orderly environment; should the latter be prior and preferred?[50] In the obvious sense that an outright end to nuclear coexistence would mean annihilation for us all, this is clearly true. Any disposition less than this, however, will convey and defend the preferred values of one social group rather than another, and we are obliged to consider what distribution of values such a disposition defines. There still exists a widespread bias among students and practitioners of world affairs toward a reified, denatured concept of 'order', and it is no accident perhaps that global elites tend to subscribe to the same idea. 'Order' is of 'primary' or 'elemental' concern, while justice is residual, to catch as catch can.

It is a familiar task to trace the way social struggles became domesticated over the last century or so with the spread of nation-states. We are still less familiar, however, with a picture of the social continuities that crystallised, in most cases after World War II, between the 'old' states and the 'new'. Class struggles, which tended to disappear in the face of rivalry, began to re-emerge again though in a global context this time. Much of the pattern of present world politics has to do with their second sublimation. E.H. Carr wrote before this pattern was apparent, but he demonstrates a perceptive awareness of the fact that conflicts of this kind 'cannot be resolved without real sacrifices, involving in all probability a substantial reduction of consumption by privileged groups and in privileged countries. There may be other obstacles to the establishment of a new international order. But failure to recognise the fundamental character of the conflict and the radical nature of the measures necessary to meet it, is certainly one of them'.[51]

In conclusion it may be worth pointing out that there is the distinct possibility of a deeper malaise again. Behind the moral claims for social justice put forward in the 'first', 'second' and 'third' worlds on behalf of the 'fourth' may lurk psychological motives hardly discerned. Freud once drew attention to the sense of guilt that was, he said, a decisive concomitant of 'civilisation' and grew in equal strength as it did. From his theory of instincts, and his own estimates of growing unease in industrialised societies, he argued that the 'most important problem in the evolution of culture', and the 'price of progress in civilisation' is the 'forfeiting [of] happiness through the heightening of the sense of guilt'.[52] This thesis seems unconvincing, however, given the capacity of the affluent and powerful to ignore the plight of those less well placed than themselves, and to remain unapologetic about it. His one-time colleague, Carl Jung, pushed into a parallel, in some ways more interesting vein. In a letter to Freud, dated 1910, he wrote that '. . . only the wise are ethical from sheer intellectual presumption – the rest of us need the eternal truth of myth . . .'[53] The problem is that 'Northern' man in particular seems to have divested himself of sustaining myths at an alarming rate:

> . . . he has abandoned his animism; his Ptolemaic astronomy that assured his position in the center of the universe; his faith in a hereafter that endowed him with eternal life; his belief in the supreme and infinite worth of his person that assured him a position of isolate dignity in an otherwise meaningless and impersonal world; and even perhaps his faith in a God whose attributes, under the impact of man's rationalistic scrutiny, became ever more abstract until He vanished in the metaphysical concept of the Whole. The shedding of these inestimable illusions may be merely stages in his diminishing stature before he himself vanishes from the scene – lost in the icy fixity of his final state in a posthistoric age.[54]

Presumptive ethics may comfort the wise as Jung assumed, but what of the rest? Can they be made wise in time too, or do they have to generate new myths to steer by, or are there other options, hardly apparent to us now, which will emerge in due course? To contemplate answers to questions like these is to contemplate the purpose of the human enterprise as a whole, which is an aspect of the discipline of world affairs, if not positively trivialised, then at least largely ignored.

Notes

1. D. Easton, 'The New Revolution in Political Science', *American Political Science Review,* vol. 63, no. 4 (Dec. 1969), pp. 1051-61.
2. The *deontologist* (or at least his/her ideal type) will consider moral precepts as radical, cardinal, prime — as imperious objects in their own right. Such a stance tends to see an 'additional component of meaning outside nature. Plato located it in a realm of abstract Forms, Christianity in the will of God, the intuitionists in the direct recognition of the quality of rightness, the moral-sense theorists in the feeling of approbation'. It reveals, that is, those 'prescriptive aspects of moral concepts that are independent of prudential considerations'. Raziel Abelson, 'History of Ethics', *The Encyclopaedia of Philosophy* (The Macmillan Co. & the Free Press, NY, 1967), vol. 3, p. 100. The *teleologist,* on the other hand, will want to consider *consequences* and whether such precepts foster the 'good' things any moral system permits, and inhibits the 'bad' that it forbids. He/she tends to define ' "good" and related concepts in terms of observable criteria, such as fulfilment of natural tendencies (Aristotle), satisfaction of desire (Hobbes and Spinoza), production of pleasure for the greatest number (utilitarianism), conduciveness to historical progress (Spencer and Marx), or efficiency of means to ends (Dewey)'. This reveals 'various ways in which ethical judgement is grounded on the fulfilment of biological and social needs' (loc. cit.). Unless one is merely mouthing moral absolutes any human act will situate a moral proposal in a social context where there are consequences. The separation is an analytic one, which does not in practice obtain.
3. *Value non-cognitivists* argue that moral claims have 'no cognitive status; they cannot be *known* to be either true or false because they *are* not true or false; and they are neither true nor false because they do not affirm or deny that something is the case'. See Felix Oppenheim, *Moral Principles in Political Philosophy* (Random House, NY, 1968), p. 24. Thus they may be sentimental, declaratory, influential, and even decisive, but they are never objective or observable matters of fact. *Value cognitivists,* on the other hand, affirm that 'valuational and moral statements are assertions about objective states of affairs and have, as such, cognitive status; that is, they are, and can be known to be, either true or false'. Oppenheim, *Moral Principles,* p. 21. The 'naturalists' derive such statements from 'true descriptive generalisations', from non-moral propositions of an empirical or teleological sort, or else they simply legislate so as to define moral claims in non-moral ways. The 'intuitionalists', however, agree with the 'naturalists' that 'ethical terms refer to objective characteristics, but interpret them as designating "non-natural" or "simple" properties which cannot be further defined'. Oppenheim, *Moral Principles,* pp. 22-3. While one may agree with the non-cognitivists that behind all moral claims lurk residual meanings that may not be 'factual' in any strict sense, it also seems apparent that, as the 'naturalists' argue, valuing precepts are connected very closely with factual convictions of one sort or another, indeed may well presuppose them. Furthermore, as the 'intuitionalists' seem to say, 'the connections, whatever they may be are not

going to prove to be the philosophically favoured ones of explicit definition and logical derivation'. Arthur Danto, *Mysticism and Morality: oriental thought and moral philosophy* (Basic Books, NY, 1972), p. x. Thus moral judgements demand more than cognitive treatment since they also prescribe and recommend. But neither are they 'mere expressions or evocations of emotion, attitude, or desire', nor are they 'mere commands . . . They claim a certain authority and support; they claim to be backed by reasons which are generally valid, or at least to have certain consensus in their favor'. William Frankena, 'The Concept of Social Justice', in R. Brandt (ed.), *Social Justice* (Prentice-Hall, NJ, 1962), p. 24.

    4. B. Russell, 'On Comets', in his *In Praise of Idleness and other essays* (George Allen and Unwin, London, 1948), pp. 224-5.

    5. 'What I Believe', in *The Basic Writings of Bertrand Russell* (George Allen and Unwin, London, 1961), p. 371.

    6. In isolating common doctrines that occur at different points in time regardless of their immediate environments, common that is with respect to some general pattern of human preoccupations that seems to change only slowly and perhaps does not even change at all, I do not want to underplay the role of novel events and processes in the world or the sort of analysis, reductionist again, that identifies our contemporary predicament with that of the Greeks and overlooks the enormous variety of events that have intervened.

    7. Though Plato was by no means the first to do so. This honour he attributed to Pythagoras.

    8. This ambiguity may be much more important and productive than we generally realise. George Steiner, in his book *After Babel* (OUP, 1975) suggests that: 'The dialectic of "alternity", the genius of language for planned counter-factuality, are overwhelmingly positive and creative . . . human tongues, with their conspicuous consumption of subjective, future, and optative forms are a decisive evolutionary advantage. Through them we proceed in a substantive illusion of freedom. Man's sensibility endures and transcends the brevity, the haphazard ravages, the physiological programming of individual life because the semantically coded responses of the mind are constantly broader, freer, more inventive than the demands and stimulus of the material fact . . . Metaphysics, religion, ethics, knowledge — all derive from man's will to art, to lies, from his flight before truth, from his negation of truth, said Nietzsche . . . The relevant framework is not one of morality but of survival. At every level, from brute camouflage to poetic vision, the linguistic capacity to conceal, misinform, leave ambiguous, hypothesize, invent is indispensable to the equilibrium of human consciousness and the development of man in society' (pp. 226-8).

    9. The scope is not limitless; it has many concrete features. Moral differences, in part at least, reflect disagreements as to fact. It is, as Danto points out, through their factual components and premises that ethical concepts engage our attention, and to comprehend a moral injunction is to know at least how it might be applied (Danto, *Mysticism and Morality*, p. 11). Resolving matters of fact does not ultimately resolve matters of moral meaning. Ethical assertions pertain to social relations and social relations have 'no material existence. We can only "observe" social relations indirectly by interpreting other people's behaviour, and we can only do this if we first invent an artificial code which attaches social meaning to cultural facts'. (E. Leach, *A Runaway World?*, BBC, London, 1968, p. 55). Cracking these codes so they may be understood in terms more familiar to us is an academic trade of its own, and '[w]hatever may be the logical connections between factual and moral propositions . . . there is enough of a tie between them, so that when we reckon in the application conditions of moral beliefs, we have some basis for rational criticism and rational debate in the moral sphere' (Danto, *Mysticism and Morality,* p. 13).

10. Colin Turnbull's work among the Ik of Uganda, and published reports of life in concentration camps, indicate that under extreme conditions of cultural disarray or material privation this capacity is severely distorted or altogether lost. '[H] umanity, as we generally define it, *is* an option', Turnbull argues in 'Human Nature and Primal Man', *Social Research,* vol. 4, no. 3 (Autumn 1973), p. 530.

11. See, for example, Leach's Lament: 'If only we could come to feel that consciousness is not something which makes human beings different and sets them apart but something which connects us all together — both with each other and with everything else' (Leach, *A Runaway World?*, p. 18).

12. Note, however, the monolithic consciousness generated by fascist parties, religious crusades, and by socialist mobilisation regimes as well, perhaps.

13. Turnbull, 'Human Nature and Primal Man', p. 528.

14. Ibid., pp. 529-30.

15. Robert Merton in the Foreword to Jacques Ellul, *The Technological Society* (Cape, London, 1965), p. x.

16. Ibid., p. xi.

17. A.N. Whitehead, *Science and the Modern World* (CUP, 1946), p. 20.

18. Ibid., p. 22.

19. T. Roszak, *Where the Wasteland Ends: politics and transcendence in post-industrial society* (Doubleday and Co., NY, 1972), p. 208.

20. Ibid., p. 58.

21. M. Wight, 'Western Values in International Relations', in H. Butterfield and M. Wight (eds.), *Diplomatic Investigations* (George Allen and Unwin, London, 1966), p. 127.

22. Ibid., pp. 130-31.

23. Thus Morgenthau has attributed what he sees as a general deterioration in moral limitations upon world politics to the growth of 'nationalistic universalism', to the dissolution of the aristocratic society that for three or four hundred years caused Europe, morally at least, to cohere, and to the rise of competitive state systems that construe their moral claims in global terms. Hans Morgenthau, 'The Twilight of International Morality', *Ethics,* vol. 56, no. 2 (January 1948), pp. 88, 94.

24. A. Wolfers, 'Statesmanship and Moral Choice', *World Politics*, vol. 1, no. 2 (1949), p. 192.

25. See *The Prince and the Discourses* (Random House, NY, 1950), pp. 64-6.

26. I. Berlin, 'The Originality of Machiavelli', a paper delivered to the Political Studies Conference, Oxford, 27 March 1963, p. 1. By 'natural law' is meant the notion 'that there is some single principle that not only regulates the course of the sun and the stars, but one that prescribes their proper behaviour to all animate creatures: animals, sub-rational beings of all kinds, follow it by instinct, others attain to consciousness of it and are free to abandon it only at their peril'.

27. Ibid., p. 15.

28. Ibid., p. 17.

29. Loc. cit.

30. H.L.A. Hart, *The Concept of Law* (OUP, 1961), p. 189.

31. Ibid., pp. 190-3.

32. Barrington Moore Jr., *Reflections on the Causes of Human Misery and upon certain proposals to eliminate them* (Allen Lane, London, 1972), p. 5.

33. *Birthright of Man* (UNESCO, 1969); also Jeanne Hersch, 'Is the Declaration of Human Rights a Western Concept?', in H. Kiefer and M. Munitz (eds.), *Ethics and Social Justice* (State University of New York Press, Albany, 1970).

34. Sidney Hook, 'Reflections on Human Rights', in Kiefer and Munitz, *Ethics and Social Justice,* p. 263.

35. See, for example, A. Linklater, 'Moral Agents and International Politics', *International Relations,* vol. 4, no. 3 (May 1973), p. 299.

36. The behavioural preoccupation with the 'system', because of its preference

for scientific methodology, led away from 'value' questions, and hence any
discussion of moral claims at all.
    37. E. Krippendorff, 'Peace Research and the Industrial Revolution', *Journal
of Peace Research,* vol. 10, no. 3 (1973), p. 189. Also, Samir Amin, 'Accumula-
tion and development: a theoretical model', *Review of African Political Economy,*
no. 1 (1974), p. 23.
    38. A. Mazrui, 'Modernisation and reform in Africa', in J. Bhagwati (ed.),
Economics and World Order (The Macmillan Co., NY, 1972).
    39. J. Galtung, 'A Structural Theory of Imperialism', *Journal of Peace
Research,* vol. 8, no. 2 (1971), p. 93.
    40. Cogently demonstrated by Abdou Moumouni, *Education in Africa*
(Praeger, NY, 1968).
    41. See P. Freire, *Pedagogy of the Oppressed* (Penguin, 1972), p. 15. There is
an important question closely related to this about the place of university pedagogues
and their part in the social definition of what is knowledge – in our own case,
whether we teach the 'politics of ruling', or the 'alternative politics of mobilisation
and self-management', to use Terry Irving's phrase.
    42. M. Cranston, *What Are Human Rights?* (The Bodley Head, London, 1973),
p.22; also, Mahbub ul Haq, 'Mr. Polanski's Dilemma', in B. Ward *et al., The
Widening Gap: development in the 1970s* (Columbia University Press, NY, 1971)
pp. 278-9. Not all transfers create debts. Apart from gifts or displays, for example,
consider market ethics: all mature adults are competent to enter contracts, and
should expect no redress when they commit themselves to (as they later perceive)
their disadvantage. The process referred to in the text is not one of contract, however, but one of exploitation, and the notion of market ethics does not obtain.
    43. Implicit, if not explicit, in neo-Marxist analyses of the politico-socio-
economic structures of the present global system are prescriptions for both state
and collective-state self-reliance. These issue in part from the manifest success of
the Yenan model in post-revolutionary China, but also derive directly from radical
theoretical analyses of world affairs themselves. The literature is extensive,
including the work of the Latin American 'dependencia' theorists (Furtado, Dos
Santos, Sunkel, Cardoso, for example) as well as A. Gunder Frank, Samir Amin,
Pierre Jalee, Suzanne Bodenheimer and many more. See also, for example,
Surendra Patel, 'Collective Self-reliance of Developing Countries', *The Journal of
Modern African Studies,* vol. 13, no. 4 (December 1975), pp. 569-83.
    44. J. Caporaso, 'Methodological Issues in the Measurement of Inequality,
Dependence, and Exploitation', in S. Rosen and J. Kurth (eds.), *Testing Theories
of Economic Imperialism* (Lexington Books, Mass., 1974), p. 91.
    45. H. Bull, 'Order vs. Justice in International Society', *Political Studies,* vol.
19, no. 3 (September 1971), pp. 272-4.
    46. R. Kothari, *Footsteps into the Future: diagnosis of the present world and
a design for an alternative* (Orient Longman, 1974), Ch. 3 and particularly
pp. 68-74. See also, M. Haq, 'Employment in the 1970's', *International Development Review,* no. 4 (1971), pp. 9-13.
    47. A term used by Julius Stone throughout his *Approaches to the Notion of
International Justice,* Truman Center Publications, no. 4 (January 1970).
    48. Though ethical discourse normally fastens obligations upon individuals, it
is not uncommon in world politics for obligations to be placed between groups.
Postwar reparations are only one example.
    49. J. Rawls, 'Justice as Fairness', *Philosophical Review,* vol. 67 (1958),
pp. 164-94; also, W. Runciman, *Relative Deprivation and Social Justice* (Routledge
and Kegan Paul, London, 1966). This notion has been seriously challenged by
Rawls's fellow philosophers, for example, Alain Zaitchik, 'Just Enough', *Philosophical Quarterly,* vol. 25, no. 101 (October 1975), pp. 340-45; Brian Barry, *The*

liberal theory of justice: a critical examination of the principal doctrines in 'A theory of justice' by John Rawls (Clarendon Press, Oxford, 1973). Enough seems to survive this challenge, however, to give it the credence accorded here.

50. H. Bull, 'Order vs. Justice', p. 277.

51. E.H. Carr, *The Twenty Years' Crisis* (Macmillan, London, 1962), p. 237.

52. S. Freud, *Civilisation and its Discontents* (Hogarth Press, London, 1949), p. 123; see also, H. Marcuse, *Eros and Civilization* (Routledge and Kegan Paul, London, 1956).

53. Quoted in Anthony Storr, 'The Significance of Jung', *Times Literary Supplement,* 25 July 1975.

54. Roderick Seidenberg, *Posthistoric Man: an inquiry* (University of North Carolina Press, Chapel Hill, 1950).

2 MORALITY, INTERESTS AND RATIONALISATION

J.D.B. Miller

Morality is right conduct. It is the way we think we ought to behave, even when we do not observe it. In this paper I shall try to explain why ordinary moral considerations appear to have so little application to world politics, and to answer some questions about the relationship of the sovereign state to morality. To start with, we should keep in mind two considerations.

The first is that no system of morality is fully observed in any society. If it were, there would be no need for courts, police, and the other coercive aspects of the state, because everyone would behave towards other people as they and he thought he should. Systems of morality are only partially observed anywhere. The lack of application of moral considerations to the actions of states has numerous parallels in the domestic life of states; it is not so remarkable as is often made out.

The second is that, while discussion often gives predominance to notions of universal morality (i.e. to any man's conceivable treatment of any other), in practice most people adhere to *group* morality (i.e. a code of conduct based on one's membership of a particular group, with rights and duties flowing from loyalty to that group). From the family onwards, groups give meaning and significance to life, and provide minimum protection and opportunity. To the great mass of mankind, the dichotomy in Western philosophy between the individual and mankind is meaningless: the individual is part of a tribe, clan, sect, family, village, and the like, and this serves as the effective middle term between him and the world at large. The essence of the group is its distinction from outsiders; morality consists primarily of right conduct towards the other members of the group. The kind of violent morality practised by the Mafia and by gangs of outlaws and buccaneers is the extreme case of a general rule: that the group comes first, that it makes its own morality, and that, if others suffer, that is too bad.

We should thus not be surprised if states prescribe their own morality in relation to other states, since the same is done, to a greater or lesser extent, by all the other human groupings of which we have knowledge. Within any complex society, the groups aim at getting what they can for themselves. Their degree of ferocity, and the exclusiveness of their several moralities, will depend on the degree of scarcity in the society, on the cohesiveness of the group itself, and upon the degree of intermixing which has taken place between groups and sections, i.e. upon the success of 'melting-pot' policies, and the widening or narrowing of opportunities to emerge from 'ghetto' conditions of economic and social life. Generally speaking, groups operate so as to maximise advantage but not to pull down the temple about their own ears: they do not challenge the basis on which the society rests, but work within it to secure the most they can, consistent with a relatively peaceful life. The greater the scarcity of opportunities and material goods, the stronger is likely to be the exclusiveness of the moralities practised by groups.

Thus, in any society which goes beyond the simple village or tribe, there will be found not one, but a variety, of moral imperatives and moral orders. The kind of social and moral patchwork represented by the Turkish and Austro-Hungarian Empires before World War I was an extreme but not untypical example of what a modern state is composed of. These states often hang together because to do so is self-evidently better than to have the parts hanging separately, i.e. carrying their differences to the point of open violence. In some such cases, as in Malaysia, basic conflicts are underplayed because it suits the leaders of the groups, as distinct from the rank and file, to maintain a common interest in the preservation of the existing form of the state. In others, e.g. Northern Ireland and Lebanon, the basic conflicts may be contained beneath the surface for long periods but then break loose, in spite of the efforts of formal leaders. In all these instances one can discern, not simply a clash of groups, but also a clash of moralities.[1] One does not need to go to these bitterly divided societies to see a variety of moralities in operation within a single state: the cross-hatching of ethnic, regional and national moralities in the United States is sufficient evidence.

My point is that the assertion of 'reason of state' or 'national interest' as a sufficient basis for morality by the sovereign state is not an isolated or unusual case. One can compare it with the operation of social groups before the state was a central feature of social life, and with the operation of more or less organised groups in societies today. In all these cases the essential element is the assertion of a special morality against a universalist one, whether it is the attempt of the European state in medieval and Renaissance times to evade the morality which the Papacy attempted to impose, or the insistence of certain groups in modern societies that they will not accept the imperatives about drinking, drugs and sex which are present in the laws of the society, or the determination of Catholics to preserve their own schools in the face of bitter majority resistance in late nineteenth-century Australia. The 'universalist' morality is in each case a morality serving the interests of particular people, who may or may not constitute a majority in the society, but who usually command effective political power. If we think of each moral code as serving some people's interests more than others', we shall have a fair picture of the actual state of morality of a society. Competing moral codes correspond to competing groups, and can be used to support the perceived interests of the members of each group. Just as, in the political sphere, the groups achieve compromises and trade-offs, so in the moral sphere the moralities may be compromised one with another to produce a vague result referred to as 'the contemporary moral climate'; but if there are attempts forcibly to impose one group's morality upon another, there will be conflict. This conflict may reach the levels of violence at times, but it is more likely to be contained conflict which occasionally breaks the surface.

In the case of the sovereign state, the assertion of a separate and superior morality — 'reason of state' — can be interpreted both historically and in social terms. Historically the theory of 'reason of state', given solid form by Machiavelli, was a response by European rulers to the pretensions to absolute power of the Church. It has its religio-political sponsor in Luther. I cannot forbear to quote a long passage from J.N. Figgis, whose works are too little read:

It is in international politics that Machiavelli has had his greatest influence. With territorialism dominant, and the unity, however vague, afforded by a single supra-national religious system with a recognized code of law, at an end, the relations of States became more definitely those of the 'state of nature' than they had been since the early days of the Roman Republic. The struggle for existence or power became more keen, and less obviously subject to any rules than it had ever been before among civilised peoples. Now the remarkable point about Machiavelli (and even of his adversaries) is what he omits . . . The question at the back of his mind was . . . what rules of prudence may be garnered from history or contemporary experience to guide us here and now. What distinguishes him from his predecessors is his entire discarding of any attempt to found a philosophy of right. To speak generally, all political speculation in the past few centuries might be described as directed to that end. To Machiavelli, however, the questions which seemed of such importance to St. Thomas and the innumerable other

writers on the subject of politics, *whatever side they took,* were
beside the mark. He did not consciously omit them; it did not
occur to him to discuss them. The practical end ruled everything,
and, as has been said, 'he is the founder of utilitarian ethics'. It is
remarkable, too, that he expresses the atmosphere of the Italy
of his day. Even a writer definitely hostile to him, like Botero, in his
work *Il Ragion di Stato*, makes very much the same assumptions,
and appeals to the same kind of motives.

What has vanished from Machiavelli is the conception of natural
law. So long as this belief is held, however inadequate may be the
conception as a view of the facts of life, it affords some criterion for
submitting the acts of statesmen to the rule of justice, and some
check on the rule of pure expediency in internal and of force in
external politics. The more law comes to be thought of as merely
positive, the command of a law-giver, the more difficult is it to put
any restraints upon the action of the legislator, and in cases of
monarchical government to avoid a tyranny. So long as ordinary law
is regarded as to some extent merely the explication of law natural,
so long as there is some general conception remaining by which
governments may be judged; so long, in fact, do they rest on a con-
fessedly moral basis. This remains true, however little their ordinary
actions may be justifiable, however much they may in practice over-
step their limits. When, however, natural law and its outcome in
custom are discarded, it is clear that the ruler must be consciously
sovereign in a way he has not been before, and that his relations to
other rulers will also be much freer — especially owing to the confusion of *jus naturale* with *jus gentium* which is at the bottom of
International Law. The despots of Italy were, in fact, in the Greek
sense, tyrants, and Machiavelli did little more than say so. What
gives him his importance is that what was true of the small despots
of Italy was about to become true of the national monarchs of
Europe. To Machiavelli the State, i.e., Italy, is an end in itself. The
restraints of natural law seem mere moonshine to a man of his
positif habit. He substitutes the practical conceptions of *reason of
state* as a ground of all government action, and the *balance of power*
as the goal of all international efforts, in place of the ancient ideals,
inefficient enough but not insignificant, of internal justice and international unity. No one can deny that very largely they have been
ruling in Europe ever since; just as it was only three centuries and a
half after his day that Italy herself reached, under the leadership of
Cavour, the goal which Machiavelli had set before her, by methods

which his typical man of *virtu* would scarcely have disdained.

. . . Social justice had no meaning to him apart from the one great
end of the salvation of his country. He had the limited horizon and
unlimited influence which always come of narrowing the problem.
There is a sense in which it is true that *salus populi* is *suprema lex*; for
laws and rules suitable for ordinary times are not always suitable for
emergencies . . . Every nation would allow that there are emergencies
in which it is the right and duty of a government to proclaim a state
of siege and authorise the supersession of the common rules of
remedy by the rapid methods of martial law. What Machiavelli did, or
rather what his followers have been doing ever since, is to elevate this
principle into the normal rule for statesmen's actions. When his books
are made into a system they must result in a perpetual suspension of
the *habeas corpus* acts of the whole human race. It is not the removal
of restraints under extraordinary emergencies that is the fallacy of
Machiavelli, it is the erection of this removal into an ordinary and
every-day rule of action. Machiavelli's maxims are merely the paradoxes of self-defence . . . It is the transformation of these paradoxes
into principles, that has been so dangerous. The net result of his
writings has been that, in the long run, Machiavelli's principles have
remained, as they ought, as a mere *Deus ex machina* for internal
politics, but have become a commonplace in International
diplomacy.[2]

Machiavelli's defence, of course, would be that he was no stranger to the
idea of right, that he respected it as significant in the lives of individuals,
but that it was simply not applicable to dealings between states:

for how we live is so far removed from how we ought to live, that he
who abandons what is done for what ought to be done, will rather
learn to bring about his own ruin than his preservation. A man who
wishes to make a profession of goodness in everything must
necessarily come to grief among so many who are not good. Therefore it is necessary for a prince, who wishes to maintain himself, to
learn how not to be good, and to use it and not use it according to
the necessities of the case.[3]

Machiavelli does not think of this as simply a description of what a
prince must do to preserve personal power; he also thinks of it in
nationalist terms as what a *people* must do in order to 'save the life and
preserve the freedom of one's country'.[4] What made Machiavelli's

doctrine so readily adaptable to international relations was this nationalist element: to him, the saving of the state was paramount. Figgis is right in saying that Machiavelli disregards the idea of natural law, as it might apply to relations between states or rulers. He does not disregard it as a means of judging personal conduct; his categories here are the normal ones, involving the keeping of promises, the need for just cause when people are killed, and the like. But Machiavelli maintains that these axioms do not apply to inter-state politics (or indeed to internal politics), because in the political realm men's selfishness is boundless; one must not let oneself be sacrificed to it. One's own selfishness can reasonably be given free play in the service of one's state. It is the state, as an end in itself, that ultimately justifies the means which Machiavelli is prepared to see employed.

We do not have to suggest that Machiavelli was the inventor of 'reason of state' in order to recognise that he gave coherent expression to a doctrine which was well in evidence in his own time and has become so much more important in later times. It is useful, however, to keep in mind Figgis's contrast between the natural law doctrine and Machiavelli's, since this is what so many arguments about morality in world politics turn upon. Ultimately, some universal imperative has to be found if the people of one country are to be made to regard the people of other countries as brothers, entitled to the same consideration as themselves. Some form of the 'reason and nature' doctrine must prevail. Otherwise, Machiavelli's view that nationalist expediency is proper will be the norm from which national policies flow, whether they flow in the form of war and conquest or in that of co-operation and regulated competition. Historically, Machiavellianism has proved to be normal for all kinds of state — democratic authoritarian, new, old, capitalist, socialist, poor, rich — with certain variations of time and place.

In terms of individual societies, the state has been able to continue to put Machiavelli's maxims into practice, partly because it can use or threaten force, but also because it can go beyond force in appealing to its citizens. Here we arrive at the social reality behind Machiavelli's doctrine. If we regard the state, not simply as a mutual conspiracy of force and fraud between those who control power, but as a body which provides certain guarantees and opportunities to its citizens — especially in respect of security and prosperity — we shall have a clearer picture of why it can maintain its pretensions of internal and external sovereignty, and why its citizens so often give it loyalty in spite of its manifest injustices. I have gone into this elsewhere,[5] and shall state the

point here only briefly. States gain credibility to the extent that they
protect their citizens from external attack and internal disturbances
and deprivation. 'Their citizens' must, of course, be understood in this
context as meaning mainly those citizens who matter, in the sense of
being able to organise some effective opposition to a government which
does not please them. In a wider sense, however, the state loses its
credibility even if it satisfies the generals and politicos but signally fails
the mass of the people, as the Tsarist regime did in Russia in its mis-
management of the war and its inability to provide basic needs to
workers and peasants. Hobbes and Machiavelli, both realists, fully
acknowledged this point: in spite of Hobbes's emphasis upon one's duty
to obey the ruler, he regards this duty as nullified if the ruler cannot
protect his citizens; and Machiavelli, while recognising that 'a prince who
possesses a strong city and does not make himself hated, cannot be
assaulted',[6] sees clearly that a prince who is weak and hateful cannot
command the allegiance of his subjects.

In modern terms, while the function of security remains significant
in enabling a state to command the loyalty of its citizens, the function
of provision — of welfare services of various kinds in particular — has
increasingly become the mark of a strong state. The more that citizens
conceive they have a stake in the country, in the sense of dependence
upon the state for jobs and benefits, the more they will adhere to it as
the ultimate group to which their loyalty is given and from which they
derive their morality towards people of other countries. In brief, if the
state provides the rations, it can give the orders.

It is largely in this respect that we can apply Figgis's point that
Machiavelli's is a philosophy of emergency, siege and self-defence.
From Machiavelli's point of view, the state of emergency was so potent
and permanent that it created its own morality towards other states.
The modern state operates primarily upon this principle, with the underlying assumption that if its people are not protected against foreigners,
not only their independence but also their standard of living will fall.
Just as Machiavelli allowed for occasional combinations and alliances with
other states, in order that particular advantages might be gained, the
modern state enters into these to a considerable extent; but it does not
provide the structures thus created with supra-national power, and it
insists on its right of individual action when circumstances go against it.
Such bodies as NATO, EEC and ASEAN illustrate the point. The state's
normal posture is one of either permanent emergency or of the recognition that an emergency may occur at any time. To say this is not to deny
the possibility or the existence of co-operation between states, or to

suggest that they are all potentially in a state of war. It is simply to assert that states operate as essentially self-regarding entities which submit all questions to the standard of their own advantage as they see it. The norms, rules and associations of international life are fashioned so as to take account of this prime characteristic. If there is an international morality, it is simply that minimum degree of common acceptance which the separate moralities of the individual states will permit. There is no higher morality than reason of state; but states may agree that their reasons coincide for particular purposes and within limited spheres. The fragility of detente between the United States and the Soviet Union is not an exceptional or surprising attribute: it is merely an expression of the fact that the interests and moralities of these two mighty states coincide at only a few (though vital) points. Each, like lesser states, is able to sustain its individual posture because of the conviction of the effective body of its citizens that unless that posture is sustained they will be worse off.

In using the term 'state' as I have used it in the foregoing paragraphs, I run the risk of its seeming that I regard all states as alike or even the same, thus inviting the charge that it is absurd to treat such disparate bodies as Singapore, China, Nigeria and the United States as examples of the same thing. This particular difficulty can never be satisfactorily resolved. The point of underlying importance, in my view, is that states have agreed, for the sake of convenience, to recognise one another's existence, to provide a minimum degree of non-intervention in one another's affairs, and, in particular, to agree that what is done domestically is not normally brought to international account. This still leaves room for enormous differences between states in strength, efficiency and cohesion. What it does, however, is to enable the governments of states (i.e. the actual bodies of persons who decide and execute policy) to try to use effectively the powers which a state is assumed to possess. Some are much better at this than others. In some, a constant regime is maintained; in others, there is a succession of governments, none of which seems able to do what it or anyone else wants. But in all these cases, effective and ineffective, there is a common factor — the freedom of the state machine to fashion whatever system of protection, provision and coercion it regards as suitable for its own people. In this respect all states are alike, although in so many other respects they are not.

Another point of importance is that co-operation between states can go a long way, even though each maintains that it is concerned with national interest when it does co-operate. States may be built up on the

basis of co-operation with others (as in the case of Australia and
Britain); they may have inescapable economic ties of a buyer-seller
nature; they may be linked by a common ideology; they may have
ethnic connections which induce close relations. But their co-operation
(even when institutionalised in formal treaties) is always subject to
demur by either party, because of the fundamental assumption of each
state that it is the final judge of its own interests.

The argument to this stage may be summed up as follows: if we
juxtapose reason of state and natural law, we have two opposing conceptions of international morality, the one stressing the exclusive
character of the people composing the state, and the other stressing
the brotherhood of man at large. The latter is usually regarded as the
more 'moral'. In fact, both express moralities; but one is supported by
force and loyalty, by appeal to potent symbols of patriotism and to the
joint selfish interests of a particular group, while the other has to rest
upon a vaguer sense of common humanity. Both assert 'brotherhood',
but one is narrower in definition than the other. If we ever had a War
of the Worlds, we might find the wider brotherhood made real, in
essentially the same way as the narrower one now is. Short of that outcome, however, we have no warrant for thinking that loyalty to mankind, or to any system of morality based upon common humanity, will
prevail against the morality of the state. The fact that there have always
been some people who wanted the wider morality to prevail is no indication that it will; the weight of experience is firmly on the other side.

This analysis seems to be true of all kinds of states, and to be true in
particular whether states are authoritarian or not. Obviously the basic
Machiavellian approach can often be more easily applied in authoritarian states in which opinion can be more readily manipulated, and
censorship applied over a wide area, than in less disciplined states in
which citizens can become independently aware of what the world is
like. But the attractions of the state are such that governments can
expect them to be heeded, even if they are flawed or misrepresented.
It is a sad conclusion that unjust, corrupt and cruel states successfully
claim the allegiance of the great body of their people, and can, to a
large degree, gain assent to whatever version of morality they care to
apply to international issues; but it is correct.

Against this background, certain further questions may be asked:

(1) Why does the wider morality make so little headway, short of a
    War of the Worlds?
(2) Why, in spite of this little headway, does the sovereign state custom-
    arily borrow the concepts of the wider morality to justify its pursuit

of national interests?

(3) Why does the state, rather than class, colour, or religion, prove the deciding element in the morality pursued in world politics?

(4) Is it true that the notion of a moral order in world politics is essentially Anglo-Saxon (or, as some would say, 'Wilsonian') in character, and does not affect other peoples?

(5) In what sense does the Third World demand for economic 'justice' (as expressed in the demand for a new economic order) alter the framework of contending moral imperatives to which we have been accustomed?

(6) Is there any prospect of agreement on a wider morality than that which states now exercise?

The first question can be answered only in terms of experience, along the lines indicated above. States are, so far, the biggest and most utilitarian groups to which people belong. Because they can exercise force and pressure, both internally and externally, they can be used to procure advantage, through governmental means, by particular groups within a society, and the society can be plausibly represented as a group sufficiently distinct to make its interests appear general. These interests are assumed — rightly — to be pursued in a world of comparative scarcity and insecurity, within which the state provides advantages through such means as tariffs, trade agreements, supervision of investment, currency manipulation, alliances and armed force. In such a situation it is not surprising that a wider morality, which either invites or commands people to treat as equals those who are worse off than themselves, makes so little headway. It is an invitation to be worse off oneself. Whether this is true in the long run or not (and the point is arguable, but in no sense settled), it is not acceptable to most people. The notion that foreigners should be treated as if they mattered as much as oneself and one's fellow citizens is a moral claim which few will accept; the competing claim, that only within one's own state can a reasonable standard be attained and preserved for oneself and one's family, is intrinsically more plausible and is much more acceptable in terms of the morality which effectively applies.

Given such an explanation, how do we explain the fact that wider moral claims are often made for national policies which are clearly selfish, and intended to benefit only a particular state? Everyone knows how each warlike move is presented as a gesture towards peace; how proposals for higher tariffs are said to be good for world trade; how immigration restrictions are intended to benefit potential immigrants;

and the like. The most naked policies of national aggrandisement have
habitually been put forward as benefiting everyone.[7] One has only to
re-read the nauseous claims by leaders on both sides in World War II to
realise how ingrained is the business of saying that what is right for one's
own country will be right for everyone else.

This is essentially a matter of the rationalisation of interests. Just as
sectional claims are advertised as general in impact within a society, so
in the world at large the claims of states are represented as benefiting
mankind. In part this is because the natural law tradition of the Western
world has shown an obstinate power of survival in rhetoric, but it is
mainly because generalised statements enable the impact of specific
policies to be disguised. It is more comforting to speaker and listener
alike if statements are made in general terms. It fortifies the sense of
self-assurance, and throws the onus on the foreigner to appear to be
going against what is proper and above all moral. The more general in
application appears to be the law which we are obeying or our
opponent is breaking, the more moral our behaviour can be made to
appear. It was thus quite in character for the Allied Prosecution in the
War Crimes Trials in Japan to base its case against the Japanese upon
natural law principles which were specifically Western rather than
Japanese.[8] We are confronted, as in all cases of rationalisation, by a
mixture of levels at which argument, action and justification occur.
Although one speaks of 'hypocrisy' in respect of the more flagrant
cases of rationalisation, this is often unfair and indeed misleading, since
most statesmen appear to be quite sincere in the use of a wider
morality to justify what has been, in fact, the outcome of a morality
centred upon the interests of their own states. The process is not confined to states, or to any particular group of states, though the Western
intellectual tradition provides a firm foundation for it.

The third question is somewhat detached from the first two. It asks,
not why men neglect their common humanity as the basis of the
morality which they obey, but why they choose the state as a basis,
rather than other forms of association which go beyond state boundaries, such as class, colour and religion. The answer is that these transnational links may provide a basis for loyalties and for the exercise of a
somewhat different morality, but that this extension normally occurs
under the aegis of the sovereign state and is not allowed to progress
beyond the point at which it becomes inconvenient for those who run
the state. Pan-Arabism is a source of morality which Arab leaders
employ but which they are anxious not to have used against them: one
thus sees the kind of alternate co-operation and estrangement which has

been so notable between the leaders of Egypt, Jordan, Libya and Syria in recent years. Pan-Africanism provides a morality for use against South Africa and Rhodesia, but those who employ it are careful to see that it does not dictate imperatives for the conduct of one black African state towards another. When Nkrumah tried to turn Pan-Africanism into a movement requiring general obedience by African states to a general African government, he had few supporters. The class situation is not significantly different. Never since the Second International dissolved into national fragments at the outbreak of World War I has it been possible to pretend that a common class interest would motivate the workers of the world (or any significant part of it) to go against the orders of their several governments.

The answer would seem to be that national interests are stronger than those of class, colour, or religion, largely because they are so much more concrete, so much more capable of enforcement, and so much more agreed upon by those who are asked to support them. The sovereign state is a concrete reality of provision and command. It offers both a refuge and a boundary: to disobey it is not only to risk punishment, but to risk exchanging the concrete reality, with all its imperfections, for the untried structures of organisation and morality which may be turned against one in the interest of others. It is significant that, whenever specific proposals for a new economic order are made, they come in forms which will provide benefits within a national framework of which the state machinery is the regulator. No proposal which requires the benefiting states to submit themselves to external decisions about what they will receive is entertained. Even though the common attributes of poverty and underdevelopment are stressed in demands by developing states upon the richer countries, the answer emerges in a national form.[9]

The fact that Third World states so zealously pursue a universalist morality in their efforts to obtain a new economic order (while ensuring that this will operate in essentially inter-state forms) is sufficient answer to the claim that recourse to general moral precepts is confined to Anglo-Saxon countries. There is, however, a special kind of universalist approach which appeals to elements of opinion in Britain, the United States and other English-speaking countries, and which is viewed with distaste by others such as the French. This, as before, is a case of competing moralities which correspond largely to national interests; but it is more a matter of style and tradition than a clear contrast between a narrow and broad morality. Wilson's formulations in the Fourteen Points were extremely broad in statement, and breathed a universalist morality, but they were regarded by the British government as well as the French as primarily representing the interests of the United States. Nonetheless, they appealed to the Gladstonian and Cobdenite tradition amongst British thinkers, and helped to create pressure upon the British government for what eventually became the League of Nations. Something similar occurred in World War II in respect of Roosevelt's Atlantic Charter. Certainly, one can say that a preoccupation with universalist international morality is more marked in the Anglo-Saxon countries; one can also say that elements of this 'Wilsonian' tradition appear in the approaches of former British dependencies, such as India, to international questions. The Indian case is, however, a good example of how general moral claims can act as a cloak for particular national interests. Nehru and his successors used as much of the universalist morality as suited them, and no more.

India offers something of a test for the fifth question, that which asks whether Third World demands for a new economic order change the framework of contending moral imperatives (and of no viable universalist morality) to which we have been accustomed. The Third World claims are made in terms of justice, which is another way of saying that right conduct towards the Third World involves a fairer share of the world's goods and services. In practice, fairer shares would mean that nearly all the countries of the world — not just the rich ones — had to contribute to raise the standard of life in India. Any attempt at equality would involve so vast a shareout that the mind boggles at conceiving the machinery which could accomplish it, let alone the united will which would need to lie behind it.

In practice, however, the ideas which lie behind the demand for a new economic order are conceived in nationalist terms, so that solutions are to be achieved in ways which suit individual states. International investment is not to be carried out by a worldwide controlling authority making overall decisions on the basis of need; instead, individual states are to control more effectively the investment made in their territories by multi-national companies. Broadly speaking, the Third World economic demands since the first UNCTAD have been pursued in terms which ensure that the rich states should suffer but that there should be no shareout between the others — except that a Least Developed Country category has been worked out for the receipt of UN aid. To this latter extent, a further step towards a universalist morality has been taken; but the sums involved are small, and the approach does not affect the main problem of economic development on the grand scale, i.e. the problem of how to achieve sufficient productive investment in poor countries to bring them up to a viable standard. Third World economic demands are best viewed as strategy, not morality. They are intended to work simultaneously upon the conscience and sense of security of the rich countries, to the point at which those make concessions which provide benefits for all underdeveloped countries in some measure, and to some in large measure. But the national element remains strong, the universalist element weak.

It is true that some Third World theorists are not prepared to accept the national element in demands for justice; they maintain that the governments which make the demands are so closely linked with Western economic interests (i.e. are 'compradore' in character) that they cannot be said to represent their peoples. It is sometimes argued that if these people were 'truly' represented (i.e. by genuinely revolutionary governments), they would accept genuinely universalist solutions. Put this way, the argument is very like that which Mazzini and other European nationalists of the nineteenth century used against Austrian and Russian imperialism, and that which Lenin and the Bolsheviks used in respect of European labour movements in World War I.[10] Like those two, it can be tested by two questions: (i) what evidence is there that popular movements, left to themselves (i.e. not subject to pressure from the presumed enemy), incline towards universalism in sympthy; and (ii) what evidence is there that, if governments are constructed out of these movements, they will be less inclined to use the weapons of state, and to construct a 'reason of state' morality, than other regimes? The difficulty in answering the questions is that a 'truly revolutionary' government is like the Snark: one hunts it but finds it always beyond reach. All such governments (i.e. all declaring themselves such) have compromised their positions and have made accommodation with capitalist international economics; all have adopted strong local versions of 'reason of state', and have frequently found it more congenial to attack the pretensions of other allegedly revolutionary states than to affirm a wider morality. The matter goes further than economics; it moves into the larger sphere of power politics, as it has with the Soviet Union and China. If we take the revolutionary states which have appeared, rather than those which might be imagined to appear, then nationalist morality can be expected from them as from other sorts of state.

The sixth question will be answered by different people in different ways. A wider morality can variously be said to come from a change of heart, a universal revolution, a canalisation of religious urges, the destruction of the sovereign state, better publicity, and so on:

basically, approaches like these maintain that, if people can be made aware of their common humanity, they will accept both a universal morality and its consequences. I do not believe any of this, although I believe that there are always people to whom the universal impulse is paramount. There are not enough of them, and they normally yield to reason of state when it is applied. To someone who holds the view of international morality expressed in this chapter, the only hope of a wider morality being applied lies in the acceptance of the state as the dominant continuing force in men's lives, rather than in any attempt to supplant it. Such a hope must necessarily be limited and prudential, since the main characteristic of the state is the protection of its own interests and no one else's: this limits the possibilities of wider moral imperatives, and forces one to base any hope of advance upon the state's own view of what is prudential for it to undertake.

The key to such a possible outcome is the same as that which produces relative harmony, and a degree of common morality, in a society in which a number of groups co-exist: the notion that there should be sufficient mutual accommodation to ensure that, on the one hand, no group is entirely shut out from the good things of the society, and, on the other, that the pillars of the temple are not pulled down by groups which want more than the others are willing to provide. In other words, the problem of whether morality can be made wider internationally is much the same as the problem of war. War will be avoided if states are convinced that they will lose by it, or if they believe that in the long run they cannot gain from it. A wider morality in world politics will result, slowly and painfully, from more and more accommodation between competing interests. There are certain practical matters, such as merchant shipping and international communications, in which this kind of accommodation of mutual interests has been achieved, to such a degree that one may sometimes hardly recognise that sovereign states are involved in it. There is, in fact, a superior morality involved in posting a letter to a foreign country than in discussing arms limitation with it, although the process of negotiating arms limitation, with all the threats to survival implicit in the process, is a step on the way to what might in the end prove to be a superior morality.

Notes

1. There may often be nice examples of conflicting moralities within the one group. The IRA, while relying for its support upon Catholics, openly defies important elements in Catholic morality, replacing these by the imperatives of group loyalty.

2. J.N. Figgis, *From Gerson to Grotius* (Cambridge, 1923), pp. 74-7.

3. *The Prince*, Ch. XV. See also the notorious Ch. XVIII.

4. *Discourses*, III, 41.

5. *The Nature of Politics*, Ch. VIII, and in statements about 'state nationalism' in *The Politics of the Third World*, Chs. 1 and 5.

6. *The Prince*, Ch. X.

7. As both a relief from, and a highlight to, contemporary efforts of this kind, I recommend Lord Ivywood's speeches in Ch. II of G.K. Chesterton's *The Flying Inn*.

8. My reference here is to Brendan F. Brown (ed.), *The Natural Law Reader* (New York, 1960), p. 109.

9. This comes out strikingly in the Charter of Economic Rights and Duties of States adopted by the UN General Assembly in December 1974.

10. A neglected book in the examination of these important questions is D.W. Brogan, *The Price of Revolution* (London, 1951).

3 WESTERN CONCEPTIONS OF A UNIVERSAL MORAL ORDER*

R.J. Vincent

Morality, says Bruce Miller, in his account of why it is something that has such a small place in world politics, is about right conduct.[1] In practice, he goes on to say, the content of right conduct is determined by people's group, and especially their state, affiliation, so that the vision of a universal morality depicted in Western philosophy is not matched by the historical record. Part of the concern of this chapter will be to attempt to save the notion of a universal morality from the savaging administered by Professor Miller, and to do this in two ways: firstly, by stressing that universality is something implied by the very idea of morality itself; and secondly, by pointing out the extent to which morality, in its strong form as the good enjoining action as well as in its weak form as rights and duties requiring forbearance and abstention, is something that informs and mobilises international politics. It will be argued that morality is not simply a decoration for a cake made with other ingredients.

The chief object of this chapter is, however, expository rather than argumentative. Part One sets out those moral orders or frameworks that have been held in Western thought to enclose systems of morality, and highlights the particular moral attitudes seemingly characteristic of each system. Part Two looks at some particular moral issues that have been and remain controversial in international politics, and seeks to show the extent to which the controversy derives from a disagreement about the frameworks set out in the first part. The conclusion returns to Professor Miller and the relationship between morality and interests.

A discussion of moral frameworks should perhaps be introduced by reference to that theme in Western thought which denies the possibility of their construction. Thrasymachus' doctrine of 'justice as the interest of the stronger' allows no room for morality that is not taken up by what suits the ruling party.[2] There is not in this conception the material for building any moral framework at all, but only a name for a structure raised up on different principles. Whether this is a theme which has dominated Western thought and practice at the expense of doctrines

* An earlier version of this chapter was published in the *British Journal of International Studies*, Vol. 4, No. 1, April 1978.

that have not conceded right to might is a question which this chapter must try to resolve. Meanwhile, it can already be said that even Thrasymachus, by bothering to seek a definition of justice, pays homage to virtue, albeit that of the 'good-natured simpleton'.[3] The conception of justice as the rationalisation of interest does at least accept some form of moral constituency, however inchoate, which insists on a moral defence if not on moral motivation.[4] And this is the beginning of the idea that morality exists as a standard apart from its interpretation from the standpoint of interests. From here it is not such a long step to the positivist position which admits morality to a place in society which might indeed arise from interests but which then forms a body of imperatives which are separate from them and defended against them. But these imperatives, in the positivist account, are special to the society in which they find a place: morality is relative. A particular morality can have, on this view, no truth value, and can lay no claim to universality. This relativist position, which Bernard Williams attacks as 'the anthropologist's heresy' (though he had in mind the now defunct functionalist anthropology of a previous generation), would deny the contention that the 'element of universalization' is integral to any morality.[5] This is a contention which is characteristic of the tradition of natural law: that pattern of thought which is clustered round the view that there are certain moral principles inherent in human nature, which contain thereby the element of universalisation, and which are discoverable by the application of right reason. Morality is now no longer relativist, and the attachment of 'right' to 'reason' asserts that it is a subject which has truth and not mere emotion or opinion as its stock in trade. And if, described in this way, naturalist doctrine has a medieval flavour, it has nevertheless maintained its grip on Western thought, and its contentions are not so unscientific or metaphysical as to place them beyond the attempt at vindication by contemporary biologists.[6]

There is then a range in Western thought about morality from the denial that it has any autonomous existence whatever, to the insistence on its universality based on the ethical capacity of the individual. Marx bestrides this range by agreeing with Thrasymachus that morality is the rationalised interest of the ruling class, at the same time as looking forward to a final stage of communism in which men and nature would be in harmony in a society which conformed with the innate needs of man.[7] It is with the latter (and longer) end of this range that I am concerned in the consideration of moral frameworks and the attitudes they enclose, and what follows will look first at the state (or rather at the *polis*), and then at the individual, the society of states, and world society.

Those rights and obligations, goods and ideals that are commonly thought of as the things that morality is about are qualities that tend now to be associated with the individual. This was not a dominant tendency of Greek thought. Plato's own account of justice begins with the treatment of it as a quality which exists in a whole community. Socrates says that justice might be easier to make out at that level than at the level of the individual, and suggests that the growth of justice be observed in the construction of the state.[8] Aristotle too, thinking of wholes before parts, has the state prior to the household and the individual in the order of nature, and the achievement of the good of the state as the 'greater and more perfect good' than the good of the individual.[9] This priority of the *polis* as the framework for morality had consequences for the quality of its principles. In Plato, the discussion of social organisation is concerned with the division of labour and embraces as a result a principle of interdependence rather than independence. Such rights and duties as follow are attached to services and functions rather than to individuals.[10] The definition of justice as 'giving to every man his due' pays attention not to some *a priori* individual claim to equal treatment, but to a social measure of worth in the community. And the position is similar in Aristotle. He does accept the principle of equality in his account of justice as fairness, and it is this quality which continues to recommend him to modern writers on ethics. But in the course of establishing distributive and corrective justice he finds good reasons to depart from his original principle of equality, so that desert, or proportion, or appropriateness might each of them set equality aside.[11] Rights are assigned here to classes of people according to principles of social order, and there is little hint of the modern idea of individual rights which are prior to the rules of society. True, a fair distribution is one in which those who are equal have equal shares, but the decision about who is equal is made according to the criterion of equal ability to serve the state.[12]

Outside the *polis*, then, the good life was impossible, for virtue had a social meaning. This Greek idea of the state as the primary moral constituency was to reappear with the emergence of the modern state and to reach its apogee in Hegel.[13] In the meantime, it was a notion that disappeared with the submergence of the *polis* in the *cosmopolis* of the Macedonian Empire. And where, in this system, political power was located at some distance from the daily preoccupations of men, the speculation of moralists turned from the public to the private domain, and the virtuous individual replaced the virtuous state.[14] The retreat from the mundane that was involved in this process found its justification in the Christian gospel of individual salvation, and its unworldliness has been a more or less visible characteristic of Christianity ever since. 'When it is considered how short is the span of human life', said Augustine, 'does it really matter to a man whose days are numbered what government he must obey, so long as he is not compelled to act against God or his conscience?'[15] It was the life hereafter that mattered, and in virtue of this and its contemplation no really holy man concerned himself with the political except from his duty to release others from such concern,[16] and no earthly distinction between bond and free, or between rich and poor was of any consequence.[17] There is in this obliviousness to politics and society the material for an attack on Christianity as a 'slave morality',[18] but it was an obliviousness that gave rise to three doctrines about morality that were to have more noble consequences for the Western experience of politics.

How did these doctrines differ from their Greek predecessors? In the first place, men were confronted with a dual loyalty to the city of God and to the city of man where the Greek *polis* had required no such division. Secondly, where Aristotle had ethics as a branch of politics, the Augustinian legacy sharply separated them. And in the third place, Christian moralists, in the debate about ethics as ends or means, placed virtue in the means, the moral action itself if not regardless of ends then at least, in a moral scale, before them.[19]

The worldlessness of Augustine is, however, an extreme doctrine of what has been called 'primitive Christianity'.[20] The great medieval institution of the Church was necessarily worldly, and could not avoid a concern with society and politics. It was Aquinas who provided the theory to accompany this practice in accepting the world as an arena for the present achievement of a Christian civilisation, as well as a mere preparation for the life which was to come. The Aristotelian conception of the state, and the Roman idea of universal law, were channelled into Christian doctrine by Aquinas's use of the natural law of rational creatures. And this enabled him not merely to establish and defend a system of ethics, but also to render politics and society as Christian institutions. This achievement, however, meant a departure from Augustine's individual, and the just ordering of society came back into view. It was not until natural law became natural right that the Christian emphasis on the individual made its full political impact.

The way from natural law to natural right passes from the demise in the Reformation of the medieval notion of a single Christian common-

wealth to the eighteenth-century enlistment of Christian doctrine in the
service of political principle. The first step was taken by the Reformers
in their attack on the Papacy, which, since they accepted the divine
character of the Church, depended for its success on an appeal that had
no less claim to divinity. They thus reasserted the doctrine of the divine
nature of princely rule, and derived from it a right on the part of rulers
to control the religion of their subjects.[21] It is not this claim itself that
is important for the route we are tracing, but the one to which it gave
rise. For once the central façade of medieval unity had been breached,
and the right of the prince to religious sovereignty proclaimed, the new
problem was for the domestic dissenter to find a basis for reducing
princely pretension. And in the wake of the Massacre of Saint
Bartholomew, which had destroyed the myth of the prince as protector
of all his subjects, the New Testament, in Laski's phrase, was ransacked
for texts that might justify rebellion.[22] In this way, the Christian
attachment of importance to the individual conscience had its worldly
impact: the 'political liberty of the seventeenth and eighteenth centuries was the outcome of the protest against religious intolerance'.[23]
And this is the second stage along the route we are following – the
secularisation of a religious tradition famously exemplified by
Grotius's emancipation of natural law from divine law.[24] From here
the way was open for social contract theory, placing the origin of
society in an agreement among individuals who had natural rights, and
thence to the rights of man, on whose behalf Tom Paine could invoke,
in a style that bore no resemblance to the preoccupation with Christian
doctrine in the *Vindiciae,* the unity or equality of men as all being of
one degree from the Creation. This unity of degree, he says, is a feature
of all known religions, not merely of Christianity, and by this observation he takes natural right back to natural law.

Praise or blame for the place of the individual in modern Western
political thought has then to be apportioned between Christianity and
the tradition of natural law. Both of these were by implication
universalist: Christianity in its doctrine of the equality of all in the sight
of God, and the law of nature in assigning rights to men as men. But the
universe of individuals was not crowned by a universal state. The individual, even at the high-water mark of the doctrine of rights inhering in
him in the eighteenth century, looked to his state to protect them. Nor
was this simply a position maintained *faute de mieux.* Article III of the
Declaration of the Rights of Man and of Citizens declared that the
'Nation is essentially the source of all sovereignty; nor can any individual, or any body of men, be entitled to any authority which is not

expressly derived from it'.[25] The importance, then, of the framework of morality based upon the individual has not been that such a framework has provided for the enforcement of morals, but that it has kept alive the idea of a domain that was sacrosanct, beyond the reach of the political world,[26] and also the notion of an ideal pattern for society which lies ahead of man's present condition.[27] It is, perhaps, not a negligible framework for morality that has provided a buttress against totalitarianism, and a reason for progress.

The idea that rights and duties inhere in individuals was important for the birth of the idea of a society of states. The prince, as an individual, was no less bound by natural law than any other individual, and the obligation endured into action taken by him in the name of his realm. By this means, the idea was made possible that the realm itself was the bearer of rights and duties in an inter-state society, and it was the doctrine that international society was populated exclusively by sovereign states that became orthodox in the pages of the positivist international lawyers of the nineteenth century. In the course of this evolution, the status of the individual declined from one of full membership in international society alongside states to that of being a mere object of international law of which states took no legal notice. And with this eclipse, the idea of a morality that was special to the society of states had to find a place between, on the one hand, the position of the naturalists that there was no essential difference between the domestic and international domains — natural law applying in them both, and the position of *raison d'état*, which, in its extreme form, excluded morality with the exclusion of the individual.[28]

This middle course is first marked out by Hobbes: not indeed in his account of the state of nature as a state of war, but in his remark that the state of nature is a less miserable condition as it applies among states than it is in the relations of individuals.[29] If states in a posture of war uphold thereby the industry of their subjects, are less vulnerable to violent attack than are individuals at the same time as being more self-sufficient, and provide by their inequality the possibility of ordering their relations according to the principle that might is right, then there are in virtue of these contingencies the grounds for an international morality that has as its central feature the defence of the sovereign state as the provider of a degree of security in a hostile world. It is to be sure a morality in the weak sense of the word that we distinguished above, and it is, moreover, a morality that in comparison with our domestic expectations about justice is almost uniformly offensive: in its projection of special interests as moral principles; in its disposition to recognise *faits accomplis* as creative of values regardless of previous conceptions of right; and in the welcome it extends to war as a means of changing or policing international society.[30] Nor is this assessment much improved by the observation that, empirically, states have felt the need to act morally, or at least to justify their action in international relations. For in a decentralised system which allows no effective impartial verdict about the justice of any action, self-righteousness generated by a domestic justice constituency may be a greater hazard to international order than a self-interest which denies the force of morality in international affairs.

This is not, however, quite moral bankruptcy. It is true that the criterion of individual morality which leads us to esteem a man who takes into account the interests of another to the extent of preferring them to his own is not the hallmark of international morality.[31] But when the argument is taken a step further to the observation that we should be disposed to criticise (on moral grounds) a state for preferring another's interests to its own, sacrificing thereby the interests of its own citizens, then the idea of a *different* moral order rather than an *inferior* one begins to take shape. If the protection of the interests of individuals or groups is something which in general the state does more effectively than any more inclusive entity, then the interests of the state itself acquire thereby a moral dignity which is not automatically to be despised. 'The fundamental error which has thwarted American foreign policy in thought and action', said Morgenthau in 1950, 'is the antithesis of national interest and moral principles . . . The choice is not between moral principles and the national interest, devoid of moral dignity, but between one set of moral principles, divorced from political reality, and another set of moral principles, derived from political reality.'[32] And because it was not possible to attain a world based on universal moral principles, a foreign policy derived not from such a goal, but from the national interest, was in fact morally superior.

International morality might then be impoverished by being the outcome of a decision to prefer the order established within the state, but the defence of it rests on the assertion that any more ambitious doctrine that neglects the reality of a morally plural world is likely to undermine the international moral order rather than to protect and advance it. The unglamorous doctrine of non-intervention bears witness to the minimal unity of international society, and retains such universal validity as it has (universal that is in international society) by the acknowledgement on the part of states that most moral claims are to be made and met at a place other than in international society.[33] The framework for morality that is provided by the society of states is thus hostile to the substantial claims to justice of any individual, group or class that is not a member of that society, and there is, as Hedley Bull has said, a 'conspiracy of silence' against them.[34] For this reason, a group to whose grievance international (or strictly inter-state) society remains necessarily deaf, must base its appeal on the erosion of international society into a society based on a more inclusive principle which will then admit new members.[35]

I use the term 'world society' to describe the framework of morality that encompasses groups of this kind whose claims, not being accommodated by the society of states, are voiced in a tone which is hostile to it. It is not a wholly accurate term, for the moral order which such groups would build might stop short of a world society in the sense of some great society of mankind: their designs might be restricted to a society of nations, or to a society of states within each member of which republican government was instituted or the dictatorship of the proletariat established. A world society properly so-called might be one in which all human beings owed allegiance to one sovereign, or one in which a universal cultural pattern prevailed such that no part of the society could mount a defence against it, and I shall treat presently the view that a world society in a particular sense already exists. But between the society that has failed to move far from the society of states, and those world societies which might exist in virtue of the global achievement of a single order, there are a number of claims that surface in world politics because they do not find complete satisfaction at the state or inter-state level and which have established some form of non-state moral constituency in which they are considered legitimate: the claim of an individual to human rights recognised in regional and global institutions; the claim of a tribe or a cultural group in some sense to survive the depredations of its host state recognised if nowhere else by the class of professional anthropologists; the claim of a multinational corporation to penetrate the domain of the sovereign state recognised by those who assert the autonomy of the economic order; or the claim to recompense of an exploited class now voiced by the Third World under the title of the 'New International Economic Order' and recognised in some degree in the developed world.

This last claim arises from a view of world society as something already established. If the idea of society is conceived not according to some juridicial formula such as *ubi societas ibi jus est,* but in Marxian terms as a system of collective productive activity, then it can be argued that a world society exists and that it takes a form very different from

the account of international society that starts with the state. For in the
Marxian view, society is not something enclosed within the state, and
while the two might coincide, as in the Greek *polis*, there is no necessary connection between them.[36] The necessary connection is not
between society and state, but between system of production and
cultural form. And if the capitalist system of production is taken as the
key to the evolution of modern world society, then it is possible to
render that society in terms of the more powerful capitalist nations
grafting their mode of production on the rest of the world, of an international division of labour between manufacturing countries and
producers of raw materials, and of the creation of an international
hierarchy maintained by a structure of dependence.[37] This is not a
pluralist society of states with authority apportioned horizontally, but
an imperial society in which authority is allocated vertically. And with
the change of perspective, different moral scenery comes into view. In
particular, it is when set in this context that the moral claims of an
exploited class are at their most persuasive.

Whether or not it represents a liberal following of a radical lead,
there is also a non-Marxist account of a world society existing in virtue
of transnational relations, and of interdependence established across
state frontiers. In view of developments of this kind which mark out a
'world in which national boundaries can no longer be regarded as the
outer limits of social cooperation', it has been argued that principles of
justice ought to apply globally, and not merely within states set apart
by a principle of non-intervention.[38] According to this view, a norm
of non-intervention might suffice in a world of more or less self-contained states, but in an interdependent world reliance on such a norm
is a moral abdication. By benign or malign neglect, it has the effect of
withdrawing an important area of social interaction from moral
scrutiny. This is a point of view to which I shall return later: I merely
notice it here as a moral framework whose scope is global.

To whatever extent these renderings of world society are a reality in
world politics, there is a formula in the Western political tradition
which would enable them to be co-opted into a world moral order. The
conception originating in Stoic thought of a great society of mankind
contained in it, as we have seen, the idea of a universal law applying to
both individuals and to any institutions that they formed among
themselves — since these too were made up of individuals. It was this
doctrine (in addition to the idea of princely obligation) that enabled
natural law to be applied to states, and by the same token, it might be
applied to any entity beyond them. Indeed, this process would consti-

tute a return to the medieval conception of a *communitas humani generis* rather than being the departure from it that the idea of a society of states itself was. But the observation that natural law is in principle applicable to any kind of society that might be emerging — so that whither the framework thither the morality — is, it might be said, rather a vacuous one. The difficulty with it is the very lack of any kind of established, consensual framework that might enclose a robust morality. There is not *a* framework, but rather competing frameworks built to accompany each vision of world society, some of which as we have seen, assert the reality of world society as a structure of dependence or of interdependence, others of which merely invite us to consider world society from a certain point of view,[39] and still others of which assert the shape which world society ought to take without suggesting that it is yet a reality.[40]

And the idea of world society as constituting a moral framework is not problematical only because of the variety of Western conceptions of it. The more intractable difficulty is that, in being *Western* conceptions, they are inescapably a partial view of the world social whole. Thus, while it is true that, for example, John Rawls's *A Theory of Justice*[41] is a theory framed *sub specie aeternitatis,* applicable in principle at any time and place, to all of humanity (as his critics, but not Rawls himself, have said) or to any part of it, it does in fact arise from a particular philosophic tradition, and has an appeal which is unlikely to be felt outside it.[42]

For these reasons, the harsh conclusion about world society as a moral framework is that, like the one formed by the universe of individuals, it has nurtured some noble ideas but has not yet taken a form concrete enough to uphold them in practice. But this harsh conclusion is not the only one. The moral claims of individuals, or of tribes, or of multinational corporations, or of classes have a reality in world politics, and a more or less well-articulated constituency in which they are recognised, which are not simply to be measured as an inverse proportion of their distance from the sovereign state. And while it may be true that these claims might be stifled as claims before world society the more effectively they are met by the state, the finality of the latter community is a hypothesis denied by their appearance in world politics in the first place.

This discussion of moral frameworks in Western thought might be summarised by the remark that the individual is to the state as the society of states is to world society. The individual framework, and the framework of the state in international society, enclose rights and

duties that are prior to society, which social rules must then protect:
they assert, as it were, a private domain which is exclusive of public
arrangements. The framework of the state, and that of world society,
invert this order of priority and take virtue as a public property rather
than a private one: the good of society comes before the right of the
individual.[43] And this is the point of the proportion sum done to
summarise the discussion: on either side of it there is a swing from the
right to the good. The distinction between these two qualities is a theme
in Western thought most graphically illustrated by the debate between
the theorists of natural right and the utilitarians: the peremptory
quality of individual claims against the greatest happiness of the greatest
number. The long ascendancy of the latter doctrine has been challenged
by Rawls's expression of justice as fairness as the priority of the concept
of right over that of the good, so that the 'principles of justice . . .
specify the boundaries that men's systems of ends must respect'.[44] And
this is a blow struck not merely on behalf of natural right against
utilitarianism, but against that other long-standing orthodoxy of
positivism — since, in Laski's usage, it pits right against rights, expediency
being able to establish the latter but not the former.[45] And this is to
arrive again at the question of the sources of morality with which this
section of the chapter was introduced. I pass now from frameworks to
issues.

This section will treat three moral issues that recur in Western thought
— realism versus idealism, equality and human rights — with a view to
showing that much of the vitality of moral debate in international
politics is produced by a contest among the frameworks that have just
been described. The choice of these three issues, rather than certain
others which have a claim to be treated in a study of this kind — such
as the doctrine of just war, or the question of national self-determination, or the moral problems that are raised by the appearance of particular weapons in international politics — is not simply an arbitrary one,
but arises from their topicality: not only have they recurred historically,
but examples of them are the burning questions of the hour.

The debate between realism and idealism in international relations can
be thought of in four dimensions. In the first place, it is a disagreement
about the principles that are to direct action in international politics.
Thus, in the Melian controversy, the Athenians, having camped on the
island of Melos with a superior force, then set out to persuade the
Melians that their best course was prudently to accept the Athenian

preponderance and make their island over to Athens without the fight that would be in the interest of neither party.[46] The Athenians made no pretence to a right to rule in Melos, but merely invited the Melians to look circumstances in the face, and to aim with the Athenians only at what was possible — for the 'question of justice enters only where the pressure of necessity is equal', and 'the powerful exact what they can, and the weak grant what they must'. Against this celebration of the possible by the power with the upper hand, the Melians excused themselves to the Athenians for wishing things otherwise, and sought to persuade them to act according to right for this was their true interest. But if this should fail, the Melians would fight for principle and trust to good fortune. This course did not profit the Melians, but their failure did not decide the debate between idealism and realism in favour of the latter, for the Athenian point about might being accepted, that of right remained, attached only problematically to it.

The second dimension of the debate between realists and idealists is close to the first, and involves its contemplation from another angle: not what principles are to guide action, but the criteria by which we are to judge actions once they have occurred. A realist might admire a statesman for his prudence, an idealist for his vision, and so the ranks of commentators are drawn up in support of Athenians or Melians. In the history of the study of international relations in the twentieth century both sides have been heard, the idealists in support of a view of the subject as a vehicle for international improvement, the realists in defence of a conception of it as a chronicle of certain dismal regularities in the human experience, and I shall come presently to their place in contemporary international politics.

The third dimension of the debate relates to the origin of the rules that instruct behaviour and provide standards for its judgement, and to the basis of obligation to them. In this mode it is an argument carried on between naturalists and positivists, some of which we have already heard. The naturalists asserted rules of right reason discoverable by the use of the intellect which applied to men (and human institutions) in virtue of their very humanity, while the positivists derived rules from command, custom or treaty and thought of them as sprung from practice rather than precept. Whatever the reasons for the ascendancy of positivism in the nineteenth century — its appeal to good sense in not setting rules too far ahead of behaviour, or in observing that different societies did in fact have different moral regimes — it is a doctrine that has been challenged in the international relations of the twentieth century. The attention paid to human rights in such instruments as the

United Nations Charter, the Charter of the Nuremberg International
Military Tribunal and the Universal Declaration of Human Rights arose
not from evidence of state practice, but from a conviction about right
conduct regardless of state practice. And there are four different
grounds on which naturalism, to which these developments represent
a return, might be defended as a source of morality. In the first place,
the positivist doctrine that what is thought to be right in any society is
right, might have the effect of raising a protective umbrella over
practices that the philosophers' ordinary man might find morally
offensive: natural law, it might be said, is the ordinary man's informant.
Secondly, the unscientific quality of the naturalist formula for a universal morality — 'principles of conduct discouraged by the use of right
reason' — might be removed by converting it into a logical question
about what is necessary for social life,[47] or into an empirical question:
Are there as a matter of observation certain principles of human conduct which are universal in the sense that no society is to be found that
does not in some degree observe them? A less ambitious form of this
question might ask whether it is true to say that a capacity for ethical
behaviour is an observable characteristic of men everywhere, so that
even if the rules are different, an ethical competence is universal. These
questions take us into the domains of anthropology and biology, and
neither of them seems as inherently unsound as the propositions of
natural law sometimes appeared.

A third defence of natural law relies not on its form but on its function, and this is the essence of d'Entrèves' account of it. His argument
is that whatever might be thought of the particular pronouncements of
natural law at particular times, it is a body of doctrine that has fulfilled
three majestic functions in the Western experience of politics. It has
established a universal basis for law (the Stoics; Rome). It has provided
a rational foundation for ethics (Aquinas). And it has produced a theory
of natural rights (the American and French Revolutions).[48] Rationalism
is a thread that runs through each of these functions, and provides
itself a fourth defence of natural law. A large part of morality might be
conveyed by rendering it as something which requires that good reasons
be given for any action. This is a weak defence because it takes 'right'
away from 'reason', allowing thereby the possibility that positivism
might rule by default, but it does at least provide a protest against
arbitrariness. That the function of naturalism might be reduced to this
shows its worldlessness to be a central weakness, where its worldliness
is the weakness of positivism. Both weaknesses, as we shall see, endure.

The final dimension of the debate between realism and idealism has its appeal for academic international relations intramurally: it is a way of organising a history of thought about the subject, so that the tradition of *raison d'état* is opposed to that of universal morality.[49] The difficulty with this polarisation is that it leaves no room for a middle ground between the schools of thought which is, as a matter of observation, occupied even by those who are commonly considered as belonging uncompromisingly to one group or the other.[50] And it is a difficulty that applies in each of the other dimensions of the polarity. Thus the long and sometimes tedious argument between naturalists and positivists has been seen by an outsider as a local dispute between groups sharing a legalist ideology that is more striking for what unites its brethren than for what divides them.[51] In the matter of how events are to be judged it has been remarked that the debate between idealism and realism as it took place in the subject of international relations in the twentieth century was cloistered within the English-speaking world, and accepted a common framework of moral discourse.[52] And in relation to the principles that are to guide action, the Melians were concerned to show the Athenians that it was on grounds of expediency that a moral principle should be respected, while the Athenians, for their part, after an initial disclaimer about pretending to rights in Melos, defended as a law of nature the principle that might was right.

But it is not as though mere argument can break up these schools of thought, and they survive in each of the four dimensions outlined. In regard to the principles that are to guide foreign policy and by which it is to be judged, the 'realist' Henry Kissinger, working through the traditional agenda of the international politics – the 'structure of peace' – can be divided from his 'idealist' critics who lament his belated awareness of the new agenda of international politics – interdependence, the global crisis, systematic injustice to the Third (or Fourth) Worlds – and his failure fundamentally to take it seriously.[53] On the source of rules, it is possible to separate into positivist and naturalist categories the notion of 'law' as involving *stability of expectations* inherited from the past', and the idea of 'justice' as involving *changing expectations about what needs to be done in the future*'.[54] Law is connected realistically with stability, justice idealistically with chance. Within the discipline of international relations it is still possible to discern a debate 'gently raging'[55] between 'realists' who believe that international relations remains a state of war dominated by the concern for security, and idealists who believe that world politics are becoming more like domestic politics. And just as the realist and idealist dispensations endure in these ways into contemporary thought, so also does the

dissatisfaction with the dichotomy and the attempt to transcend it. Thus
Falk describes the domains of both law and justice as enclosed in a
states-system which it is the purpose of the world order radical massively
to subvert in order to achieve that central guidance on whose emergence
the survival of the planet might depend.[56] And the defence of this programme is not just an idealist one, but one that depends on a realist
demand for the construction of relevant utopias to guide a world that
has to escape its present predicament.[57] One of the things that might
stand in the way of such constructions is the doctrine of state equality,
and it is to this that I now turn.

The idea of the equality of states arrived in international relations
via an analogy with domestic politics, drawn first by Hobbes and
Pufendorf, but having its clearest expression in the writings of Wolff
and his follower Vattel. 'Since by nature all men are equal', said
Wolff, 'all nations too are by nature equal the one to the other . . . Just
as the tallest man is no more a man than the dwarf, so also a nation,
however small, is no less a nation than the greatest nation. Therefore,
since the moral equality of men has no relation to the size of their
bodies, the moral equality of nations has no relation to the number of
men of which they are composed'.[58] Vattel used the same image of
giant and dwarf to show that strength and weakness counted for
nothing in the attribution of equality to states.[59] States had an
absolute equality because they were states, and no factual inequality
was considered relevant.

A slightly less ambitious version of this doctrine, according to
which states, having an equal capacity for rights, are potentially equal,
has been taken as what most writers on international law have meant
by the principle of equality.[60] The objection to the principle in this
form, or in the stronger absolute form, is that in paying either very
little or no attention to the fact of inequality, it was likely to build a
system of international law that bore small relation to the actual
practice of states. And even the more tentative doctrine of equality —
which holds that for certain purposes factual inequalities between states
are not to be considered relevant, so that, for example, states are to be
thought of as at least equal before the law — has been taken as a
spurious application of a nominally democratic principle to the unsuit-
able environment of international relations.[61] Thus, in regard to the
United Nations, it might be argued that the doctrine of one-state-one-
vote that follows from the principle of equality gets in the way of the
efficient working of the organisation. It does so by preventing the writ
of the powerful, on whose support the survival of the organisation

depends, from running, and by allowing resolutions to be carried by coalitions of small states of whose acceptance in the international community at large there is little prospect. Against this it can be argued that equality of status for states that are not great powers attaches them to the purposes of the international community, an institution which they might otherwise regard as a systematic denial of their interests.

But if equality of status is all that small powers can be said to have gained in international relations, it is possible to think of the extension of the principle of equality in at least two directions. In the first place, international society might come to admit more respects in which the principle of equality is to apply, so that, in it, the same course for the doctrine might be traced as in domestic politics -- extending gradually from the sphere of ethics to that of law, then to religious belief, politics and society, and finally to economics.[62] And secondly, international society might admit institutions other than states as bearers of rights and duties in it, recognising to that extent their equality, and welcoming them into what would then have become a world society.

In contemporary international society there has been little progress in either of these directions, but that more has taken place in the first of them than in the second can be illustrated by reference to the General Assembly's Charter of Economic Rights and Duties of States. As to the first direction the references to equality in the Charter are mainly traditional and procedural, and do not in general constitute substantial demands for economic equality. The fundamentals of international economic relations which it lays down are for the most part a mild enough reiteration of principles already familiar from earlier Assembly resolutions. The rights it asserts are mainly to equal sovereignty for all states over foreign economic activities within their territories, and to equal access to such international economic institutions as exist between states. And equal access means either simply the right to engage in trade, or to join together in associations for the producers of primary products, or to participate in the process of decision-making about world economic matters.

In two senses only does the Charter require something more than mere juridical equality. Thus, in the first place, there is in the idea that the less-developed countries have more rights, while the developed states have more duties — to transfer technology, to give aid and to allow tariff preferences, and generally to take special account of the interests of developing countries — the beginnings of a notion that in international society economic goods must be distributed more evenly.

And secondly, there is in the idea that the states responsible for exploitation and depletion of, or damage to the natural and other resources
of other countries, territories or peoples, should make restitution to
them and fully compensate them,[63] the beginnings of a notion in
international society of a right of redress for economic injury. But
while these concepts of distributive justice, and of justice as compensation for injury,[64] do demonstrate a movement away from mere
juridical equality, they do not signify the arrival of substantial equality:
the former requires only that goods be distributed more evenly (not
necessarily equally); the latter requires compensation that might set
an historical record straight (but not the current record equal). Even in
these weakened senses, and however seriously these principles are
taken in the practice of international politics (and to take but two
examples, the United States does not accept a target level for development assistance of 0.7 per cent of each industrial country's GNP, nor
the notion that commodity prices should be pegged to an index of
world inflation), the idea that they should apply in international
society as well as in domestic society is itself an important one.

In regard to the second direction in which the principle of equality
might be extended involving the admission of institutions beyond the
state, there is little evidence in the Charter of any conception of a cosmopolitan justice that applies to men over the heads of governments.
The Charter is concerned mainly with states, and refers to entities other
than states ('peoples', 'territories') in a language which is used in the
Assembly to refer to the remnants of colonialism. For other men and
institutions waiting in the wings of international society, and making a
case for entry into it on such a basis as, for example, class, the Charter,
as a state's Charter, is no comfort at all. And in the practice of the
United Nations this represents a retreat from the Universal Declaration
of Human Rights, and from the International Convention on Economic,
Social and Cultural Rights, in both of which the individual was himself
a bearer of economic and social rights and duties.

In the matter of human rights, which is the twentieth century expression[65] for those natural rights which, as we saw in the last section, arose
from the importance attached in Western thought to the moral claims of
individuals, there are signs of a return in this century to pre-positivist
conceptions of the place of the individual in international society. Thus
Lauterpacht, in virtue of the recognition of the fundamental rights of
the individual in the Charter of the United Nations, and in other international instruments, argues that he has now been constituted a subject
of international law whose rights and freedoms states have a duty to

observe.[66] The primary difficulty with the assertion of this doctrine
as a tenet of positive law agreed between states and largely observed
by them, as distinct from a natural law which embodies principles that
international society ought to observe but cannot be said yet to have
accepted, is the prospect of its enforcement. For while it is true, as
Lauterpacht says, that this is a difficulty which attaches to international
law in general, and which should not therefore be used to bring down
human rights in particular, it can be said that there is more prospect
of even the smallest state enforcing its rights than there is of the
individual doing so. This is the more true if Article 2(7) of the United
Nations Charter — the clause reserving domestic jurisdiction against
any intrusion by the international organisation except in the case of the
enforcement of peace and security — is taken seriously, as it is by
Lauterpacht, and not regarded as an outworn dogma. And in this
respect, the practice of the United Nations since Lauterpacht wrote
has been to reinforce domestic jurisdiction rather than to give greater
recognition to the individual. Thus, the covenants on human rights
passed by the United Nations General Assembly in 1966, retreating
somewhat from the language of the 1948 Universal Declaration of
Human Rights, envisaged only states petitioning the human rights
committees provided for in them, so that, there being no direct access
for individuals, it was up to a state to take up the cause of an individual
within another state.[67] And if states are to be made thus the guardians
of human rights within each other's territories, any expectations about
their performance in this area have to be measured against their un-
promising record in the area with which the Charter was primarily concerned — that of the maintenance of peace and security in international relations.

Nevertheless, it is the idea that states do have duties in the area of
human rights that has informed the traditional doctrine of humanitarian intervention, so that if a state by its behaviour outrages the
conscience of mankind it should not be entitled to invoke the principle
of non-intervention. Thus it is argued that states had not only a right
but a duty to intervene in order to protect the Jews against Nazi
persecution, and a parallel is drawn and similar conduct urged against
apartheid in present-day South Africa. The problem with this doctrine
lies not in its identification of the evil to be removed, but in the trust
it must place in those who are to act for international society. The
moral case for non-intervention even in the face of outrageous conduct
within the state stems partly from the lack of such trust, and partly
from fear of the consequences of intervention. I shall deal first with the

general defence of a principle of non-intervention against any principle of intervention and then with the argument that there are certain special circumstances which should set it aside.[68]

The moral basis for a principle of non-intervention in international society might be said to arise from a criterion familiar from the account of morality among individuals. Just as persons are to be treated as having ends of their own, and are not to be interfered with so long as they do not themselves interfere with the equal rights of others, so, it can be argued, states as 'associations of individuals with their own common interests and aspirations expressed within a common tradition' are entitled to the same treatment.[69] But this is a general criterion for morality that might be applied to groups such as families, or tribes, or classes, or nations, as well as to individuals and states. The particular moral claim of the state to have the principle of non-intervention attached to it rests not on any intrinsic moral superiority on its part compared to these other groups, but on its potential provision of a framework of order within which justice might be achieved. It is to be defended then, on moral grounds, for what it makes possible rather than for what it is, it being hard to see justice provided for except through the agency of order. It is true that, in any instance, this order might play host to injustice, but the general defence of the state as a platform of order does not fall by reference to particular injustice. For the moral defence of the state to fall, and with it the principle of non-intervention, it would have to be shown that its affront to justice was systematic, and not merely possible.

There is a weak and a strong version of the doctrine that the state is a systematic denier of justice. An advocate of the weak version, by referring to such arbitrary patterns of authority as were imposed on Africa by the colonial powers, might reject any moral claims of the state now succeeded to that authority on the grounds that it was in no way an expression of interests and aspirations within a common tradition. Non-intervention here would be a defence of arbitrariness. An advocate of the strong version, by referring to the structure of dependence that was discussed earlier as a description of world society, might reject any moral claims of the state on the grounds that its territorial jurisdiction was over a hollow shell, emptied of any moral content by a pattern of production designed elsewhere. The principle of non-intervention here stands guard over a void, and in the process turns its back on the real subject for moral concern.

Of the advocate of the weaker version of this doctrine, it might be said that his protest is not against the state as such, but against the boundaries in which it is presently confined. If those boundaries were redrawn to coincide with tribal or national boundaries, his protest might be met, and the doctrine of non-intervention restored to moral respectability. Of the advocate of the stronger version of the doctrine, it might be said that while his protest against the moral shortsightedness of the principle of non-intervention is a persuasive one, it is not one that is accompanied by an equally convincing account of a moral order (as distinct from moral claims) that could make up for this lack. This is a question to which I shall return at the conclusion of this chapter, but the point here is that the moral case for non-intervention relies not on the perfection of the state, but on the absence of any substantial competitor for its role as a community within which morals might be enforced.

In this regard, the presumption against the morality of intervention has two aspects. In the first place, there is reason to doubt the impartiality of the state that intervenes in the internal affairs of another, to question the expectation that it can remove with surgical precision the evil that caused the intervention and then withdraw. And while it may be true that the intervention might realise a moral purpose at the same time as securing some other interest, there is no guarantee of such a coincidence. Secondly, even if impartiality could be guaranteed, intervention is likely to be unwelcome simply because it comes from outside, because it is alien to whatever common culture unites the citizens of the target state. The moral purpose of the intervening state, selfless and beyond reproach according to its own ethical lights, might have a different interpretation in the perspective of the target state: impartial perhaps, but within a partial morality. This lack of a coherent and pervasive morality to transcend international frontiers, of a 'justice constituency' in Julius Stone's phrase,[70] which might then not only inform and justify particular acts of intervention, but also make their success a likely outcome, is an important reason for preferring a principle of non-intervention.

But in such cases as the ones I have mentioned — Nazi Germany and South Africa — and in others which might be included in which the charge of genocide has been made, it might be argued, to insist on the purity of the motives of the intervening state, or to draw attention to the lack of a well-developed common morality, is grotesquely out of place. For here, it might be said, the conscience of mankind is outraged, and there is a justice constituency articulate enough to recognise such glaring cases. But if this is so, then not only do the less worthy consequences of any intervention have to be tolerated along with its good effects (so that, for example, a power might aggrandise itself at the expense of a disagreeable neighbour while intervening on purportedly humanitarian grounds), but also the possibility that the intervention might escalate into a full-scale war adding further moral outrages to the one that led to intervention in the first place.

Even in such cases, then, it may not be grotesque to agree with the 'realists' that the inter-state principle of non-intervention is to be preferred, in a moral scale, to a doctrine of humanitarian intervention based on a more inclusive ethic. And though the cases might not always be as pressing, this choice is a classical one that confronts each generation of statesmen. On the contemporary question of detente and human rights for Soviet citizens (and others), President Carter, without going to the lengths of Senator Jackson's assertion that economic concessions to the Soviet Union should be linked with freer Jewish emigration, has declared a commitment to the rights of individuals which distinguishes him from the previous administration. Dr Kissinger's view to the contrary was that making an international issue of something that the Soviet Union regarded as a domestic matter was not only unlikely to succeed, but would also place at risk the structure of peace under construction in areas that did not trouble the Soviet Union domestically. Kissinger's argument for non-intervention was not one that, in his view, surrendered morality to interests, but one that subordinated what was judged to be the lesser moral claim to the greater. There was not perhaps a 'conspiracy of silence' about the rights of Soviet Jews, but these were not to direct the course of relations between the superpowers.

But such a choice need not empty the notion of human rights of any meaning, nor need it indicate the adoption towards them of the scornful attitude of Bentham. The language of human rights, as Maurice Cranston has said, provides some form in which a person can convey that a wrong is being done to him, and that something he ought to have is being denied him.[71] Moral claims that make use of this language are heard in world politics, and their hearing might assist in the building of a transnational justice constituency which might then improve conduct within states by a means more civilised and dependable than intervention.

Involved in each of the issues just dealt with is a disagreement about frameworks for morality. The argument for non-intervention chooses the framework of the society of states, while the case for humanitarian intervention, asserting human rights that states have a duty to observe, derives from the framework of the individual. The argument that the doctrine of the equality of states should apply to economic matters arises within the framework of the society of states, but borrows from the structural dependence model of world society insofar as it asserts a duty on the part of colonialists and neocolonialists to redress past and present injuries. And when the argument for equality is pressed on behalf of individuals — a reasonable outcome of the choice of that framework — it is one that must abandon altogether the 'society of states', and come to grips with the hierarchical account of world society. The debate between realists and idealists, in each of the dimensions discussed, is a disagreement between those who accept the framework of the state, and the society of states, and attempt to work within it, and those making no such concession, who would pull international society towards one or another conception of world society.

This chapter has found more to say in defence of the conventions of diplomacy than its search for a universal morality might have suggested. This is not because of their manifest moral superiority to claims that arise from the hierarchic account of world society, discussed above, or to claims that derive from our common responsibility as travellers on 'spaceship earth', or to any claim that originates outside the society of states, but because they provide a framework of order within which moral claims might be met, and not merely a vocabulary in which they might be articulated. The claim of a peripheral, exploited class in the third or fourth worlds for recompense for injuries received at the hands of central, imperialist powers derives from a hierarchic description of world society, and it might be part of a moral case that is undeniable. The ecologists' case for 'central guidance' might be equally convincing. And there are other claims. But these claims are not matched by a constituency in which they might be met. It may be true that they derive from, in some sense, the reality of world society, but there is no community in which they can be weighed and disposed of. Instead, claims are lodged in the society of states. Their reception there has not been tumultuous, for they present maximalist demands to a society which has been unresponsive to minimalist ones. But the argument here is that there is nowhere else to go: the conventions of international society are accepted because of the absence of any alternative. And this is the difficulty with the assertion that 'the state-centred image of the world has lost its normative relevance because of the rise of global economic interdependence'.[72] It may or may not be true to say that the factual basis for a society of states is being eroded, but this society remains 'normatively relevant' so long as the justice constituency which exists in virtue of a *sense* of community is more visible within state frontiers than across them. Indeed, with reference to the notion of a trans-state hierarchy, it may be that the state-centred image of the world is to be defended as a normatively relevant means of challenging it, since it is arguably the state aiming at self-reliance and self-sufficiency that can detach itself from a structure of dependence. It is in this regard that the case of China is celebrated.

These words on behalf of the states system and the diplomatic conventions that sustain it do nothing to save the notion of a universal morality, and the argument is not yet distinguishable from Bruce Miller's 'rationalised interests'. One way of dignifying international, or strictly interstate, morality that has been noted more than once in this chapter is to find in it, with Morgenthau and Kissinger, not merely an alternative moral framework, but a superior one, so that a conception of right which takes reality into account is to be preferred to one that insists on certain courses of action regardless of circumstance. The difficulty with this view is that in making realism the touchstone of what is moral, or of what is morally superior, it allows the content of morality to be determined by the convenience of princes, for it is they who, in marking out the boundaries of political possibility, determine what is realistic. Rules arrived at in this way might be prudential but never moral except by accident, since unless conceptions of morality put forward a view of what is right universally, independent of any particular interest or convenience, it is a mistake to think of them as moral conceptions at all.[73] In this sense, universality is implicit in morality, and the expression 'universal morality' is a tautology, albeit a helpful one in unseating the idea of morality as rationalised interests. In another sense, as was seen above, universal morality, a universal moral order, is a term that describes not the nature of moral concepts, but a particular moral order among others, the framework for morality which encompasses the globe and has the great society of mankind as its constituency. In Western thought a principal support for this framework has been natural law, whose strength in turn derives from its appeal to what by nature is common to all men as distinct from the artificial obligations of states which divide them. Rules of right reason which apply to men as men set a universal standard against which all working moral orders are measured and their shortcomings noted. The positive side of this relationship is that at the same time as being an index of failure, natural law is a wellspring of ideas for international improvement so that, for example, the moral issues considered in this paper — idealism, equality, and human rights — each derive from the inspiration of natural law. The power of natural law is as a source of right, and of interstate morality as a record of what has been achieved. There is no good reason to reduce morality in international politics to the latter.

Notes

1. J.D.B. Miller, 'Morality, Interests and Rationalisation' in this volume.
2. Plato, *The Republic,* Book 1, Ch. III.
3. Ibid., Book 1, Ch. IV.
4. Bruce Miller concedes more than this when he defends statesmen against the charge of hypocrisy, and allows their sincerity in invoking a morality beyond the nation for policies that in fact derive from a national morality.
5. Bernard Williams, *Morality: An Introduction to Ethics* (Harmondsworth, 1973), pp. 34-9. I should draw attention here to a possible confusion between universalisation as application to all members of a particular class (citizens of Rome), and universalisation as application to all members of the human race (citizens of the world). That Williams means the latter and not the (relativist) former is clear from his remark that morality involves internalised norms that 'cannot merely evaporate because one is confronted with human beings in another society', ibid., p. 37.
6. See, e.g., C.H. Waddington, *The Ethical Animal* (London, 1960), *passim.* I return to naturalism vs. positivism in Part II below.
7. For Marx as a moralist in the tradition of natural law, see Paul E. Sigmund, *Natural Law in Political Thought* (Cambridge, Mass., 1971), pp. 165-6. For a trenchant denial of this view, see Allen W. Wood, 'The Marxian critique of Justice', *Philosophy and Public Affairs,* vol. 1, no. 3 (Spring 1972).
8. *The Republic,* Book II, Ch. VI.
9. *The Politics,* Iii; The *Nicomachean Ethics,* Iii.
10. See George H. Sabine, *A History of Political Theory,* 3rd edn (London, 1948), p. 60, who notes the absence in Plato of the modern notion of right.
11. *The Nicomachean Ethics,* Viii and Viv.
12. *The Politics,* IIIxii and IIIxiii.
13. I should add here that while the *polis* might have been the primary moral constituency in Greek thought, it was not the final one. Maurice Cranston begins his discussion of the history of human rights with Antigone's defiance of Creon's edict that her brother Polynices should remain unburied on the battlefield because he had fought traitorously against his own city. See *What are Human Rights?* (London, 1973), pp. 9-10. Antigone's forum is one of conscience not enclosed by the state.
14. Bertrand Russell, *History of Western Philosophy,* 2nd edn (London, 1961), p. 240. I shall return later to the distinction between individual and collectivist ethics.
15. *City of God,* Book V, Ch. 17.
16. Russell, *History of Western Philosophy,* p. 329; Hannah Arendt, *The Human Condition* (Chicago, 1958), p. 60.
17. The worldly consequence of this doctrine was, however, the failure to translate equality for slaves in the early church into an improvement in their civil status, and as Reinhold Niebuhr says, to this day the churches pride themselves on being able to transcend economic and social inequalities within their walls without it following that they should move vigorously against them. *Moral*

Man and Immoral Society (New York, 1948), pp. 77-8.

18. This is Nietzsche's phrase, but I do not meant it here in his sense. His objection to Christian morality was that its doctrine of equality before God pulled down the worthy to the level of the worthless, and prevented thereby the noble and artistic from 'fashioning man'. Slave morality was the triumph of the worthless. See *Beyond Good and Evil*, trans. Helen Zimmern (Edinburgh and London, 1909), pp. 84, 117, 227-32. The attack on Christian worldlessness that I have in mind in using the phrase 'slave morality' is the one to which I have already drawn attention — that equality stopped at the church door: slave morality as the continued oppression of the humble not their triumph.

19. Russell, *History of Western Philosophy*, p. 190.

20. By A.P. d'Entrèves, *Natural Law,* 2nd edn (London, 1970), Ch. 3, on which the following discussion of Aquinas is based.

21. Harold J. Laski, *A Defence of Liberty Against Tyrants*, (London, 1924), introduction, p. 2.

22. Ibid., p. 23.

23. Ibid., p. 27.

24. *De Jure Belli ad Pacis*, Prolegomena, para. 11.

25. *The Rights of Man,* Everyman edition, pp. 42-3. And just as Paine shows thus his emancipation from Christian dogma, so in a different way does the tract against which his was a protest. In founding society on human wants, and on interdependence, rather than on individual rights, and in preserving the differences of degree which Paine made a unity, Burke inclined more closely to the Greek account of society than to one that was dependent on a Christian view of the relations of individuals. See *Reflections on The Revolution in France*, in E.J. Payne (ed.), *Burke: Select Works*, vol. II (Oxford, 1898), pp.70-71.

26. 'The Christian', says Herbert Butterfield, 'is particularly called to carry his thinking outside that framework which a nation or a political party or a social system or an accepted regime or a mundane ideology provides.' *Christianity, Diplomacy and War* (London, 1953), p. 4.

27. This is a recurring defence of natural law in d'Entrèves, *Natural Law.*

28. Nor is this a primitive doctrine of old-fashioned 'Machiavellism'. Hans J. Morgenthau, though this is not a view he holds consistently, does declare that 'the reference to a moral rule of conduct requires an individual conscience from which it emanates, and there is no individual conscience from which what we call the international morality of Great Britain or of any other nation could emanate'. *Politics Among Nations,* 4th edn (New York, 1967), p. 240. E.H. Carr's answer to this point of view is that the attribution of personality to the state, so that it might be thought of as subject to moral rules, is a necessary fiction in international society, just as the notion of the corporate responsibility of a joint stock company is a fiction necessary to municipal law. *The Twenty Years' Crisis,* 2nd edn (London, 1946), pp. 148-9.

29. See *Leviathan,* Ch. XIII, and Hedley Bull, 'Society and Anarchy in International Relations', in Butterfield and Wight, *Diplomatic Investigations,* pp. 45-8.

30. It is this moral offensiveness, or so it seems to me, that renders somewhat out of place the liking among some English writers for the cosy simile of the club in describing this aspect of international society. Thus Butterfield: 'It was certainly true that, though the international order [after the Treaty of Utrecht] performed its function, aggression was not eliminated, and the nations still often came into conflict with one another. But it was as though the members of the international club were competing for the best armchairs, or the best service at dinner — jockeying one another, shall we say, to obtain the best room in the house . . .' *Christianity, Diplomacy and War*, p. 81.

31. See Niebuhr, *Moral Man and Immoral Society,* pp. xi-xii.

32. 'The Mainsprings of American Foreign Policy: The National Interest vs. Moral Abstractions', *American Political Science Review*, vol. XLIV, no. 4, (December 1950), pp. 853-4. I return to this argument in Part II, and in the conclusion.

33. I say most rather than all, for the assertion of a principle of non-intervention is itself a moral claim as I shall argue in the next section of the paper.

34. 'Order vs. Justice in International Society', *Political Studies*, vol. XIX, no. 3 (September 1971), p. 275.

35. This is true even though a new entrant, having made a claim of this kind in order to gain admission, might want to revert to the old principles once successful. I have in mind the group that would be a state basing its claim to such status on the principle of national self-determination, but then having become a state, insisting on the principle of state sovereignty to deter further disintegration.

36. See Wood, 'The Marxian Critique of Justice', *Philosophy and Public Affairs* (Spring 1972), pp. 251-5.

37. See Harry Magdoff, 'Imperialism: A Historical Survey', *Monthly Review*, vol. 24, no. 1 (May 1972), pp. 4 and 12.

38. See Charles L. Beitz, 'Justice and International Relations', *Philosophy and Public Affairs*, vol. 4, no. 4 (Summer 1975), p. 374. Though Beitz does not deal with this aspect of it, the argument for world justice to accommodate transnational relations involves a judgement about their importance compared to inter-state relations, as well as the mere observation that they exist (or have expanded) and are norm-creating. As Raymond Aron has said, transnational relations have been regulated in all periods by custom, or convention, or by a specific code. The question, as Aron puts it, is one between public and private international law – whether in, for example, contemporary international politics, the heterogeneous inter-state system divides transnational society. *Peace and War* (London, 1966), p. 106.

39. See George Modelski's layer-cake model of it in *Principles of World Politics* (New York, 1972), Ch. 13.

40. One thinks here of the use of the domestic analogy in international relations, asserting that what is required for the establishment of a world political society is the same single sovereign that was established within the state. A modern version of this doctrine asserting the need for a 'central guidance mechanism' is Richard A. Falk, *A Study of Future Worlds* (New York, 1975), Ch. 4.

41. (London, 1972).

42. Rawls says that his aim is to generalise and carry to a higher level of abstraction the familiar theory of the social contract as found in Locke, Rousseau and Kant, *Theory of Justice*, p. 11. It is the difficulty of applying this 'familiar theory' to non-Western societies in which it is not familiar, in my view, that those who argue for the global application of Rawls's principles of justice have failed adequately to confront. Thus Beitz, for example, notices that different principles may be appropriate for different societies, but does not give this the central place in his analysis that it seems to me to require, 'Justice and International Relations', p. 377, note 24.

43. I am not here making the silly point that two of the moral frameworks are for individuals, and the other two are for societies, for morality is a notion that presupposes society. Nobody, as Marx said, seen in his isolation produces values, and nobody, as Hannah Arendt adds, in his isolation cares about them – things, or ideas, or moral ideals 'become values only in their social relationship'. Arendt, *The Human Condition*, p. 165.

44. Rawls, *Theory of Justice*, p. 31.

45. Laski, *A Defence of Liberty Against Tyrants*, p. 27.

46. See *Thucydides,* Jowett's translation (Oxford, 1881), vol. I, pp. 398-407, from which the quotations following are taken.

47. As in H.L.A. Hart's 'minimum content of Natural Law' derived from his truisms about human nature. See *The Concept of Law* (Oxford, 1961), pp. 186-95.

48. These three form the structure of d'Entrèves, *Natural Law.*

49. See Graham Evans, 'Some Problems with a History of Thought in International Relations', *International Relations,* vol. IV, no. 6, November 1974.

50. Thus, for example, E.H. Carr's realism did not prevent him from defending the idea of an international morality.

51. Shklar, *Legalism, passim.*

52. Bull, 'The Theory of International Politics 1919-1969', in Brian Porter (ed.), *The Aberystwyth Papers* (London, 1972), p. 37.

53. See, e.g. Falk, *What's Wrong with Henry Kissinger's Foreign Policy?,* Policy Memo. No. 39, Center of International Studies, Princeton University (July, 1974).

54. Falk, 'The Domains of Law and Justice', *International Journal,* vol. XXXI, no. 1 (Winter 1975-6), p. 5.

55. Stanley Hoffmann, 'Choices' *Foreign Policy,* no. 12 (Fall, 1973), p. 7.

56. Falk, 'The Domains of Law and Justice', pp. 6-9.

57. Falk, *A Study of Future Worlds,* Ch. 1. A decade or so earlier, and in another context (that of the problem of civil war), Falk wrote that 'a contemporary Machiavelli perceiving the novel necessity for a community of mankind, might be dismissed by the best minds as recklessly utopian'. 'The International Law of Internal War', in *Legal Order in a Violent World* (Princeton, 1968), pp. 114-15.

58. Christian Wolff, *Ius Gentium Methodo Scientifica Pertractatum,* 1764, trans. J.H. Drake, 1934, rept. (New York, 1964), Prolegomena, para. 16.

59. E. de Vattel, *The Law of Nations or the Principles of Natural Law,* 1758, trans. Charles E. Fenwick (Washington, 1916), Preface, p. 7a.

60. See E.D. Dickinson, *The Equality of States in International Law* (Cambridge, Mass., 1920), pp. 4-5.

61. J.L. Brierly, *The Law of Nations,* 6th edn, C.H.M. Waldock (ed.) (Oxford, 1963), pp. 132-3.

62. David Thomson, *Equality* (Cambridge, 1949), p. 147.

63. Article 16.

64. And with these concepts we are back to Aristotle. For their relationship with the idea of equality see Hart, *The Concept of Law,* Ch. VIII.

65. See Maurice Cranston, *What are Human Rights?,* p. 1.

66. H. Lauterpacht, *International Law and Human Rights* (London, 1950), pp. 4, 33 and 147-54.

67. As Maurice Cranston says: 'There is indeed something deeply absurd in an arrangement by which something so personal and individual as the rights of man should be settled in committees to which only governments have access; it is a situation worthy of Lewis Carroll.' *What are Human Rights?,* p. 81.

68. The outline of the argument here is borrowed from my *Nonintervention and International Order* (Princeton, 1974), Ch. 9.

69. S.I. Benn and R.S. Peters, *Social Principles and the Democratic State* (London, 1959), pp. 361-2.

70. 'Approaches to the Notion of International Justice', in Richard A. Falk and Cyril E. Black (eds.), *The Future of the International Legal Order,* vol. I, *Trends and Patterns* (Princeton, 1969), pp. 425-6.

71. *What are Human Rights?,* pp. 15-16.

72. Beitz, 'Justice and International Relations', *Philosophy and Public Affairs* (Summer, 1975), p. 383.

73. For an exposition of the logic of moral argument in the context of International Relations, see Hidemi Suganami, 'Why Ought Treaties to be Kept?', forthcoming in the *Year Book of World Affairs.*

4 HUMAN RIGHTS AND WORLD POLITICS
Hedley Bull

My purpose in this essay is to raise three questions:

(1) What are human rights, and what place has been and can be occupied by attempts to recognise or to realise them within international politics?

(2) What are the special issues raised by the debate about human rights at the present time, in the context of the international politics of the 1970s?

(3) What, broadly, should we do about human rights? Are there any human rights, and if there are, what steps can be taken, at what risk to other objectives that may be regarded as desirable, to promote them?

Human Rights

Human rights are rights attaching to human beings as such, rather than to this or that class of human beings. They are thought to be enjoyed by all human beings, to be enjoyed by human beings only and to be enjoyed by them equally. The notion that someone has a right, in my view, generally implies that someone else has a duty, and vice versa (although we may note in passing, without pursuing the issue, that this is sometimes disputed). The notions both of a right and of a duty pre-suppose the notion of a rule. Thus if there are rights belonging to human beings as such, so also are there duties.

When we say that a man or woman has a right to freedom from arbitrary arrest or to security of employment or to racial equality we mean that he or she should be able to enjoy these things not as a favour bestowed or privilege extended, but as entitlements conferred by a valid rule. When we say that such rights are human rights we mean that persons are entitled to these things by virtue of being human beings, that there is a valid rule which establishes such entitlements for the class of human beings as a whole. Such rules, however, may be of different sorts.

Sometimes what we mean is that there are *moral* rights enjoyed by all human beings: that whether or not human beings are accorded these rights by positive legal instruments, and whether or not they actually enjoy freedom from arbitrary arrest, security of employment or racial

79

equality, they are morally entitled to them. One form of this view is the doctrine of 'natural rights', such as that formulated by Locke and reflected in the American Declaration of Independence, the French Declaration of the Rights of Man and of the Citizen and similar documents. It is possible to embrace a form of natural law position that recognises 'natural rights' without subscribing to the whole package of doctrines which were put forward on the subject by Locke and his school, for example that these 'natural rights' are self-evident (or evident in the light of reason and revelation), that they derive from a pre-contractual state of nature, that they are inalienable, that they include rights of property the protection of which is the proper end of government, and that they provide the basis of a right of revolution. Moreover, it is possible to maintain that there are moral rights attaching to all human beings while at the same time rejecting any belief in 'natural rights' or, more broadly, in natural law at all. Nevertheless, the doctrine that there are human rights in a moral sense, and the doctrine that there are 'natural rights', are hard to separate. For the core of what is meant by those who contend that certain rights are 'natural' is that they are inherent in the nature of human beings, more particularly in their 'rational' nature. And those who hold that there are human rights of a moral kind are generally found to adopt the position not merely that all human beings have these rights, but that these rights are an essential part of men's and women's humanity, that is, of their 'nature'.

Sometimes, however, when we speak of human rights, we are referring to *legal* rights that are incorporated in some system of positive law, domestic or international. Domestic legal instruments, such as constitutions, basic laws or bills of rights, seek to establish merely that certain legal rights are enjoyed by the citizens or subjects of the countries concerned. However, in some cases – for example, the 1949 Basic Law of the German Federal Republic, or the Canadian Bill of Rights of 1960 – they refer to 'human rights', just as the American Declaration of 1776 and the French Declaration of 1789 referred to 'natural rights'. But even where – as in the case, for example, of the British Bill of Rights of 1688 or the United States Bill of Rights of 1791 – no reference is made to rights other than those of citizens of the countries concerned, these may be interpreted as efforts to give local effect to rights believed to be valid for human beings at large. In the case of international legal instruments, which we shall examine below, particularly those which have a universal import, the concern is to establish particular human rights as part of positive international law.[1]

It is important to recognise that neither when we are talking about

the moral rights to which human beings as such are entitled, nor when
we are referring to legal rights proclaimed in some constitution or
international convention are we necessarily talking about rights that are
actually implemented and enforced. The fact that rights of freedom of
thought are proclaimed in the Constitution of the USSR of 1936 and
in the International Covenant on Civil and Political Rights of 1966 is
no more evidence that citizens of the Soviet Union actually enjoy
rights of that kind than is any belief we may have that since citizens
of the Soviet Union are human beings they are morally entitled to
them. Alongside human rights in the moral sense and in the legal sense
we need to recognise a third category, rights in the *empirical* sense,
rights that we know from experience and observation to be observed
and implemented. It is worth noting, incidentally, that just as human
rights in the first sense fall within the province of moral philosophy,
and human rights in the second sense come within the scope of constitutional and international law, human rights in the empirical sense are
now the subject of detailed studies that belong to political science or
sociology rather than to philosophy or to law, of 'human rights conditions' in various countries. While studies of this sort have long been
undertaken by organisations such as Amnesty, the recent American
human rights initiatives (dating from before the Carter administration,
but much stimulated by it) have had as one of their by-products a
burgeoning of highly professional, academic studies of this kind, dealing
not with particular violations of human rights, but with the record of
countries in relation to a comprehensive array of human rights over a
period of time.

Before we leave the subject of the meaning of human rights there is
a further matter to which we must allude, because it will dog our path
later. Human rights are enjoyed by human beings: but do they enjoy
them only individually, or can they also be enjoyed collectively? Our
Western conceptions of human rights, like the seventeenth- and
eighteenth-century ideas of natural rights from which they derive, are
deeply impregnated with the political philosophy of individualism: the
rights of which we speak are above all rights possessed by human beings
as individuals, and are intended to limit the rights of society or the
state. But, of course, even the American Declaration of Independence
and the French Declaration of the Rights of Man and of the Citizen
refer to the rights of peoples, as well as to those of individuals. Behind
the French Revolution stood the Janus-like figure of Rousseau, who spoke
not only of men who were born free but also of a general will that was itself
a moral person and that expressed the will of all. The German Romantic
theory of *Volksgeist* and *Volksrecht* asserted the rights of the nation

to unity and liberty but in the same breath asserted the primacy of these rights over those of the individuals of whom the nation was composed. Many of the international declarations and conventions that are taken to convey the content of human rights as they are understood today deal with the rights of groups rather than individuals – nations, racial, ethnic or religious groups, labour organisations and even states. Nor can there be any appeal to the tradition of natural law thinking before the Enlightenment to substantiate the idea that human or natural rights concern only the rights of individuals; this tradition is much concerned with the rights and duties of groups and corporations, so much so that its chronicler Gierke was able to treat it in terms of the history of the right of fellowship, *Das Deutsche Genossenschaftsrecht.*[2]

It is possible to regard the rights of groups as deriving from the rights of individuals, as Locke saw the rights of government as deriving from the consent of the governed, and as J.S. Mill or Woodrow Wilson saw the right of a nation to self-determination as founded upon the rights of individual members of that nation to representative or democratic government. But this is emphatically not how the rights of oppressed nations, states and classes are conceived by some of those who believe that the latter is the core of what is meant by human rights today.

Modern international society has provided – and, I think, continues to provide – a framework of international politics that is basically inhospitable to the idea of human rights, or at least to the idea that they should be internationally recognised and protected. This is most clear if we consider the European states system in its mature period, from the time of Vattel until that of World War I. According to the legal norms which then prevailed states alone were subjects of international law, while individuals and groups other than states were mere objects of it. That is to say, states could enter into agreements that concerned individuals and non-state groups (as they did, for example, in relation to extradition or political asylum or the suppression of piracy) but individuals and non-state groups were not themselves directly the bearers of rights and duties in international law.

International society was a society whose members – or at least whose direct and immediate members – were states; individual persons and groups other than states participated in it only indirectly, through the relationship in which they stood to states. The foundation of this society of states was their mutual recognition of one another's sovereign jurisdiction, and a corollary of this was their acceptance of the obligation not to interfere in one another's internal affairs. In an international society of this sort, which treats the maintenance of order among states as the highest value, the very idea of human or natural rights (like the idea of human or natural duties) is potentially disruptive. For if human rights come to assume not merely a moral but a legal form, and if it comes to be held that one state can interfere within the sovereign jurisdiction of another to uphold the human rights of its citizens, the basic rules of the society may be undermined.

It is true that in the nineteenth and early twentieth centuries appeal was sometimes made to a right of 'humanitarian intervention', for which one could cite the authority of Grotius and other natural law thinkers who wrote at a time when the states system had not yet reached its maturity, and normative conceptions bearing upon international relations were still deeply marked by the legacy of the Christian republic. Such a right was treated as part of positive international law by many European and American authorities; it was said to have been exercised, for example, by Britain, France and Russia when intervening in Turkey on behalf of the Greek insurrection in 1827; by France, authorised by the European Concert and Turkey, in her intervention in Syria on behalf of the Maronite Christians in 1860; and by the United States in Cuba in 1898. Leaving aside the question how far considerations of the protection of human rights actually motivated these and other purported examples of 'humanitarian intervention', we may note that the latter provide some clue as to the conditions under which, in a system of legal rules concerned essentially with the preservation of order among states, a crack may be left in the door through which some element of concern for the protection of human rights can creep. One condition is that the state intervening to uphold human rights should be acting not unilaterally, but with the agreement of the society of states as a whole, or at least of the great powers. If intervention to promote human rights proceeds on the basis of a consensus in favour of it among the society of states as a whole, then we may imagine that the intervention can take place without endangering international order. The other condition is that the political entity being intervened against should be a weak state, an entity whose credentials as a state are uncertain, or — better still — not a state at all. The promotion of human rights was, of course, a cardinal justification of European expansion and imperial government. The classic examples of purported 'humanitarian intervention' in the nineteenth century — the interventions endorsed by the European Concert to protect the Christian subjects of the Ottoman Empire — met both these conditions.

The international society that has evolved since 1919 seems at first sight much less inhospitable to recognition and protection of human rights. Beginning with the attempts in the League of Nations period to set standards in such fields as minority rights, forced labour and the responsibilities of Mandatory powers, and rising to a flood in the period of the United Nations, there has been a great development of general treaties, declarations or resolutions of international bodies and adjudications that set standards of human rights in international law. At the centre of this development is the work done or sponsored by the United Nations itself: the provisions of the Charter relating to human rights, the Universal Declaration of Human Rights of 1948; the two Covenants of 1966 — one on Economic, Social and Cultural Rights, the other on Civil and Political Rights; the Convention on the Prevention and Punishment of the Crime of Genocide of 1948; the Declaration on the Granting of Independence to Colonial Countries and Peoples of 1960; and conventions dealing, among other things, with slavery, refugees, stateless persons, women, religious intolerance and racial discrimination. To this one has to add the declarations and conventions of the ILO and UNESCO, the Council of Europe, the Organisation of American States and the Organisation of African Unity.

What is perhaps more impressive than this multiplication of legal or quasi-legal obligations entered into by states with regard to human rights is the evidence that has accumulated that individual persons and groups other than states are now thought to be subjects, and not merely objects, of international law. The Nuremberg and Tokyo international military tribunals witnessed the charging of individual persons with 'war crimes' and 'crimes against the peace'. The machinery developed to implement the European Convention for the Protection of Human Rights and Fundamental Freedoms affords an individual person the right of access to an international court. Non-governmental organisiations now have various kinds of access to international organisations, and enjoy various kinds of international status or recognition as participants in the international political process. Western expositions of international law now often proclaim the arrival of a world society, whose members include individuals and non-state groups, that has replaced the former society of states. Soviet international legal authorities, while they are more conservative in their attitude to the states system, argue that nations are subjects of international law as well as states.

But are these developments evidence of the majestic progress of the prevailing norms of world politics 'from international law to world law', the birth-pangs of a world society or community that is replacing the society of states? We have to note that the legal standing of many of the declarations and resolutions in which standards of human rights are proclaimed, is in dispute. With the important exception of the European Convention, the instruments that have been developed are without effective procedures for implementation and enforcement. There is a great gap between the standards proclaimed and actual 'human rights conditions' in various parts of the world (a gap made more apparent by the great increase that has taken place in our awareness of the latter). It is clear that despite the 'convergence' of values with regard to human rights that one might infer from the proliferation of treaties and declarations (and the arguments for the general similarity of the main principles of human legal systems put forward by C. Wilfred Jenks in *The Common Law of Mankind*) there are divergences of the most fundamental kind as to what these values are.[3] We have to note that human rights standards in international law, for whatever they are worth, rest chiefly on treaties entered into by sovereign states; claims that they express not the consent of states, but 'the general will of the world community', are an aspiration rather than a description of actual trends. Human rights, conceived as legal rather than moral rights, and accompanied by effective procedures for implementation and enforcement, might be expected to gain a firm foothold in a developing world society or cosmopolis. In a society of states, as Kant argued in *Perpetual Peace,* cosmopolitical law can find only a limited expression.[4] The society of states which provides international political life today with its uncertain foundation shows more signs of disintegration than of increasing integration, at all events if we consider it globally rather than regionally; and present contention about human rights, to which I shall now turn, is one of these signs.

There is a certain tendency in the Western countries to believe that human rights are valued and enjoyed only or chiefly in these countries, that the Western countries are the custodians of human rights in the world today, and that the human rights problem is essentially the problem of how the Western countries are to use their influence to bring the Socialist countries and the countries of the Third World into line on this matter. Indeed, one can say — particularly, although not exclusively, with regard to the United States — that the public appeal of human rights as an objective of foreign policy derives in large measure from this belief that the guardianship of human rights in the world as a whole is the special vocation of the Western countries. It helps to restore our flagging conviction of our own virtue, and at the same time enables us to give vent to long-pent-up feelings of frustration and aggression towards our critics in other parts of the world. I think it is perfectly possible that this belief is quite correct, but it does depend on a very particular view of what human rights are, and it neglects to recognise that beliefs about human rights, in one sense or another, are deeply and passionately held in all parts of the world community today.

The Western peoples are inclined to think of human rights principally in terms of the civil and political rights of individuals. They are the countries in which these rights were first achieved (although here one has to recognise that 'Western' is a loose and shifting term, and that the experience of the Anglo-Saxon democracies and France is radically different from that of Germany and again from that of the countries of southern Europe). They correctly believe that they are the countries where these rights are best enjoyed. It is true that since the 1940s they have given increasing attention to economic, social and cultural rights, but they see these rights as a broadening and filling out of civil and political rights previously established. In their experience the civil and political rights were established first; the advances achieved in economic, social and cultural fields took place without serious infringement of civil and political rights, and indeed as a consequence of their exercise. Rights to economic security, to racial equality, or to education are seen as having been established through, and as dependent for their continuance upon, rights of freedom from arbitrary arrest, of freedom of speech and political association.

It is true also that the Western countries recognise not only the rights of individuals but also the collective rights of peoples or nations. The idea of the rights of nations to self-determination is part of the Western moral legacy in terms of which the rest of the world formulates its demands. But an important theme in the Western complex of attitudes to national self-determination (it has to be admitted that there is a counter-theme: here one must set the Founding Fathers, Mazzini and Wilson against Herder and Hegel) is that the right of a nation to become a state is an expression of the right of a people democratically to choose its government.

For the Soviet Union and the socialist countries, or at least for their rulers, human rights are seen primarily in terms of economic, social and cultural rights. They believe that the reality of economic and social security and well being is available to their citizens, and there is truth in their claim, at least in relation to some of the indices, that their citizens are better provided for in these respects than those in Western countries. Civil and political rights that are not built upon economic and social foundations they regard as the sham of the bourgeois democracies. The Soviet Union and the east European countries apart from Czechoslovakia have had little experience of civil and political rights as these are understood in the West, and the economic and social gains that they believe themselves to have made were achieved through a ruthless suppression of those whose civil and political rights stood in their way, which they believe to have been entirely necessary and thoroughly justified by its results, even if they now acknowledge that excesses took place in the Stalin era.

It is true that in their domestic constitutions and in the international undertakings into which they have entered they commit themselves to the maintenance of civil and political rights. But they do not see either these, or the economic, social and cultural rights to which they attach such prominence, as limiting the powers of government. To preserve the gains of the revolution, and continue its forward march, what is necessary is that the working class through its agent, the communist party, should keep a firm grip on the helm of the ship of state, and to concede individual rights that would be used by the enemies of the working class to loosen this grip would be a betrayal of the revolution.

For the countries of the Third World the human rights that are important are collective rights -- of subject peoples to be liberated from colonialism, subject states from neo-colonialism and subject races from white domination. National liberation is a moral imperative that does not presuppose readiness for self-government in a Western sense, or depend for its validity upon a plebiscitary act of choice. The liberation of formally independent states from the economic subjection of neo-colonialism depends not upon standards of minimum welfare or economic justice applied within poor countries or to the world as a whole, but on a redistribution of wealth, and along with it a redistribution of power, as between rich states and poor, a 'Charter of the Economic Rights and Duties of States' in which the rights of individuals receive no mention, and the duties are imposed only upon the rich states and the rights conceded only to the poor. Racial equality is above all a demand for the liberation of coloured peoples from subjection to white rule in southern Africa and elsewhere.

The Third World ideology embraces a great variety of political doctrines and attitudes, and we cannot find within it any uniform hostility or indifference towards the civil and political or the economic and social rights of individuals. In some Third World countries, and above all in India, the governing elites are deeply affected by a regard for human rights in a Western sense. The common platform of the Third World coalition, however, is that collective rights have priority: without liberation from colonial, neo-colonial and white supremacist domination, the rights of individuals can have no meaning. To those who argue that freedom from colonial rule has led not to an increase but to a decline in respect for civil and political rights, that transfer of wealth from rich countries to poor has merely benefited the rich in the poor countries at the expense of the poor in the rich, or that the economic conditions of blacks in South Africa are the best in the African continent, it can be replied that racial and national dignity represent a more vital human right than any of these things, even if those who have always taken them for granted find this hard to grasp.

It would be wrong to conclude from this very simplified account of the differences in conceptions of human rights which mark the current debate that no common ground exists among them at all. There are certain elementary rules — touching, for example, restrictions on violence, the protection of property and the keeping of promises, and much celebrated by the philosophers — that all societies do in fact endorse.[5] President Carter has been at some pains to show that his policies in this area have been directed not towards bringing other countries to emulate American or Western institutions, but rather towards promoting the observance of what are called 'basic' human rights. Torture, cruel or degrading treatment, and denial of a fair trial are sometimes mentioned as examples of infringements of such 'basic' human rights, and it is true, as United States spokesmen are wont to say, that there is 'nothing parochial' about the insistence that such practices are wrong, however widespread they may be. It is also notable that President Carter has sought to found his policies not upon any uniquely American or Western doctrines about human rights, but on treaties and declarations — the Universal Declaration of Human Rights, the American (that is, the Inter-American) Declaration of the Rights and Duties of Man, the Helsinki Accords — to which the countries he admonishes are parties.

However, these treaties and declarations mask the extent to which the main groups of states in the world are divided on the human rights issue, not merely over the tactics of it or through reluctance to have the bone pointed at themselves but over basic matters of principle. President Carter may have made a correct observation when he said to the UN

General Assembly in April 1977 that 'the basic thrust of human affairs points towards a more universal demand for basic human rights', if by this he meant that the sort of restlessness and turbulence, and striving after new forms of political self-expression that since the eighteenth century have characterised the history of Europe and America, now characterise the world as a whole. But there is no reason to assume that the result of this process will be that other parts of the world will move closer to the social and political practices of the Western countries, rather than further away from them.

The discussion of President Carter's human rights policy has tended to concern only the issues of its cost and its effectiveness. Does the attempt to promote human rights in the Soviet Union involve too high a price in terms of political detente or co-operation in arms control? Does it actually have the effect of advancing the enjoyment of human rights by Soviet citizens, or of retarding it? These questions do not go to the heart of the matter. The basic question that we need to ask is: do human rights of a moral kind exist at all?

In the sense of rights established by some *a priori* moral rule that can be shown to be objectively valid, there are no human rights. Not only is it not self-evident that men are born free and entitled to life, liberty and the pursuit of happiness: these are propositions for which there is no foundation whatever. There is no way of showing that human or any other rights or duties somehow exist objectively in the nature of things rather than in our own attitudes and preferences.

If our conceptions of human rights are rooted not, as the eighteenth-century declarations proclaimed, in the nature of things but only in our own attitudes and preferences this does not mean that our choice of them is capricious or arbitrary. The moral attitudes we take up are the authentic expression of the ways of life we lead, and reflect our own history and character. Because different societies and individuals lead different ways of life and have different histories, disagreement about moral values is a natural and inevitable feature of human life. Theories which impute a natural or objective quality to moral values obscure this fact.

It is true that despite the immense variety of ways of life human beings nevertheless have certain experiences in common as human beings. These common experiences give rise to very widely shared attitudes of support for certain elementary rules of social life, to which reference was made above. It is the absence, or virtual absence, of disagreement about these elementary rules that makes plausible the notion that certain human rights are natural or objective. There is not a natural right to security of the person, or to have one's property respected, or to have contracts honoured, but because *a posteriori* we know these rights to enjoy something like universal support, it is possible for practical purposes to proceed as if they were natural rights.

But such nearly universal attitudes of support relate only to this area of the most elementary or primary rules of social life. They do not obtain in relation to the complex of civil and political, economic, social and cultural rights that are taken to provide the content of human rights today. We know that in China and Central Africa, in Pakistan and Saudi Arabia, it is not merely the case that human rights in the Western sense are not enjoyed; it is also the case that these rights are not regarded as morally valid. The idea that the universal validity of human rights is self-evident in the light of reason is an eighteenth-century illusion, as even President Carter's policy tacitly acknowledges.

It is possible that the area of shared moral attitudes and preferences in world society as a whole will grow. Those who believe that there is occurring at present a process of social and political convergence or homogenisation, giving rise to a greater uniformity of ways of life, can reasonably hold also that this is likely to find increasing expression in a convergence of attitudes towards the rights that all human beings should be accorded. There is, in President Carter's human rights policy, an implicit cosmopolitanism, a belief that a more homogeneous world culture is developing, or can be encouraged to develop. This may or may not be so: evidence can be adduced that points in both directions. Nor is it easy to say whether such a homogeneous world culture, if it is developing, will lead towards Western conceptions of human rights or away from them. What we can say, however, is that in the absence of any striking new tendency of ways of life to converge, the appeal to a conception of human rights that expresses the ways of life simply of our part of the world is not likely to evoke a response elsewhere.

Notes

1. For these and other documents to which reference is made see Ian Brownlie (ed.), *Basic Documents on Human Rights* (Clarendon Press, Oxford, 1971).

2. See Otto von Gierke, *Natural Law and the Theory of Society 1500 to 1800,* trans. E. Barker (Cambridge University Press, 1934).

3. See C. Wilfred Jenks, *The Common Law of Mankind,* 1958.

4. I refer here to Kant's third Definitive Article for a Perpetual Peace: 'The

law of world citizenship shall be limited to the conditions of universal hospitality'.

5. For a perceptive account of these elementary rules, see H.L.A. Hart, *The Concept of Law* (Clarendon Press, Oxford 1961).

5   JUSTICE: NATIONAL, INTERNATIONAL OR GLOBAL?

W.H. Smith

This chapter will look at some of the problems encountered in applying ideas of justice outside the nation-state. Traditionally, political philosophy has dealt with justice in the context of the *polis* or of national societies. This tradition remains important but the intensification of international politics, the development of a global economic system and the shift to thinking in terms of world politics have presented a conceptual challenge in recent decades. Must justice remain bound to the nation-state? What sort of justice is possible between sovereign states? Are we moving toward a notion of justice tied to an emergent world society of which all human beings are members?

Particular attention will be paid to the way that worldwide economic inequalities bear upon questions of justice. Much of the contemporary debate about justice in world politics focuses on this issue: it claims at times not only to be a new item on the agenda of international politics but to have produced a 'new agenda' altogether. How much this reflects the concerns of developed countries and the interests of Third World *governments* is touched upon in the chapters by Professor Miller and Ralph Pettman. Whatever the politics or psychology of the new agenda, however, it poses some crucial questions. Can economic justice be considered in isolation from a wider conception of justice? If not, as I believe to be the case, what importance should be attached to economic issues? And, more philosophically still, what precisely is it about economic developments that raise doubts about our established notions of justice? In considering such questions what I have to say will, I hope, be relevant to other, more traditional issues of justice in world politics, such as war and intervention.

Justice I take to be a quality of social groups. It refers to the way in which goods — defined in the widest sense to include rights and privileges as well as material possessions — are distributed among members of that group.[1] A concept of justice will normally contain principles about which goods — not necessarily all — are to be distributed and principles about the claims of various classes of people to various kinds of goods. Justice, then, looks at the overall picture so that one can say, given agreement on principles, that a particular society is just or unjust (or somewhere in between). It is clearly important not to assume at the outset that world society, however defined, necessarily constitutes a proper context for justice. As will become apparent, there are arguments for thinking of justice only in the context of the state and arguments about how justice in different kinds of society may or may not correspond.

Justice is, of course, related to the question of right conduct for individuals — 'morality' in perhaps its most usual sense. But there is much room to disagree on how they are related. Many philosophers have noted a general reluctance to accept that a right (moral) action could produce injustice or that a wrong action could promote justice. In such cases an attempt is usually made to depict the 'right' action as not really right in view of all the circumstances — and vice versa.[2] This is a feature of the utilitarian approach to justice. It takes justice — or, more widely, the general good or 'the greatest happiness' — as the standard for judging the rightness of individual conduct. An act is right if it promotes justice, more right than another act if it promotes greater justice.

To put this in the context of world politics, it might be argued that global justice requires — as an absolute minimum — the sparing of as many human lives as possible and that the moral injunction against killing others is (and ought to be) tailored to this end. Now from this conception of justice it may be argued that any involvement in activities which cause death or cause more to die than would otherwise be the case must be accounted immoral; thus support for a business enterprise which pays unduly low wages to its employees in an under-developed country is prohibited to the individual on moral grounds.[3] Global justice and moral behaviour are thus intimately related. Yet this connection is difficult to sustain for two reasons. It is open to the objection that individual acts cannot have any influence on the alleged injustice of business operations or of economic organisation in general. But the more fundamental objection is that such an argument does not correspond with the way people (and many philosophers) normally think about moral rules.

Moral principles are usually identified with individuals. The morality of an act will depend on various factors associated with the actor: his intentions, his reasons for acting, his circumstances, his relationship to the person or persons directly affected. There is a focus on acts such as killing, lying, stealing, which in themselves have little impact beyond those directly involved; their moral or immoral character is such that their ramifications need not be further explored. Norms of conduct, moreover, are frequently regarded as in principle relevant to all men. John Vincent's chapter traces the development of this line of thought in Western philosophy and it is not infrequently found outside Western culture. Moral rules are easily universalised, it would seem, because they deal with the relative simplicities of specific, small-scale events rather than the complexities of social institutions.[4]

These fall rather into the province of justice which looks at the way in which goods ought to be distributed among members of a group. It provides standards by which to judge the competing claims and interests of numerous individuals. The focus is not on motives or immediate circumstances but on the impact of policies, laws, institutions, traditions on a society. In contrast to principles of morality, those of justice take heed of geographical boundaries for they mark off the area in which social interaction occurs. It is precisely because national boundaries appear to some to have been transcended in some areas that the prospect of a wider justice has been raised.

Now a concept of global justice does not seem necessary in order to justify giving aid to the needy and starving. Many individuals feel a moral obligation to give to those less fortunate regardless of national boundaries or political and economic structures. It may well be the case that individuals have a moral duty to assist the needy.[5] As well, some governments are sometimes prompted to give aid by citizens who have a sense of moral duty. Of course, governments may believe that such aid serves their national interest but it would be difficult to prove that this is always the reason for aid or, indeed, that such a reason was necessarily incompatible with genuine humanitarian concern on the part of some decision-makers.[6] The basis of such aid, in short, is morality, not necessarily justice.

But much of the contemporary debate goes beyond this. It is said not to be enough to give even a generous amount of aid, even with the best of intentions. And the reason is not simply the inadequacy of the amount that might be forthcoming. It is rather that the whole economic framework which distributes global resources is unjust. Humanitarianism serves merely as a distraction from this fact and as a palliative which further degrades the dignity of those who receive. What is needed is radical reform of existing institutions, perhaps even their overthrow.[7]

What I have said so far will perhaps have indicated the unwisdom of applying rules of individual conduct (moral principles) to the actions of states, of asking, for example, whether the foreign policy of a particular state is moral in some degree. This may have been appropriate when a nation could be identified with its prince; policies could be examined *in foro conscientiae* and measured against the natural law held to govern all men. But Machiavelli early stressed the special demands of princely office and the prince's need 'not to be good'. The question to be asked of a state's policy is not whether it is moral but whether it is just: how does it affect the distribution of goods among the members of the appropriate society, whether national, international or global?

In domestic policy we are accustomed to judging laws and policies according to principles of justice rather than morality. It is, of course, possible to say that a particular law is immoral (or moral) but this is likely to mean (i) that the law amounts to an immoral act, e.g. provides for capital punishment; or (ii) that the law encourages or discourages individuals in matters of moral behaviour, e.g. laws on prostitution or pornography. It may also be possible to identify certain laws or policies with particular individuals who have taken initiatives or pushed strenuously for change.

In foreign policy, however, these possibilities virtually disappear. Policy and *a fortiori* international law originate rarely from individuals, most commonly from complex and impersonal decision-making organisations or processes. Certain kinds of foreign policy, e.g. war and intervention, do invite moral judgement because they involve individuals in actions, such as killing, against which they are normally enjoined by moral codes. And while it is sometimes possible to identify particular acts of immorality in a war, e.g. those of a Lieutenant Calley, the invitation to moral judgement of a state's policy should in general be declined: firstly, because it blurs the distinction between simple and complex acts and, secondly, because the admission of some acts of foreign policy to the realm of morality is likely to lead to the indiscriminate entry of all.

None of this exempts the individual decision-maker from the demands of his moral conscience. He must attend to these as best he can in the circumstances of his office and he may find that, whatever his decision, he cannot help having dirty hands.[8] What he ought not to do is confuse morality and justice. For this is to deal with groups of people and aggregate interests in the same way as individual and particular interests. An attempt to introduce the latter approach into politics is likely to meet with a flat rejection and a monistic realism. Concern with humanity, with mercy, can be brought into politics only as an integral part of a concept of justice whether within the state or beyond it. Moral vision, in fact, may be necessary to genuine political action.[9]

In politics, then, morality is a second-order concept, subordinate to justice. The question is not, for example, 'Is Chinese foreign policy moral?', but 'What are China's conceptions of justice as evidenced by her policies and objectives?' The concept of 'just war' embodies the correct approach despite its medieval origins: it is concerned not so much with the moral virtue of princes but with the impact of their policies on other princes and peoples. A further example concerns refugees where it is easy enough to see the moral response — and if numbers are small this may be a practical response — but in dealing with larger numbers deeper problems arise. We come up against the interests of groups and their potential impact on other groups, all matters where no simple answers are possible. Similarly, the suggested human right to settle anywhere in the world (or even to emigrate from one's country) asserts a moral principle with total disregard for the rights and interests of groups.

I may be accused at this point, if not earlier, of the sin of states-centrism. But the distinction between the individual and the collectivity — and the principles to govern their behaviour — holds in my view whatever the nature of the groups and whatever the nature of the relations between them. If the world consisted simply of two or more social classes or if there existed dominant and subordinate groups, the dichotomy between the individual and the collectivity would remain. We may wish to develop new concepts of justice to deal with a changed situation but the purpose of introducing moral principles into the debate must be to provide the requisite moral impetus — Weber's 'passion' — not the substance.

The substance of justice must originate with some idea about the nature of those who are the subjects of justice and about the relations between them. In most cases this means beginning with the nature of man. Discovering the true essence of man is, of course, notoriously impossible however essential the search may be. In recent years, moreover, we have come to understand (perhaps to re-learn) that we cannot be certain even about the moment when individuals begin and end their earthly lives.

Now philosophers seek man not only as he is but also as he ought to be, as he once was and as he will be. The first of these approaches identifies a goal or *telos* toward which man ought to move. The second seeks an insight into man's nature by conceiving of an earlier condition, perhaps a state of nature (pleasant or unpleasant), perhaps a time of innocence. The third approach is determinist. It sets out laws of necessity, not principles of moral obligation or eternal justice. Thus Marxism recognises the concept of justice only as the creature of a particular historical epoch; justice is relevant to its own time and cannot be applied to any other epoch. Moreover, since justice is seen by Marx as a formal, juridical and state-bound concept, justice in this sense will have no place in a truly communist society.[10]

There are clearly problems in defining the nature of justice and in identifying the subjects of justice. Of relevance here is the possibility that the subjects of justice may be other than individual human beings. In particular, it can be argued that states — as distinct entities — are capable of creating a special kind of justice amongst themselves, i.e. international justice.[11] A more pessimistic version has it that the intrinsic nature of states leaves no scope for justice at all. The possibility of international justice *per se*, then, arises only with those philosophers who interpret the state not (or not merely) as an institution ordained by God or constructed by men, but as a natural, organic being. The classic statement of the organic view can be found in Aristotle.

For Aristotle the state or *polis* was the supreme institution. It aimed at the supreme good; it was self-sufficient where other associations were not; it was prior to the individual and the household, a whole prior to its parts. As much as man himself, the state was an organism, a creation of nature. Within each community a particular justice could be established based on the precepts of equality and subjection to the law.[12] But Aristotle's conception of justice also transcends the boundaries of the state for it is ultimately founded on reason. Where reason is, so too is justice. Hence in dealing with other states, Aristotle argued, it would be 'completely unreasonable . . . if the work of the statesman were to be reduced to seeing how he could rule others with or without their consent. How could that be regarded as statecraft or lawgiving which is not even lawful in itself?'[13] In practice, of course, as Aristotle well knew, men were not usually inspired by reason, feeling no compunction about dominating other states in a way they would regard as unjust were their own state the victim.

Aristotle's organic view of the state may have created the possibility of a special kind of inter-state justice. But his philosophy stressed rather the role of the state in creating its own justice and where it did go beyond the state it relied on a cosmopolitan conception of men as capable of reason (though some classes of men were, in Aristotle's

view, not capable of reason and therefore fit to be ruled by others).
Other philosophers such as Rousseau and Hegel who have interpreted
the state as in some sense an organic being have stood firm on the
national basis of justice. Rousseau was decidedly pessimistic about
international relations;[14] while Hegel at least saw certain virtues in
conflict between states.[15]

   A concept of international justice, it would seem, cannot stand on
its own.[16] It must derive from cosmopolitan ideas or from national
conceptions of justice; and is likely in practice to combine some por-
tion of both. It is true that both sources may undermine international
justice but it is also true that these sources will provide its strength
and resilience. Being derivative does not necessarily mean being weak
and insubstantial. For many purposes international justice can be
thought of as existing in its own right just as international society is
conceived to be a working, if fictional, society. David Hume regarded
justice as an artificial virtue for it is not one of the feelings naturally
found in men.[17] This virtue is acquired readily enough within the state
but in relations between artificial persons justice must be accounted
doubly artificial. The following sections of this chapter will look at the
nature of this artifice within states, among mankind as a whole and
between states.

Traditionally justice has been regarded as a quality of politically
autonomous institutions. Such an organisation holds final authority
over the individuals and lesser groups within it, a sovereignty which is
self-contained and exclusive of the authority of other organisations.
It is in the state that problems of distribution perennially arise. The
social and economic co-operation that facilitates the creation of goods
of all kinds takes place largely within states. In many societies, moreover, the distribution of these goods is something which the central
government can significantly influence. Government, in other words,
offers one means of creating justice at least within its own boundaries.

   The business of social co-operation is highly complex, giving rise to
many rights and duties among those participating in the enterprise.
These rights and duties are 'special' in the sense that they are held not
by all individuals but by specific individuals by virtue of the association
or connection between them.[18] Each society, while perhaps accepting
the idea of general rights, will determine for itself what particular rights
and duties (as examples of goods in general) ought to be distributed and
what rules of distribution ought to be adopted. As Hume observed in the

Inquiry Concerning the Principles of Morals, the content of rights and duties varies from society to society and the fact that they exist at all is not a necessary but merely a contingent fact.[19] Only when men come together for some purpose does the possibility of justice arise and then it is limited to that specific group.

It is the stuff of political philosophy to speculate on the nature of political association among men. Explanations are, in the broadest terms, based either on a social contract or on convention. Both approaches seek to account for the fundamental principles which govern a society and must therefore find a place for concepts of justice. This is not the occasion to go over the classical theories, although I shall refer to some of them here and there. I shall instead look at two contributions to the theory of justice — one based on contract, the other on convention — which are of recent date and might be expected to throw some light on the more contemporary issues.

The first work is John Rawls's *A Theory of Justice* which, in the author's words, 'generalizes and carries to a higher level of abstraction' traditional contract theories.[20] For Rawls justice is 'the first virtue of social institutions' (3). It is concerned with 'the way in which the major social institutions distribute fundamental rights and duties and determine the division of advantages from social co-operation' (7). Rawls envisages the basic principles of justice being chosen by free and rational individuals who are willing to co-operate yet concerned for their own interests. In this 'original position' the parties are equal in terms of bargaining power but, most importantly, ignorant of the position which each will occupy in the social structure for which they are drawing up rules. From behind this 'veil of ignorance' two principles are said to emerge. The first states the requirement of equality in apportioning basic rights and duties; the second holds that inequality is justified only if it produces benefits for the whole society, in particular for those least favourably placed. This latter principle Rawls terms the 'difference principle' and adds to it provisions concerning equality of opportunity to enjoy whatever privileges do prove necessary.[21]

Rawls's theory is far richer than this summary might suggest. Two important qualifications which Rawls makes need to be noted here. The first is that justice is not the only prerequisite for a viable society since problems of co-ordination, efficiency and stability must also be solved (6). Secondly, Rawls assumes a society which is more or less self-sufficient (4). It is not altogether clear what Rawls means by this. A community that is self-sufficient both economically and politically certainly fits the description. The whole notion of a contract suggests political autonomy but the consequences of extensive foreign relations and interdependence are not spelled out (though it is only fair to observe that Rawls does not see his theory as complete).

In the tradition of contract theorists Rawls demonstrates the crucial connection between social co-operation and the possibility of justice. Each society requires some notion of justice for without it conflict and coercion will prevail over co-operation. But the creation of justice is necessarily something that sets one group of individuals, the parties to the contract, apart from the rest of humanity. And by uniting with some, as Rousseau has it, we become enemies of mankind.[22] Rawls's theory is also a tribute to the long tradition in Western philosophy which has sustained a vision of the perfectly just society and has thereby provided standards by which to measure existing societies. It is also typical of the Greek inheritance which tends to relegate foreign relations to an afterthought. Rawls's attempt in this direction will be considered in a later section.

The alternative approach to political association relies not on a contract, real or notional, but on the historical fact that groups of human beings have come together for common purposes and have developed through custom and convention principles to govern their relations.[23] This approach bestows the blessing of history rather than of reason on the connection between society and justice. It begins by noting that in no society was there any initial distribution of goods in the sense of a deliberate parcelling out of rights and benefits. Men come together possessed of all kinds of resources and talents, some well endowed, some barely endowed at all. There is no call to justify this state of affairs, however randomly Nature or God might appear to have dealt out the good things of the world. Personal worth or merit has no significance for these initial holdings.

Individuals, furthermore, are free to use or dispose of their resources as they wish: to employ them, for example, to create more resources or to give them away to anyone they choose. The crucial provision governing such changes in holdings is that they do not take place in unfair or immoral ways. As long as this provision is observed, an initial just distribution of goods can only lead to other just distributions, never to an unjust distribution. Those who at any point argue for a redistribution must demonstrate that some goods have been improperly acquired; otherwise they are themselves in a position of infringing moral rules by depriving certain individuals of the freedom to use their resources as they choose. For Nozick, then, a theory of justice has three main components: an account of how goods came to be held in the first place, rules governing the transfer of holdings, and principles for rectifying unjust transfers.[24]

The strength of this approach is its rootedness in history rather than any vision of the future. It may employ various theories to account for the origin of private property, but stresses the natural liberty of men to acquire it, use it and transfer it. If men have different talents, abilities ˙ and inclinations in these respects, then some will have the means to secure more benefits than others. To prevent individuals from achieving this sort of superiority is to interfere with their natural liberty. As with men, so with states. If individuals can claim exclusive rights to certain goods, so must a group of individuals be able to enjoy possession of common goods to the exclusion of other groups.[25] The shift from individual to group is not automatic but it is reasonable and corresponds to the practice of groups in their relations with one another. It is, significantly, a major embarrassment to Marxist theory in that a communist state in a less than communist world must find itself asserting exclusive property rights over its territory and resources.[26]

A strategic redoubt in the position which sees justice as bound to the state is the historical function of the state in eliciting effort and dedication from individuals. In one way or another the state serves to channel the activities of individuals toward the welfare of the collectivity – but the national rather than the global community. An important exponent of such ideas was Friedrich Meinecke, particularly in his work *Cosmopolitanism and the Nation-State.*[27] For Meinecke the state was the ideal form of political organisation for the realisation of human values; no other community more deserved description as 'man writ large'.[28] Each nation developed in its own particular circumstances. Not reason or natural law but geography, family, common fears and so on determined the nation. And each nation, as an expression of its many individual members, represented an expression of humanity as a whole.[29]

Cosmopolitan ideas such as natural law halted before this 'abyss of individuality'.[30] A worldwide community would be both inferior to national communities and unsatisfactory in itself, and it could in any case only be achieved by conquest. Hence international relations had to be seen in national rather than cosmopolitan terms for the latter distracted the statesman and weakened his state. It was not that Meinecke rejected the ethics of cosmopolitanism; he rejected its apolitical nature and its tendency to reduce events and issues to absolutes.[31] Cosmopolitanism saw links between men where none were in fact possible and therefore provided no adequate foundation for justice.

To maintain that justice is essentially national in origin is not necessarily to deny that justice has no place in international relations. One school of thought, epitomised in various ways by Hegel, Machiavelli and Hobbes, does see justice stopping at the water's edge. For them states are morally separate and cannot subordinate themselves to any common principles of justice. Hegel, while recognising universal principles, argued that they could only be made real through the individual state. Similarly, Machiavelli accepted the existence of principles of right and wrong but maintained that they had to be overridden by the demands of the state. Only Hobbes represents a purely positivist view: such moral obligations as exist derive from the command of the sovereign and extend only to the limit of his authority.

But the other school of thought, in which the liberal realist tradition is firmly planted, does see a certain limited scope for justice. States pursue their own interests but, by virtue of a measure of overlapping interests among some or all of their number and of their longstanding interrelationship in a single system, they are able to find room for certain rules of behaviour, including principles of justice, in their relations with one another. What distinguishes the realist from the idealist is simply the extent to which each sees national interests as overlapping. The idealist can discern, actually or potentially, a perfect harmony of interests.

The national approach to justice also finds much support in the practice of states, including many who are vocal in condemning the injustice of contemporary international relations. The principle of sovereign equality has become an axiom, asserting the right of each state to manage its own affairs and hence to create its own principles of justice. Third World states in particular are anxious to confirm their ownership of resources within their national boundaries regardless of their ability or inability to exploit them. Similarly with the world's oceans, states are looking more to expand national control than to an international regime. Demands for justice, it must also be noted, are couched in terms of aid to governments rather than to individuals. For each state wishes to retain control over the manner in which goods are distributed within its boundaries.[32] And while it may be true that this is a demand of governments made for the sectional purposes of a ruling elite, it does not follow that the citizens of such governments would lightly abandon the idea of national autonomy for the sake of an improvement in their food consumption.

Justice, on this view, is founded in the state so that the mere fact of contact between states does not mean that new concepts of justice must replace the old. On the contrary, global economic interdependence has led to a reassertion of the demand for national autonomy. It is leading not to a world society with its own principles of justice but must rather be taken as a warning against the erosion of independence.

It is possible to take issue with the idea of national justice in two ways: by tackling the theories of justice as such or by arguing their applicability to some society other than the state. In recent years the main exponents of this latter line of attack have looked to a broader basis for justice than the state. This will be our focus here, although the tradition of thought that sees salvation in smaller groups is far from extinct.

The arguments against taking the state as the matrix of justice need only be summarised here. They relate, on the one hand, to doubts about the capacity of the state to perform the functions expected of it, e.g. the provision of security against attack and the maintenance of minimum economic standards. Without trying to resolve these issues, it may be noted that they reflect Western anxieties more than global concerns; they are the worries of states which have known security and prosperity but have lost them rather than of states which have never known these blessings. On the other hand, a powerful volley of arguments has been launched by those who stress the changing nature of world economic activity. Modern production, it is claimed, can no longer be walled up within the state; traditional political barriers have been scaled or have been pushed down for the benefit of economic man. Two trends are emphasised: the interdependence of national economies and the dependence of some economies on others.

This is not the place to debate the facts of global economic developments. The conclusions to be deduced from them are another matter. For some the emergence of global economic relations (whether of co-operation or exploitation) necessitates a new basis for principles of justice. No longer can states be regarded as autonomous; they are bound by economic ties and in many cases this means by political ties as well. Others, however, do not reach the same conclusions. Economic interdependence, among states as among men, is seen to breed 'not accommodation and harmony but suspicion and incompatibility'.[33] It is no answer to say that this simply demonstrates the need for a wider conception of justice. The creation of justice, moreover, has typically been possible only when men have submitted themselves to a common political authority. In the absence of world government, global justice appears to be beyond man's grasp.

Nonetheless, speculation about principles of global justice may still be worthwhile. It may offer some vision of the future and also help to explain why the vision is so remote from reality. One such approach to global justice can be developed from Rawls's theory.[34] If we imagine men in the 'original position' who are charged with finding principles of justice to govern the whole of mankind, it is questionable whether they would opt for having states at all. Assumed to be ignorant of their future nationality, they would face an odds-on chance of finding themselves in a country which could barely provide subsistence living.

Surely free and rational individuals would choose a global structure which would ensure a reasonable minimum for all, even if some groups were highly privileged. With this approach to global justice the present momentous accident of birth into one state (and plenty) or into another (and hunger) would be eliminated. Those inequalities that remained would have to be justified on the grounds that they provided the necessary incentives and rewards for those more able to contribute to the general welfare, including that of the least well-off. Inequalities might also serve to improve the efficiency of the system of distribution.[35]

Now one difficulty with this conception of global justice is that it assumes away the importance to men of their sense of nationality. We do not know what sacrifices men would be prepared to make in order to retain the multitude of national groups. An indication may perhaps be found in considering how mankind in the 'original position' would deal with nuclear weapons — on the assumption that they could not be wished away. The problem is to find how such immensely destructive power could be placed in the hands of a group of men without their fellows feeling extreme unease, if not outright fear. A world government could only use nuclear weapons against its own subjects. If placed in the hands of several groups, nuclear weapons would surely promote antagonism between them. In the present international system states always (as far as we know) direct their nuclear weapons against foreign targets. The fact that citizens of some states are nuclear targets of other states serves only to reinforce their sense of nationality.

A second fundamental criticism of this approach to global justice is applicable to many theories of justice. It is not that the principles of justice are unworkable or difficult to uphold but rather that they demand the realisation of a set pattern, a particular distribution of goods. No deviation from the pattern, e.g. equality, can be permitted except as provided for. Nozick contends that such 'patterned' principles of justice focus on criteria for deciding who shall receive goods ('recipient-justice') while ignoring the rights of those from whom goods must be taken. In the standard formula 'to each according to his —

from each according to his —', the first part tends to be carefully spelled out, the latter simply asserted.[36]

Some system, then, would have to be found both for determining who merits assistance and for distributing the world's goods in the right proportions. And, more problematically, some grounds must be found for depriving others of goods which they already have in their possession. The problem of deciding 'why' as well as 'what' and 'how much' is difficult enough in a national society; it promises to be impossible in a world where men have different cultures, religions and outlooks even if they have lost their nationality.

A chief characteristic of this contractual approach to justice is the attempt to nullify inequalities that have arisen through chance or historical fate. The approach to justice based on natural liberty, however, sees no reason to move from the fact of unequal distribution to the norm of equality; redistribution is warranted only in order to rectify the consequences of unjust behaviour in the past. Again, we do not know where men stand on this question: what price are they prepared to pay for natural liberty? If they do prefer natural liberty to a contract providing for equality, it is difficult to deny the right of individuals to form associations for the promotion of their common interests. And we are back to the state as the repository of justice. If the choice is for a contract and equality, we must doubt its credibility in the light of man's longstanding addiction to nationality. Any concept of justice, it would appear, must reckon with the existence of the nation-state.

If principles of international justice arc to bc found thcy must recognise the existence of national 'enclaves of justice' which block 'that access to the demands of men and women of all nations which is required for bringing them into a single justice-constituency'.[37] Justice within the state is at once a contribution to global justice and a barrier to it. But international justice cannot ignore the claims of mankind as a whole. For this would be to overlook the strength of cosmopolitan conceptions and to disregard the historical record such as it is. Here I shall look at two contemporary approaches to international justice: one in the tradition of Christian Wolff's *civitas maxima* based on some form of contract between states, the other in the tradition of Vattel emphasising the natural liberty of states.

The chief merit of Rawls's theory of international justice is that it takes the state as the subject of justice. Indeed, Rawls does not even discuss the question of how a community is to be defined for the

purposes of his theory of justice.[38] Using the device of a 'veil of
ignorance' Rawls would have states confer about the rules to govern
their relations without knowing their future identity, whether, for
example, there were to be Chad, India or the United States of America.
Barry's argument that they would not choose a states system at all loses
its force if it is established that states desire to create their own internal
principles of justice and are prepared to accept considerable sacrifices
to this end. So too does Barry's claim that states meeting in these
circumstances would favour strong forms of international organisation
possessing a monopoly of weapons of mass-destruction or an effective
system of collective security.[39] What states in the 'original position' are
likely to agree upon, in Rawls's view, is a series of principles which look
remarkably like those which international society has already developed:
non-intervention, *pacta sunt servanda,* self-defence and the rules of *jus
ad bellum* and *jus in bello.*[40]

One fundamental criticism of this approach is that it does not work
in a world of states which are somewhat less than self-sufficient. For
interdependence benefits some more than others and, in adding to the
world's stock of goods, raises the question of how these goods ought to
be distributed. 'In an interdependent world', Beitz argues, 'confining
principles of justice to national societies has the effect of taxing poor
nations so that others may benefit from living in "just" regimes.'[41] On
such a view promoting justice at home takes priority over aid to foreign
peoples in need. The benefits which the originally advantaged states have
gained from international transfers remain in their hands and there is
nothing — save compassion — to oblige them to surrender any part of
their possessions.

This is precisely the point which is applauded by those who conceive
of state relations in terms of natural liberty. They assert that states, like
men, own what they produce or gain through trade. Without security of
possession there is no incentive to produce goods, no basis on which to
mobilise the citizens of a state; for states, again like men, depend on
certain material goods for their survival. In international dealings there
are no grounds of justice for wealthy states to accept a lower price for
their produce or pay a higher price for others' produce than they need
to in the market-place. All are entitled to their holdings, large or small,
provided only that they have not been acquired by unfair or immoral
means.

An attempt may be made to qualify this line of argument by saying
that the better off are obliged to redistribute only that component of
their wealth which is due to trade with others, or at least a certain part

of that component. But this is in effect to tax international trade which will remain worthwhile only so long as some element of profit remains. It is clear too, that any level of tax would serve to discourage trade so that both richer and poorer lose the incentive to make exchanges they would otherwise have made. Moreover, even if the principle of redistributing gains from international transfers were accepted in some measure, the great difficulty would remain of determining the size of the component to be redistributed. Any figure produced would certainly smack of guesswork and arbitrary choice.

A further objection to the natural liberty approach is that vast differences exist and have existed in the natural resources with which states are endowed. What each has, furthermore, appears morally arbitrary, reflecting neither moral worth nor desert but the vagaries of nature. Hence some states happen to be favourably placed to improve their position in cumulative fashion, while others are unable to make improvements and simply fall further behind. It was these 'contingencies and biases of historical fate' that Rawls's notion of an international contract was intended to nullify.[42] Now one response to this objection is to treat natural resources as comparable to human talents. These also differ greatly as between individuals and must be recognised as given. It is absurd to demand that a person justify his possession of great musical gifts or cricketing ability. So with states it is pointless to require them to justify their natural endowments.

But then the objection may be pressed further by arguing that 'unlike talents, resources are not naturally attached to persons'.[43] Whereas no man can be deprived of his talents in the sense that they can be taken from him and given to another, natural resources can for the most part be easily transferred once problems of transport and storage have been solved. Depriving a man of his talents would be a monstrous act (unless they were talents of evil) for they are intrinsic to his personality. The same, it is argued, cannot be said of the natural endowment of the state.

Against this, the libertarians would reiterate the case for a concept of private property for both the individual and the group and would emphasise the need to guarantee security of property. A Lockeian would claim that natural resources require labour in order to make them useful and that the citizens of a state in applying their labour to such a purpose create property rights over their product.[44] The life of a community depends on its possessions, natural and acquired, a significance reflected in the widespread notion of motherland or fatherland.

Moreover, says Locke, 'he who appropriates land to himself by his

labour does not lessen but increase the common stock of mankind'.[45]
But Locke also assumed that in appropriating what was originally
common to all there remained 'enough and as good' for those still
unprovided for.[46] This assumption may have been valid for the greater
part of human history but recent decades have furnished reasons for
doubt in two respects. Here perhaps are arguments which will justify
the restriction of natural liberty and necessitate new principles of
justice.

First of all, there are some natural resources which are still held in
common by the earth's population — notably the resources in and under
the oceans. These may be appropriated by states which have the capital
and technological capacity in such a way as to fail to leave 'enough and
as good' for the rest of mankind. This argument, then, might distinguish
between resources which states happen to be sitting on within their
national boundaries and resources which do not as yet fall within such
boundaries. There are some reasons to quarrel with this distinction since
national boundaries have always been subject to determination by
agreement (or disagreement) between states; if states can establish
boundaries on land, what is to prohibit them from doing so at sea? The
distinction looks firmer, however, in the light of a second global
problem.

This is the possibility — some would say certainty — that the sum
total of the earth's resources will one day be exhausted. Those who
exhaust irreplaceable resources today, it is said, are failing to leave
enough, even if not as good, for some future generation. And here the
advantaged states, the high-consumption societies, appear to be chiefly
responsible for bringing closer the point of global scarcity; though it
must not be forgotten that the populous states, the less developed of
which are striving hard to increase their per capita consumption, must
also shoulder some responsibility.

Since these problems are necessarily global, the argument runs, the
natural liberty of states must be restrained according to wider principles
of justice. Rawls could do this by making states in the 'original position'
ignorant of the generation to which they were going to belong or by
having representatives from all generations. Rational men would agree on
a 'just savings rate' which each generation would maintain for the sake
of its successors.[47] Rawls, for some reason not altogether clear, does
not follow this approach but requires that a single generation in the
'original position' must care for its successors.[48]

This is in fact the sort of assumption which the libertarian would
make: man has a pride in and an incentive to provide for his children

and his children's children. A vital aspect of his property rights is the right to transfer or bequeath goods to whomever he chooses. On the basis of what Hume would call a 'natural temper', then, men will provide for their descendants. But the difficulty here is that some in providing for their descendants — whether men for their children or states for the next generation — are likely to do so at the expense of others for whom 'enough, and as good' will not be left. And it remains true that concern for future generations is almost invariably focused on one's own nation. The division of mankind into national groups has until now assisted in the provision for future generations. Whether mankind can continue to provide for its future in this piecemeal fashion has now been brought into question.

While a contractual approach to international justice, particularly one that included some principle of equality, would necessitate major redistribution among states, an approach based on natural liberty does not necessarily produce this conclusion. What is required first is a demonstration that illegitimate transfers have occurred in the past. In the language of the present debate: what was and is exploitation? how can those exploited be paid back? I shall look briefly at some of the problems raised by these questions, although it is my view that ultimately it is more desirable to look forward than to look back.

Exploitation has meaning *either* in the sense of immoral acts committed by individuals against other individuals *or* in the context of agreed principles of justice. In the former case one thinks of enslavement, brutalisation, indiscriminate slaughter and so on, acts of which many early and not so early colonisers were guilty. They may not have thought themselves in the wrong, although it might have occurred to them — as it did to some social critics — that they were acting in ways they would not contemplate in dealing with members of their own nation or race. Such people no doubt lived in societies which generally found such behaviour acceptable, even desirable, and in which it would have taken considerable moral courage to behave otherwise.

Yet even if a verdict of morally guilty is reached it is hard to see what consequences result for the present. The descendants of those who committed such acts cannot be held responsible for deeds they had no part in. The only moral duty they have is that of helping all who have suffered wrongs or who are suffering as a result of past wrongs; and this is an obligation which is shared by all men regardless of what their forebears did. It is on grounds of morality, therefore, not justice, that recompense ought to be made.

The questions raised by earlier injustices perpetrated by states —

more precisely, in the name of states — are yet more difficult. Colonisation is now recognised as an international injustice but it was not so regarded in the past. On the contrary, it was frequently seen as a contribution to the welfare of native populations and as a means of bringing to them the benefits of economic progress. Although some voices were raised against colonialism, they were little heeded until after 1945. Colonialism was outlawed *post hoc*. But the anti-colonialists at first remained forward-looking, seeing independence for non-self-governing territories as their primary goal. And with political autonomy was expected — for some reason — economic independence. It has been the failure to achieve the latter which has given rise to the concepts of neo-colonialism and its cousin structural dependence and which has led to demands for restitution.

The argument is that even if colonialism was not unjust in the past, it is unjust now for states to benefit from the economic transfers that occurred under colonial regimes. And it is a *fortiori* unjust if certain states continue to exploit others, colonies or not. In the case of past exploitation there may be some difficulty in determining who must accept responsibility and who ought to be compensated. The Western colonial powers have generally retained their identity over a period of centuries so that it could be meaningful to talk of the present generation of Britons, for example, benefiting from capital transfers that took place within the Empire. But the same cannot be said of their colonial subjects. Many Third World states are creations of their colonial masters. If their governments have any claim to compensation it is in trust for the various surviving tribes and ethnic groups that experienced colonial rule.

The next problem is to calculate the measure of recompense. Should it be set at the total amount of capital extracted? Or should the net figure be determined by deducting the capital inflow? The latter course would be more in keeping with the idea of compensation. Once figures are calculated, moreover, it will presumably be necessary to convert the sums involved to current prices and there is endless scope for argument as to how this should be done. The final sum reached, however, could well prove quite impractical for one of two reasons: it could turn out to be so great that payment would involve intolerable burdens, or so small that it would not meet the actual needs of the underdeveloped countries.[49] Yet more complex are claims for compensation in respect of spiritual losses. By what criteria could past assaults on human dignity or on traditional ways of life be recompensed?

It will be clear that the concept of compensation does not really address itself to the problems that it is supposed to solve. If economic advancement is the objective, assistance ought to be calculated in terms of what is required now rather than what happened in the past. There will also be states in need of economic aid which have never been colonies. The argument for compensation, as Stone observes, assumes a willingness to make major sacrifices on the part of some states and a great capacity for forgiveness on the part of others; but if these conditions exist the parties concerned could be expected to co-operate amicably on the basis of existing needs and future objectives.[50] The idea of compensation is thus not so much a step towards international justice as a means of focusing attention on global issues.

For the foreseeable future the most effective principles of justice will be those found within the nation-state. There is no simple way in which they can be extended to mankind at large. But while national justice is not a direct contribution to global justice and in fact makes the latter more difficult to attain, its merits ought not to be overlooked. There is a common assumption that settling for justice on a national rather than a global basis is something to be deplored, that it is to settle for second-best. Yet it does seem that part of man's nature is a sense of belonging to an exclusive group, a sense which cosmopolitanism seeks to stifle. On the other hand, the very notion of morality — moral rules which individuals as individuals ought to follow — suggests that man also has a sense of the universal. It may posit unrealisable goals but it, too, ought not to be suppressed.

The role of international justice appears to be that of mediating principles of both national and global justice. To be sure, the former will predominate, but global justice has not been ignored altogether. There is some notion of an obligation on the part of states to aid those individuals who are in the direst circumstances; but states naturally remain reluctant to accept principles which involve international redistribution of resources for this would open the door to all manner of claims against them. This emphasis on retaining autonomy is one that is shared both by the wealthy states and by those states which at present condemn the dominance of the rich.

As for economic inequalities in the world, these are indeed enormous. But the market-place perhaps offers more hope of reducing these differences than any principles of international or global justice. In the past political power that could be extended overseas gave certain states the capacity to create and maintain economic advantages for themselves. If it is the case that power is becoming more dispersed throughout the globe and more difficult to deploy abroad, then some economic imbalances may be reduced. Again, recent developments have shown that the sources of supply of many raw materials and primary products are widely spread. This will also serve to redress economic inequalities in some degree. And the more interdependent the world economy, the greater the bargaining power of those with goods in short supply.

The most intriguing question of all is how long the total stock of the earth's resources will hold out. If global shortages begin to bite they could lead to a much greater sense of a common predicament for man. Principles of justice to govern the distribution of resources in limited supply might become more appealing. But global shortages could also produce competition between states and present some countries with the opportunity to exploit a monopoly position. If what I have said about the persistence of national outlooks is correct, this more gloomy prospect also looks the more probable.

Notes

1. See W.K. Frankena, 'The Concept of Social Justice', in R.B. Brandt (ed.), *Social Justice* (New Jersey, 1962), pp. 1-3.

2. Ibid., pp. 4-6.

3. For an argument along these lines see Onora Nell, 'Lifeboat Earth', *Philosophy and Public Affairs,* vol. 4, no. 3 (Spring 1975).

4. There are many reasons for treating moral rules as universal and for rejecting relativism. See, for instance, B. Williams, *Morality* (Harmondsworth, 1973), pp. 17-51.

5. P. Singer, 'Famine, Affluence, and Morality', *Philosophy and Public Affairs,* vol. 1, no. 3 (Spring 1972).

6. The issue of humanitarian intervention raises similar problems. For obvious reasons humanitarian aid tends to encounter fewer objections from governments.

7. For a utilitarian, by contrast, the distinction between humanitarian aid and the demands of justice is a second-order one. C.R. Beitz, 'Justice and International Relations', *Philosophy and Public Affairs,* vol. 4, no. 4 (Summer 1975), pp. 360-1.

8. M. Walzer, 'Political Action: The Problem of Dirty Hands', in M. Cohen, T. Nagel, T. Scanlon (eds.), *War and Moral Responsibility* (Princeton, 1974).

9. '. . . the problem is simply how can warm passion and a cool sense of proportion be forged together in one and the same soul? Politics is made with the head, not with other parts of the body or soul. And yet devotion to politics, if it is not to be frivolous intellectual play but rather genuinely human conduct, can be born and nourished from passion alone'; Max Weber, 'Politics as a Vocation', in *From Max Weber,* H.H. Gerth, C. Wright Mills (eds.) (London, 1948), p. 115.

10. On Marx and justice see A.W. Wood, 'The Marxian Critique of Justice', *Philosophy and Public Affairs,* vol. 1, no. 3 (Spring 1972), esp. pp. 257-8, 271.

11. Important here is the idea that only similar entities can be members of the same justice-constituency. Thus men's relations with animals, e.g. hunting or raising for slaughter, are not generally seen as giving rise to questions of justice, although men might be said to have a duty to treat them humanely.

12. '. . . it is preferable that law should rule rather than any single one of the citizens . . . he who asks Law to rule is asking God and Intelligence and no others to rule; while he who asks for the rule of a human being is bringing in a wild beast . . . In law you have the intellect without the passions', *Politics*, Book III, Ch. 16, trans. T.A. Sinclair (Harmondsworth, 1962).

13. Ibid., Book VII, Ch. 2.

14. For an exposition of Rousseau's ideas on international relations, see S. Hoffman, 'Rousseau on War and Peace', in *The State of War* (New York, 1965).

15. S. Avineri, *Hegel's Theory of the Modern State* (Cambridge, 1972), Ch. 10.

16. Julius Stone reaches the same conclusion by a different route, viz. denial of the domestic analogy: 'The aggregate of state entities cannot *as such* constitute a meaningful justice-constituency'. 'Approaches to the Notion of International Justice', in R.A. Falk, C.E. Black (eds.), *The Future of the International Legal Order*, vol. I (Princeton, 1969), p. 435.

17. *A Treatise of Human Nature*, Book III, part ii (London, 1972), pp. 210ff.

18. For the distinction between special rights and general rights see H.L.A. Hart, 'Are There Any Natural Rights?', *Philosophical Review*, vol. 64, no. 2 (April 1955), pp. 183-8. General rights are held by men regardless of any special relationship and are essentially defensive in character, requiring non-interference on the part of others.

19. See W.N. Nelson, 'Special Rights, General Rights, and Social Justice', *Philosophy and Public Affairs*, vol. 3, no. 4 (Summer 1974).

20. (London, 1972), p. 11. Page references in the text are to this work. The main ideas of Rawls's theory are set out on pp. 11-17.

21. For a full statement of these principles and rules of priority see *Theory of Justice*, pp. 302-3.

22. *Discourse on Inequality*, cited in Hoffmann, 'Rousseau on War and Peace', p. 67.

23. The present account follows Robert Nozick, *Anarchy, State, and Utopia* (Oxford, 1974), esp. Ch. 7. A standard exposition can be found in Hume, *Treatise of Human Nature*, Book III, part ii.

24. *Anarchy, State and Utopia*, pp. 150-3.

25. Ibid., p. 178. Nozick does not give any full argument for this shift. This is a potential weakness since the holding of property in common could be said to justify a government with extensive rights over individuals. The whole thrust of Nozick's argument, however, is towards a minimal state.

26. This paradox is pursued in R.N. Berki, 'On Marxian Thought and the Problem of International Relations', *World Politics*, vol. XXIV, no. 1 (October 1971).

27. Trans. R.B. Kimber (Princeton, 1970); the original German edition, *Weltbürgertum und Nationalstaat*, first appeared in 1907.

28. R.W. Sterling, *Ethics in a World of Power: The Political Ideas of Friedrich Meinecke* (Princeton, 1958), pp. 10, 32-3; Meinecke, *Cosmopolitanism*, p. 15.

29. Sterling, *Ethics in a World of Power*, p. 45.

30. Ibid., p. 34.

31. Ibid., pp. 59-60; Meinecke, *Cosmopolitanism*, pp. 20-1.

32. The Chinese concept of aid at grass roots level challenges this view. One may doubt whether governments really welcome this form of aid.

33. Hoffmann deems this 'one of Rousseau's deepest insights, one that shatters a large part of the liberal vision of world affairs'; 'Rousseau on War and Peace', p. 62.

34. Rawls in fact takes a different path, one that leads to *international* justice —see below. The procedure outlined here is proposed by Brian Barry, *The Liberal Theory of Justice* (London, 1973), pp. 129-30.

35. Frankena, 'Concept of Social Justice', p. 16.

36. Ibid., pp. 155-60, 167-73.

37. Stone, 'Approaches . . .', p. 435.

38. Barry, *Liberal Theory of Justice,* p. 128. Rawls's criterion is perhaps implicit in his assumption (admittedly ambiguous) of more or less self-sufficient associations.

39. Ibid., pp. 132-3.

40. Rawls, *Theory of Justice,* p. 378.

41. Ibid., p. 375.

42. Ibid., p. 364

43. Beitz, 'Justice and International Relations', p. 368.

44. 'Whatsoever [man] removes out of the state that nature hath provided and left it in, he hath mixed his labour with, and joined to it something that is his own, and thereby makes it his property . . . it hath by this labour something annexed to it that excludes the common right of other men', John Locke, *The Second Treatise of Government,* J. Gough (ed.) (Oxford, 1956), p. 15 (para 27).

45. Ibid., p. 20 (para 37).

46. Ibid., p. 18 (para 33).

47. Ibid., p. 291.

48. Ibid., p. 292. See the comments in Barry, *Liberal Theory of Justice,* p. 131.

49. It might be pointed out here that the burden of payments could well fall most heavily on the poorest classes in the states concerned.

50. Stone, 'Approaches . . .', p. 442.

6 INJUSTICE AND EVIL IN THE POLITICS OF THE POWERS*

A.L. Burns

In free societies we have some apprehension of injustice in power politics — enough, as Calvin put it, to leave us without excuse — but little
apprehension of evil. Ignorance of the evil in ourselves is itself partly
evil; but it is also partly innocence, an uncovenanted blessing which
obtains just because we are unaware of it.

In the theory and analysis of international relations, including the
corpus of international law, the idea of justice and injustice can have
factual application, though in no facile way: many annexations, exploi-
tations, the unjust levying of war, and long-term distributions of
resources and power which are inequitable and nowadays styled 'structural violence', can sometimes be designated quite objectively as unjust
and wrong. After two centuries of the is-ought, the fact-value
dichotomy, we can now see it as a philosophers' error of perspective,
and recognise that despite it civilised societies since the Middle Ages have
increased the discrimination and the range of their judgements of justice
and injustice. The societies have not necessarily become more just in
themselves; but the codes they subscribe to have progressed in definition and sensitivity.

Thus, a doctoral thesis questioning the justice or otherwise of some
internationally significant act[1] would be a possible enterprise. The
actuality of evil in power-political and other situations on the other
hand, though palpable, is not subject to scholarly demonstration in the
same way, except insofar as it has been expressed in specific injustices.
Yet profound historical and similar writing can reveal it, as Thucydides'
account of demoralisation in Athens does. And of course works of high
imagination, such as the great tragedies, paintings and sculpture, are the
chief secular teachers of the knowledge of good and evil. But above all
that knowledge is made the burden of the Old and New Testaments,

---

* This chapter is in tribute to Stephen Yarnold, formerly Moderator of the
Presbyterian Church of Victoria, and for more than 40 years a powerful and
liberating influence, as teacher and pastor, upon his pupils, students and
congregations, and many others. He has imparted a sense of history's informing
the present moment, and of the depths of the moment. Matt. 16:1-3; Eccl. 11:1.

from Genesis to Revelation. I hope to show how intimately that scriptural theme is related throughout to the politics of the Powers, even in apparently so remote an aspect as the forbidding of idolatry and polytheism.[2]

Evil, then, is a purely subjective or a specially religious concept? So it was taken, by a leading international scholar whose work is known worldwide for its shrewdness, lucidity, and sharpness of perception, on the occasion of this chapter's first presentation. His argument was that whereas the principles of justice (right and wrong) were rules and arrangements by which people ordered their relations with each other, evil and good appertained to the individual's attitude to the devil and to God (as in Graham Greene's *Brighton Rock*) and so were concepts not relevant to international relations, nor of much help to non-believers.

One would indeed expect a sharper sensitivity in these matters from believers than from non-believers (given always equal experience; for in our fortunate societies, traditional believers have often been sheltered, at least until the present decade). But it is not credible that the non-believer has no perception of evil in our terrible twentieth century. Yet the international expert could certainly argue that his analyses need not refer explicitly to good or evil, much as a psychiatrist might use precisely the same approach and methods in treating a saintly person with an intermittent psychosis (a number of saints, we are told, have suffered episodes of mental illness) and a horrid psychopath. Further, there is a level of relationship between Powers to which questions about degrees of evil characterising particular Powers — or for that matter their several injustices — are not immediately pertinent. The civilian strategic expert who said

> . . . what king, going to make war against another king, sitteth not down first and consulteth whether he be able with ten thousand to meet him that cometh with twenty thousand? Or else, while the other is yet a great way off, he sendeth an ambassage, and desireth conditions of peace[3]

though hardly an amoralist, well understood the relative distinctiveness of this level of relationship. But analyses that not only begin but also end at that level, without ever entering the ethical dimensions, are unrealistic and wrong-headed.

Injustice has its place solely in the dimension of actions and institutions; but evil belongs also to the dimension of disposition, and indeed has its source there. Two recent reports of evil incidents may bring this out. In one, a crowd chanted, 'Jump, jump, jump!' to a man standing on a high window-ledge. In the other, another crowd shouted, 'Do your own thing!' and 'Right on, sister!' to a girl preparing to slash her wrists. Both crowds were of evil disposition but also did wrong (or injustice in an extended sense); but the element of evil would have been just as great had each member of the crowds *wished* what he did sitting solitary in his room watching television.

From another angle, stark injustice can be done, in a kind of invincible ignorance or error, by pure and even noble characters: there may even be some amongst the murderous Provisional IRA. Tragic paradox, however, is bound to afflict such people, as bitter remorse or as clinical insanity or most often as gradual infection and corruption by self-exculpating anger. Most men and some women, looking within, will be aware of this. It arises from the general disposition to give one's allegiance to some nation, organised movement, state, class, tribe, creed, gang or faction (once, as in the blood-feud, to an extended family) that is or has in it to become a Power, i.e. a group capable of collectively exercising armed force against 'outsiders'.[4] These Powers, into which we have such a tendency to group ourselves, are by their constitution morally ambiguous: the sources of the paradoxical 'well-intentioned' injustices mentioned above, but also now and then of internal justice and freedom; susceptible to overwhelming possession by evil, but also to partial conversion, if not to unqualified goodness, at least to a human decency.

Injustice, even when done in error, is always of course an evil, but evil is not merely injustice only worse: it is not as though the young fiend proceeding to his baccalaureate of wickedness needs only injustice for a pass but must take the course in evil for an honours degree. Reflection will show further aspects of the distinguishable dimensions of the two. As we shall see, for instance, rational progress in the recognition of injustice is possible and has been made. The knowledge of evil comes instead from personal experience. Injustice can sometimes be redressed by action, and free men are under constant obligation to do so. Evil can only be redeemed.

Evidently evil is not an appropriate subject for research. To look for causes of such phenomena as crowds clamouring for suicide, for gladiatorial deaths in the arena, and so on, is beyond the scope of fundamentally historical investigation, such as international politics; for it seems often to arise of its own accord. But there are other and great manifestations of evil for which historically-evolved structures can sometimes be found.

The structures principally considered here are the Powers, which now hold all but universal sway. But from others, whose members each see their particular structure not ambiguous, as in a Power, but instead positively good, great evil may arise, e.g. from churches. One thinks of the Salem witch-hunts, the burning of Servetus in Geneva, the church-encouraged holocausts of witches and heretics, elsewhere and earlier. Precisely because the churchmen more or less responsible for such atrocities usually conceived of a warfare against the forces of darkness (and were not always wholly mistaken as to their victims' intentions: a few of the would-be witches did aspire, like the moor murderers and the Manson family of our day, to wield diabolical powers; some of the heresies were destructive), they could be utterly ruthless in good conscience.

Often, churches could persecute only by compact with the civil Power, so that a structure's giving rise to evil is just another instance of what this chapter chiefly deals with. But more to the point, ecclesiastical sources of evil reveal the importance of fundamental *belief* in its genesis, when some social structure is also present. (To repeat, this is not *necessary* for evil, which often exists willy-nilly.) An example from pagan religion is the belief alleged to have been held by the Aztecs: that the sun would cool and go out if not continually fed with living human hearts torn out of prisoners of war.

Consider that 'belief'. On the one hand, it was not an imaginative figure of speech expressive of some other belief, as in William Blake's

If the sun or moon should doubt,
They'd immediately go out.[5]

Apparently it was literal fact for the people. Yet to us it looks like a blatant rationalisation of the Aztec drive toward conquest and exploitation. We cannot understand how its falsity could remain unrecognised, and suppose the priests must have put it about deliberately as propaganda. But the latter is a naive supposition: the most destructive and lying nonsense in our time has been promulgated by those, e.g. most of the Nazi leaders, who really did believe it themselves.

Not all false beliefs are malignant. From Elizabethan times it was popularly believed that English law made it impossible to tread English soil and remain a slave. The late eighteenth-century lawyers who opposed Grenville Sharp on the slavery issue seem to have been correct at law in denying this popular belief. Thus the Mansfield judgement beneficently validated what may well have been historically false.

Whether our own complex of beliefs are on the whole benign or rather generate evil is a vastly more intractable question. It should be plain from what has gone before that the most careful answers to it cannot be accredited as the products of academic research. Also there are the obvious traps of self-observation; and the ruling beliefs of Western societies form such a complicated structure that one can hardly tell which component is responsible for what. Nevertheless we shall concentrate on one widely-held belief, that the balance of terror guarantees peace at least between the Super-powers and is, because of that, justifiable and necessary. The 'balance of terror' here means the reciprocal deterrence of major and mainly nuclear attack by the known capacity for mass destruction ('counter-resource strikes') in response to the other's most effective 'counter-force strike'. Though actual possession of the weapons that yield this capacity is both necessary and sufficient for ability to deter (no doctrine is really needed beyond a bald description of such weapons and what they can do), each nuclear-weapons Power does spell out its doctrine in its own terms: the US-SU agreement of mid-1972, concluding SALT ONE, generally presupposed the American policy of Mutual Assured Destruction (MAD), though the Soviet Union publicly envisages, in the worst case, all-out war employing all forces, conventional as well as nuclear. The French used to speak of being able to 'tear off a limb' — an expression which has at least candour to its moral credit. The Chinese and the British doctrines are much less explicit, since their strategic situations involve the capacities of other nuclear-weapon states as well as their own, and are better not spelt out.

The balance of terror and all doctrines expressing it inescapably imply a national will to acquire the nuclear forces that would make the nation able to commit an appalling crime against humanity; yet in some cases (China is a clear one) national leaders may well judge that failing to acquire such forces would be committing just such a crime against their own people.[6] It is as though the sole means available to parents for preventing their children being molested were the ability to torture to death the would-be molester and ten of his nearest relatives. Suppose also that those were the sole methods available to a householder of protecting his liberty, house and property.

That comparison immediately suggests a major countervailing difference: dependence upon the balance of terror is far from direct for the private person whose country is assuredly or possibly under some nuclear umbrella. The doctrine of nuclear deterrence does not so affect his everyday conduct as to reduce him at once to a state of savagery in the way that re-adoption of the *lex talionis* in the above comparison would do. All the same, the general assumption of the validity and application of the balance of terror (i.e. fundamental *belief* in it, and in the existence of the Powers that operate it) amounts to some acceptance of evil; and anyone who has seen a generation of children grow up under its shadow will have perceived the rarely expressed but crippling despair which it creates.

Another effect, combining with that of the televising of the Vietnam and similar conflicts, has been to promote condonation of, if not positive support for, terroristic ventures. If the president of the United States can hold scores of millions of foreigners hostage for the prudent conduct of Moscow and Peking, why should not the PLO or the Red Army or the Angry Brigade or the IRA make hostage, for their several objectives, plane-loads of passengers? Though terrorism was by no means an invention of the 'sixties, what is rather new is the proliferation of these trans-national and ephemeral Powers, ephemeral insofar as, unlike full-blown territorial Powers, they do not control a producing economy, or at least not yet. Eire, Israel, Kenya, Algeria and Greek Cyprus are all now fully territorial Powers (the last not quite so) which to some extent or another '*grew*' out of the barrels of terrorist guns. Those of the contemporary organisations, e.g. PLO and IRA, with connections to particular countries and peoples, may and sometimes do persist through several generations, turning youthful idealists into brave and fanatical murderers persuaded that they deserve the status of military combatants. (And why do they not? — Because they are propagating a national ideal, trying to bring a territorial nation into existence, and working to redress what they see as historic injustices, not defending family and home. Legal distinctions between combatant and civilian, and concomitant obligations to prisoners of war, have come to be recognised in the West because the waging of war came to be seen as at best a necessary evil for citizens in a polity, whereas when done by revolutionaries it appears to be a gratuitous act, almost as though it were a mere crime. I can now see a great deal of sense in that interpretation.) Yet actual evil, in its *extent*, correlates inversely with the degree of irresponsibility of its perpetrators: criminal gangs can do less than idealistic terrorists, and they far less than responsible statesmen.

The balance of terror epitomises evil at this time, not by being worse in itself than anything before — consider the imperialism of the ancient Assyrians, for instance — but by its worldwide application and its possible worldwide effects. We have seen that it is also a moral infection that seems to abet terrorism in lesser forms. Therefore any adult who lives in a country protected to some extent or other under a 'nuclear umbrella' is despite himself implicated in the evil of the balance of terror. The nature and necessity of this implication takes some understanding. Is one, for instance, similarly implicated in the torture of prisoners of war, should some Australian soldier commit that crime? — No; for it is no part of that nation's defence policy. On the contrary, it is strictly forbidden, and their code of military law has the contrary intent.

Our strategic doctrine and defence policy, on the other hand, predicate a Western nuclear deterrent. We cannot claim, for our conventional military forces, that they depend in no way on the balance of terror. Indeed, the implication of the nuclear umbrella provided by some other Power is morally no different from that of having nuclear weapons of our own. Hence the strong attraction, for Christians and others brought up in a tradition of conscience, of pacifism and withdrawal from an inescapable evil world.

Not only has this way of life been a major influence amongst Eastern Orthodox and Roman Catholics since the third century, when the decline and corruption of Classical civilisation appalled Christian minds who withdrew as anchorites and later as monks and nuns: the earliest biblical stories tell of other, non-celibate, withdrawals such as Abraham's departure from Ur of the Chaldees, and of returns to the nomadic, wilderness existence from time to time in the history of Israel. Under the New Testament dispensation, obedient to the command to render to Caesar what is Caesar's and to God what is God's, there have not been wanting those who, not retreating to the desert, have nevertheless renounced Caesar's protection and defied his power, e.g. the present-day dissident Baptists and Evangelicals in the Soviet Union. Nor have these witnesses all been people who did not really understand the workings of power politics, e.g. not the late Martin Wight, who throughout World War II was a Christian pacifist.[7] As indicated below, evil sometimes so pervades a society or parts of it, e.g. Nazi-occupied Europe, that not only is just treatment unavailable to the individual, but also wholly just action is not open to him as a member of that society. In such cases personal integrity seems to leave no option but withdrawal of social commitment, even though withdrawal may well bring martyrdom.

An argument against withdrawing in order to be in no way responsible for evil which pervades one's country is that one may thereby fail to redress injustices. Suppose you are a citizen of a nuclear-weapon state which has a treaty of military assistance with a smaller non-nuclear state. The latter is attacked without provocation by a more powerful non-

nuclear state. Your government decides to go with conventional forces
to the aid of its ally. But it also deploys, publicly though quietly,
nuclear delivery systems which, though they *could* be used to attack
centres of population, have the obvious purpose of deterring the aggres-
sor from massing either invasion forces or strategic strike forces. The
strong presumption is that these deterrent forces will in any case *not* be
used, because of the powerful inhibition everywhere against being the
first actually to use nuclear weapons since Hiroshima and Nagasaki.
Your nuclear weapon state in fact achieves a satisfactory conventional
victory quite without employment of its nuclear forces; but no one
is prepared to claim that the mere presence of the latter had not affected the outcome. In this instance (contrasting with the actual purpose
of nuclear deployment — to deter *conventional* attack), the terror of
nuclear attack upon mass populations was possible and is of background
moral significance, though admittedly remote.

   Even more poignant situations arise when a Power committed to
evil can be effectively resisted only by introduction of some other,
potentially evil, resources. The United Kingdom's (and later, combined
Western allies') project to develop the atomic bomb in order to forestall
Nazi Germany's doing so had its justification in the conscious diabolism
of Hitler's creed and regime, discussed below. (This is not said in miti-
gation of the Allies' mass destruction by conventional weapons, nor doe
it apply directly or in the same way to the other issue of the bombing
of Hiroshima and Nagasaki.) Evil sometimes gets built so thoroughly into a society that there may be call to stop it by force. In contrary cases,
e.g. religious persecution as discussed above, there is either magnificatior
or total misperception of the 'evil' to be overcome, while the injustice,
or indeed the evil, of the means proposed to overcome it is not perceived at all. R.H. Tawney, noble and generous of spirit, once summed
this up, saying that war must be either a crime or a crusade.

   If only that were so! Often, undoubtedly, it has been — and much
more often a crime than a crusade. But there have also been other cases
the English Civil War within England itself providing a clear example,
when each party has had some right on its side and each would have
felt themselves treacherous if they had not resisted. As usual in civil
wars, the one people of England became for the time two Powers, with
a third Power, the Scots, to the north. For armed forces of its day, the
New Model Army campaigned with considerable restraint in England
itself; but in Ireland, where Cromwell and his Roundheads believed the
were combating the Romish Antichrist, the tale was merciless.

   Thus even in this exemplary case of the English Civil War as a tragic conflict between causes both of which could lay claim to justice and even to public benefit, the transition to evil and to a kind of lunacy was a short one. And whereas the evil of war with no quarter given has persisted in Ireland to this day (though much moderated now), from the English 'tragic conflict' a development through two and a half centuries of civil liberty, free political institutions, legal justice and, at last, welfare and some small degree of equality can be historically traced. Other societies, in Europe and in the New World, developed similarly, so that from the turn of the century, though interrupted by the terrors of the two world wars and the paradoxical catastrophe — 'poverty in the midst of plenty' — of the Great Depression, an atmosphere of somewhat banal innocence began to prevail in such societies, often contaminated by racial injustice, and always by economic injustice,[8] yet discernible enough.

That atmosphere of innocence had one perilous effect upon those who lived in it: they did not recognise the devil immediately upon meeting him. (There are other, worse effects: one often hears now of many driving past accidents, or stopping only to peer and pry. This used to be rare, with the average person offering help as a matter of course, even at personal inconvenience. I am not thinking of the heroism, sometimes displayed in almost any society, where, say, someone who could have armed himself talks a homicidal maniac who has taken hostages into giving up his weapon instead of picking off the maniac in justifiable self-protection and protection of the hostages. The latter heroism is an instance of the redemptive action.) Specifically, they (or we) did not recognise Hitler.

Melbourne schools in 1939 dealt in one of the history courses with totalitarian ideologies and the contemporary dictators. The textbooks had not been written, so perforce we depended upon original works, including *Mein Kampf*. Its nastiness of tone was at once apparent. We were already informed about Hitler's militarism, employment of crowd hysteria, destruction of liberty and free institutions, use of pan-German nationalism in foreign conquest, and anti-Semitism (though not of the depth and extent of the last), all of which were certainly unjust enough. A very few had learnt of sources of indigenous resistance, e.g. of the Confessing Church and its Barmen Declaration against 'German Christianity', which more than venerated 'the man Adolf Hitler'. But what I for one could not credit were the book's quite explicit indications of his purpose of conquest at least Europe-wide and of establishing a Faustian totalitarian Power based on sheer race. It seemed unbelievable that a society should utterly eliminate the very possibility of public justice, corrupt children and friends into denouncing parents and friends, and worship instead blood, soil, and the Führer. We had been taught that injustices could and should be redressed one by one according to conscience, by what Karl Popper later styled 'piecemeal social engineering'. The actuality of evil was beyond our experience.

Our failure was a failure of imagination. Yet after the event the actuality of evil can be conveyed even to the culpably innocent. A former colleague of Jewish parentage had spent her years from seven to thirteen (1939-46) in and around Warsaw. Her detailed account of experiences was instructive, but even more the sense conveyed of the atmosphere of a society in which public justice was impossible, and '. . . the blast of the terrible ones . . . like a storm against the wall'.[9] The evil could be withstood, but at a high cost in risk incurred, and with little hope. The peril and the fear which battle or a natural disaster bring, though doubtless as intense, are of a different and less pervasive order. Borrowing the terminology but not the philosophy of ancient Gnosticism, Paul sets out that contrast:

> We wrestle not against flesh and blood but against principalities, against powers, against the rulers of the darkness of this world, against spiritual wickedness in high places.[10]

Those mysterious, supernatural and evil Powers were thought of as transcending but participating in the earthly 'Powers that be . . .', which in turn were the scene of a warfare between God who had ordained them and the Powers of Darkness. When the latter had temporarily prevailed, they were represented in idolatrous form by the gods of the nations. Hence, from the Mosaic epoch onward, the prohibition upon idol-making and image-worship, and the Hebrew, later Iconoclastic and Islamic, recoil from great but idolatrous works of art as from uncleanness.[11]

By a strange paradox, the allegedly 'subjective' perception of evil is sometimes stronger and more vivid, and sometimes tells one more about the state of a society than can the 'objective' analysis of the material facts. Often, this is because an evil regime destroys the evidence of its misdeeds, as does the Ministry of Truth in Orwell's *Nineteen Eighty-Four*; or it fails to produce, and if produced cannot command, the free enquirers who can assess the evidence from day to day. This partly explains the widely remarked-on difficulty of evil regimes having no continuous history, while civilisation and the religious communions have. (Some secret societies such as the Mafia may be exceptions, though most of them have not been precisely 'regimes'.) To express some notions barely half-baked: progress in good, such as the step-by-step abolition of slavery and serfdom (by which we modern pygmies have been advanced beyond such giants as Plato and Aristotle) has no mirror-image in any progress of evil, though an illusion of such 'progress' may be given by evil's being parasitic upon good. The Assassins of the ancient Islamic world, and *thuggee* as a worship of Kali in India, could not 'advance', but at most merely recrudesce, as they and even Nazism may yet do, even in sterile and artificial forms like the contemporary recrudescence of witchcraft. But progress in good — say, in civilisation considered as 'the diminution of the *traces* of original sin' — can never be guaranteed to be once-for-all: to believe otherwise is to accept the *myth* of progress.

That evil can be and is parasitic ephemerally upon good shows up in the use of the blessings of current psychiatric medicine for purposes of intellectual and political repression, purportedly done for the benefit not only of the whole community, but even more of the 'patient' himself. It is at this point that the myth of the Antichrist lends its perspective: upon the occasions of many advances in good, evil men take up as pseudo-saviours the very advance itself and, worse, persuade otherwise decent and well-meaning people to accept them as saviours (nevertheless, there is no identifying the historical pseudo-saviour as *the* contemporary Antichrist in the way, for instance, that the antipopes might once have been identifiable). But in parts of the world, e.g. parts of Asia, where the Messianic conception is not native, the Antichrist myth has of course no application. Nevertheless it would be unsurprising if Eastern traditions with some sense of history should turn out to have comparable ideas.

Insofar as a society, e.g. a nation-state, continues to afford the possibility of significant redress of injustice, it remains not wholly subject to evil: one mark of the nation-state wholly subject to evil is that it makes impossible the recourse to ordinary, everyday, demonstrable justice. Redemption in the latter case is worked, if it is worked at all, by the martyrs and the small martyr-communities, many of whom will never be known; and no political arrangement can prepare beforehand to provide and train martyrs. But before a society gets to that pass, politics and law can do much to set up a structure of freedom and justice.

Justice and freedom are interrelated, for the essentials of just procedure, logically prior to and more important than apprehension, charging, adjudicating or sentencing, are the means of publicly establishing the truths of the matter; such means are available only where the truth can be elicited by free enquirers from free witnesses.

The conditions for a society in which there is a good prospect of truth's being thus elicited include a recognisable and accepted body of law, and in particular the principle that no-one can be detained or penalised except according to law. These conditions do not necessarily include electoral or representative democracy in the sense of 'one man, one vote'. The latter, however, is a near-necessity for the further structure that guards against the seizure of power by any single movement, evil or otherwise, by its fragmenting of state power. Though (under the Westminster system, for example) the leader of a governing party has, as prime minister, considerable power, that power is limited in extent by law and by the constitution, and in time by the requirement periodically to face the electors; and *their* power, jointly sovereign, is severally minute. Furthermore, a polity is free and democratic when similar constitutions and systems are accepted, not only at the level of national government, but even, for instance, in private associations and clubs. All the citizens of such a polity could, admittedly, succumb to evil at the same time, in which case the free and democratic polity would soon be overthrown; but that is much less likely than in a concerted and corporate society.[12]

Along with the rather uninteresting innocence and ignorance of evil referred to at the beginning of this chapter, we labour under an unawareness of our freedom: for us it is, and it should be, taken as much for granted as the air. Yet though it is not perhaps directly detectable, its absence is. If you cannot leave the society, that nation-state is not free. The greatest political difference in the world is between those Powers that maintain their frontiers only to keep outsiders out, and those which also and even more maintain them to keep insiders in.

Notes

1. E.g., the UN Congo forces' closure of airports and the radio station in Léopoldville on 5 September 1961, following the former Prime Minister Lumumba attempted deposition of Kasavubu, the Head of State. In that instance the rights and wrongs of the action, by no means immediately clear, could be disentangled, with care: see A.L. Burns and Nina Heathcote, *Peace-Keeping by U.N. Forces: from Suez to the Congo* (Praeger, New York, 1963).

2. No derogation is suggested of the scriptures of other religions, such as Islam, Zoroastrianism or Buddhism, with which we are much less familiar.

3. Luke 14:31-2.

4. This idea is pursued further in A.L. Burns, *Of Powers and their Politics* (Prentice-Hall, Englewood Cliffs, 1968), especially pp. 85-90 and 267-80.

5. William Blake, *Songs of Innocence and Experience.* The belief Blake refers to is that 'the just shall live by his faith', faith being thought of by him as creative energy, which resembled the physical energy that radiates light from and to natural objects.

6. This dilemma is considered at length in A.L. Burns, *Ethics and Deterrence: a nuclear balance without hostage cities?*, Adelphi Paper No. 69, International Institute for Strategic Studies (London, 1970).

7. Hedley Bull, 'Martin Wight and the theory of international relations', *British Journal of International Studies* (1976) vol. 2, p. 103.

8. Economic injustice, and the nihilistic power-hungry evil which often arises from it, are not dealt with in this essay, principally because it is a distinct theme and, even more, because I have no substantial knowledge of it. But it does seem that one can distinguish two phases of exploitative evil — the first, in which labour is exploited, without a qualm about injustice, by virtue of the scarcity of the necessities of life (a situation currently perpetuated in totalitarian regimes by the causing of 'artificial' scarcity of these necessities); and the second, the notorious consumerism, in which new demands are elicited for novel goods by methods amongst which advertising is only one, and the workers who produce such goods are also given a vested interest in the sustaining of demand for them. The two phases of course often co-exist, as in the major capitalist economies nowadays. When, in the first phase, some compunction about wage injustice is shown, and when, in the second phase, exploiters hold back to some extent from eliciting demand for destructive or debilitating 'goods', a hope can be entertained for reform. But when in either phase the exploitation is sheerly nihilistic, then it often combines with the evil of unbridled power-politics to cause, say, the Opium Wars.

9. Isaiah 25:4.

10. Ephesians 6:12. It is odd that this dark saying, when received as a depiction of the history of the last 60 years, seems merely matter-of-fact.

11. See further G.B. Caird, *Principalities and Powers* (Oxford, 1956), and the present author in *Of Powers and their Politics*, pp. 77-85. The foregoing paragraphs do not invoke Scriptural authority on behalf of a particular interpretation of international politics; they assert a mainly biblical origin for the concept of 'the Power' as an international actor; and they attempt to show how the historical international order appears from a biblically-formed perspective. Concepts like 'the Powers' and 'the Antichrist' are not abstract ones under which to find specific historical instances, as Aristotle found many such instances under his abstract concept of '*the constitution* of a city-state': to attempt to find instances leads straight to the literalist millenarianism which seeks the identity of the current Antichrist or the Book of Daniel's Fifth Monarchy. These biblical concept-images are generative ideas that set and (I believe) widen and deepen a perspective upon history and upon today's world, and that stimulate one's analyses.

12. The fragmentation of power is not the same as (the illusion of) pluralism. Free democracy comprises a strong, strict and rather narrow set of values, but in matters indifferent its principle is to remain indifferent. Matters indifferent are the illusory realm of pluralism.

PART TWO: PRAXIS

7 RACE, CONFLICT AND LIBERATION IN AFRICA

Jan Pettman

In the late 1950s and early 1960s colonialism and racism appeared on the retreat before the triumphant demands of African nationalism. The retreat was halted at the Zambesi, leaving white Southern Africa in a strong defensive stance against the black north. Confrontation included liberation wars within the white preserve. In 1974, the *coup* in Portugal found Africa's oldest imperial power acknowledging the right of its colonies to independence. With the frontiers of white power contracting, South Africa joined forces with Western governments to legitimise a moderate form of majority rule in Rhodesia and the 'independence' of Namibia, and began to seek acceptance within the continent as an African state.

In the years that separate the two stages of African decolonisation, the political, economic and ideological forces in Africa have changed profoundly, and with them the bases for moral claims[1] made on behalf of African peoples. There is some continuity in the assertion of African identity, since shared colonial experiences and being judged by others as 'Africans' led to feelings of common victimisation,[2] but in the mid seventies the issues have become decisively more complex. Previously, African leaders claimed rights on behalf of their fellows against their colonial masters, and demanded control of their own destinies. These demands were articulated in terms of race, colour and access to wealth and power, and were summed up in slogans of anti-colonialism, anti-racism and rights of national self determination. Africans did not seek to establish rights of a new kind or on a different philosophical base from those already accepted within the Western tradition, but required of Europeans that they extend these rights to Africans, and so close the gap between the liberal rhetoric and the colonial reality. Africans asserted the universal applicability of these rights, and denied the legitimacy of alien rule, and of a privileged caste system based on race. They thus claimed the right to rebel, to resort to violence in the face of their continued exclusion from the political processes of their country.

In this way, African leaders not only pursued claims on behalf of their fellows, but saw themselves as a moral force, 'teaching' the decadent, inconsistent European powers to live by their own moral principles. This dimension, an added self-righteousness, stemmed from

the African self-image as being the most victimised of peoples.[3] A sense of
injury, and of innocence as victim compared with the guilt of the
aggressors, helped fuel the struggle against colonialism.

By the mid seventies, however, the debate had become much more
complicated and critical. The key issue is no longer the challenge to
formal colonial rule, but rather the very nature of the post-colonial
state in Africa, and of its relations with the wider, Western-dominated,
economic, political and cultural system. The lines of conflict are no
longer simply black against white but reflect deep divisions within the
black ranks. Many African leaders, both of independent governments
and of aspiring political movements in Southern Africa, continue to
couch their claims in terms of majority rule and political independence.
They are countered by others who speak of liberation and social
revolution, of armed struggle and the need to create alternative structures within the state, to create new relationships capable of sustaining
and defending the rights of Africans against those who continue to
deny them. These rights are no longer claimed for Africans *per se*, or
for those within a certain territory, but for those who are in an exploited, subordinate position. The claims are made as much against the
African elite as against outsiders. The issue has become 'who speaks for
whom?', with competing spokesmen representing different kinds of
interests and competing notions of the good society, with its consequent
rights and duties.

There remains a considerable moral element, no longer seeking
morally correct behaviour from the colonial powers, but rather recognising the psychologically crippling and morally compromising effects
of colonialism on the colonised.[4] In this sense, liberation becomes a
search for African moral regeneration, the rediscovery of integrity
through assuming responsibility for self, and establishing African
autonomy.

The overwhelming facts of 'independent' Africa's existence are its
extreme weakness, and subsequent vulnerability, and its profound
dependence on external forces. All the black African states are poor,[5]
insecure, dependent on their military forces for internal use, and
lacking the instruments or basis for economic development or effective political control. State borders do not on the whole coincide with
ethnic, racial or cultural frontiers, but are the creation of colonial
regimes whose legitimacy has now been denied. At independence, all
the units of the polity – the government, the state and the nation –
were underdeveloped and, in the last case, almost non-existent. In this
situation 'it is not the country that is in danger of attack or conquest,

but the government that is in danger of overthrow or collapse. Insecurity is thus endemic, inherent, and political, rather than specific, external and military'.[6] Anti-national threats are often internal, sub-national ones — from tribal, ethnic or regional groups, or stemming simply from alternative elites like the military. Government rests on so slender a base that little power is necessary to topple it.[7]

This weakness has crucial implications for the external relations of African states. A dissatisfied group within the country may, through external support, provide itself with the means to overthrow the government. This support may take the form of a covert guarantee from the ex-colonial or dominant external power that it will not intervene against the *coup*-makers. But the government is vulnerable to other kinds of intervention or outside influence — to the threatened withdrawal of a desperately-needed loan, or insistence on changes in domestic policy as a precondition for the loan; to a fall in prices for the principal export crop, since the export-dominated, externally-orientated economy of most African countries is mono-cultural; or to the advice and aid of 'experts' whose guidance may be sought voluntarily by governments appalled at the gap between policy formulations and the instruments which are available for government action.

At independence, then, African leaders found themselves charged with responsibility for pursuit of the 'national interest'. Because the government was obliged to create the nation, as much as assert its independence, national security was often defined in terms of the survival of the government. Defence of both the state and its government led, therefore, to attempts to argue and implement the rights of state sovereignty and continental hegemony, to protect the country against intervention by either African neighbours or extra-continental powers.

Independent Africa's search for its own ground-rules, for consensus on the rights and duties of African states, thus reflects African vulnerability and fear of intervention. The Organisation of African States, an all-inclusive grouping established in 1963, has attempted to regularise intra-African relations, based on such norms as non-interference in the domestic affairs of others, and the peaceful settlement of disputes.[8] The functioning of these rules depends upon coexistence and compromise, on values of good neighbourliness and mutual forbearance, thus guaranteeing the status quo. Hence only four African states recognised Biafra's right to secede, despite its claim to national self determination, a moral claim viewed as universally valid in the colonial context.[9] So the anti-colonial movements, on becoming successor governments, assert the legitimacy of colonially-drawn boundaries, and accept the Western international law bases of state sovereignty and non-interference.[10] Such a mutually agreed-upon stand-off thereby allows governments to turn their attention, and their minimal resources, to the more urgent threats to their security, that is, internal opposition, and extra-continental penetration and manipulation.[11]

Calls for African unity do reflect the emotional identification which comes from shared colonial experience and racial humiliation. They also reflect awareness that the 'Balkanisation' of Africa, now divided into over 50 countries, invites further external intervention.[12] However, lack of ideological consensus, lack of clearly-demonstrated short-run economic advantages, and the unwillingness of any existing leaders to surrender what power they do have, makes the commitment to unity little more than rhetorical. No leader, except possibly Nkrumah, seriously considered jeopardising his state's sovereign rights in an all-African supra-national government. What African unity does assert, however, is Africa's claim to continental jurisdiction — that Africa has the right to solve its own problems, without external intervention.[13] Thus African unity represents not an attempt to challenge state sovereignty, but to bolster state sovereignty by mutual collaboration to insulate the continent from those external forces which would exploit Africa's vulnerability for their own ends.

Such a defence, through alliances and organisations and the assertion of on-going rights of self-determination, is a desperate attempt to manipulate symbols and so convince others to forgo their comparative power advantage.[14] The moral rights of the poor and downtrodden must be legitimised and recognised for the poor lack the resources to defend themselves against the strong. Such pleadings are unlikely to succeed, both because Africans have no sanctions to enforce their claims, and because Africa is already so deeply enmeshed in the global capitalist system that intervention is everywhere an on-going, structural and total reality. Every 'independent' African state is profoundly shaped by external forces, tightly linked into relations of dependence, and thoroughly penetrated by patterns of unequal economic interchange.[15] The non-autonomous nature of African states results from their role as periphery, integrated into and shaped by wider systems of trade, investment and direction. Thus Zambia, one of the 'richest' and comparatively strongest African states, depends on copper for 96 per cent of its export income, and 64 per cent of its government revenue.[16]

Lacking administrative, technical or financial resources to do more than paper-nationalise the main assets of the country and to demand a slightly larger share for its elite, the government is itself a peripheral mechanism, a transmission belt through which the wider economic and more potent political directives may sometimes flow. To this extent, not only the state's independence but the government itself as little more than a fiction, and the right of national self-determination is removed from the realm of reasonable political possibility. So weak is the government, and so dependent itself on external support and finance, that the cry of non-intervention is either a convenient disguise, or a plea against hostile anti-government intervention, or, at best, the desperate claims made on behalf of an exploited people, in no position to assert their rights or interests against foreign interests.

In the two decades since the first advances of African nationalism, the realities of the wider international system and the distortion of African forms through integration into that system have acted to deny the very rights which African leaders thought they had won. The earlier claims for national self-determination, against alien rule and racial injustice, were gradually replaced by attacks on neo-colonialism.[17] For most African leaders this simply meant that political independence was not enough, and did not, in fact, exist if every important aspect of the economy remained in foreign hands, or was shaped by external forces far more powerful than the new African governments. Africa's right to control its own destiny then became more an issue of economics, no longer couched in Lockean terms of moral rights to individual freedom, or dignity, or humanity, but in terms of material claims, rights to the control of national resources for the national good, and the rights of Africans to a more equal share in the wealth of the world. Development replaced freedom, and the vocabulary and terminology shifted subtly from that drawing on the rhetoric of the former colonial masters, rhetoric in the liberal-democratic tradition, to that loosely selected and adapted from another alien source, Marxism.[18] Exploitation became the greatest evil, although exactly how to define the corresponding right, and how to base and justify it, was less certain. Thus a changed political situation fostered an evolving ideology which incorporated alternative definitions of rights, and different assessments of those against whom these rights were claimed. Morality became a function of ideological purity, and of recognition of the conflicting sectional and class interests of various groups.

Here, the confused nature of contemporary African political claims became evident, for while many African leaders used Marxist terms, they did not accept the logical implications of their rhetoric, nor the assumptions which they appeared to articulate. The most common response was to blame the international capitalist system for Africa's exploitation, but few (except, perhaps, Tanzania)[19] seriously tried to insulate themselves from this system. More often, they attempted to improve their position, within the rules of the system's game, seeking an economic development based on diversity of exports and import substitution which might make the state, or at least its elite, marginally more wealthy. At the same time, African Socialism was redefined, moving from its earlier version — asserting the value of African traditional communalism as an indigenous and valid form of political and economic organisation — to a policy of selective nationalisation and elaborate state planning through parastatal and government bodies (usually staffed and directed by expatriates, often the former owners or administrators, now richly compensated and bearing management contracts).[20]

Franz Fanon predicted, at the beginning of African independence, that African rights and freedoms would not be guaranteed by formal political statehood. He foresaw the subversion of African rights through the nature of African leadership, the succession governments — the intermediary elite.[21] This elite was racially representative of its people, perhaps, but was the creation of the colonial system — of its values, its education system, and its allocation of administrative and other occupational roles. The elite was not only created by the alien 'other', but remained dependent upon it for its continued existence. Lacking its own independent power base, as well as its own, or national, values or goals, it did not act to transform the polity or economy, but acted as the agent for outsiders, who continued to monopolise effective power and decision-making. Such a group might resent its inferior status, or wish for a larger share in the national wealth, but it lacked the popular base, the authentic nature, the national or ideological integrity, to pursue claims on behalf of indigenous interests and so challenge the deeprooted colonial structures. Thus independence localised the political system — and, less so, the economic management — but it did not alter either the domestic power realities or the imperial connection.

'The problem of the nature of the state created after "independence" is perhaps the secret of the failure of African independence.'[22] Nowhere in the first round of African independence did governments oversee a structural revolution of the sort necessary to create national forms able to establish and defend national independence, or even define its objectives in terms that represented a substantial break with the colonial past and neo-colonial present. Growing awareness of this fact has coincided with and reinforced another, the radicalisation of some segments of the liberation movements in Southern Africa, and the shift of claims from majority rule to liberation, from political independence to social revolution .

The liberation movements began, as did most African nationalist
movements, as mass parties committed to non-violent protest and
constitutional demands for political rights. In the early sixties, Southern
African parties found the road to peaceful change closed, their leadership decimated, their followers harassed, their demands denied all
political or moral legitimacy. They became, by default, parties of
revolution. They claimed the right to rebel, labelled their own violence
'defensive' and justified because they were given no choice but surrender
or revolt.[23] So they became clandestine, seeking the external support,
internal strategies and ideological justification for armed struggle. Some
movements, especially the MPLA in Angola, Frelimo in Mozambique,
and ZANU in Zimbabwe, developed an elaborate definition of African
realities which was far more radical than any represented by independent African governments. The role of ideology was stressed, not only
as an essential component in raising peoples' consciousness, as part of
the mass mobilisation necessary for successful guerrilla warfare, but also
to guard the movements against the pitfalls of moderate African
politics — to clarify priorities and to identify the enemy more
rigorously.[24]

Not all liberation movements have a commitment to thoroughgoing social revolution. The ambiguities of their origins are aggravated
by continuing ideological, as well as political and personal, divisions.[25]
However, the issues are no longer framed in terms of black and white,
but also, and except in South Africa itself, mainly, as a conflict
between competing African views of the good future society, and
differing definitions of social, as well as racial, justice.

The radicalisation of some segments of African politics led to the
cry for liberation, for the total destruction of the structures of
dependence and exploitation, which have proved so strong. But liberation still appears remote. When Frelimo's leader Samora Machel became
President of Mozambique, he said: 'the State is always an organized
form through which a class takes power in order to fulfil its interests'.
He went on: 'We are aware that the apparatus we are now inheriting is,
in its nature, composition and methods, a profoundly retrograde and
reactionary structure which has to be completely revolutionized in order
to put it at the service of the masses'.[26] The process of radicalisation
has led, then, to the articulation of new moral claims, and the identification of far more thoroughgoing obstacles to these claims than Africa's
early independence leaders ever suspected. But still the priorities
stemming from this alternative view of Africa's lack of freedom must

be reconciled, in government, with Africa's lack of power and dependent status. Thus Frelimo, while at war, cried: 'Smash Caborra Basa', and condemned any connection at all with South Africa. After independence the Frelimo government allows Portugal to manage Caborra Basa, and pays for the hydroelectric scheme by selling electricity to South Africa, and announces that it will still send workers to South Africa. Such phased disengagement sounds little different from statements by the Zambian government in earlier independence. Even the more morally rigorous and radical leaders, then, have been forced to compromise in the face of the objective realities of African weakness and dependence. Yet the rhetoric, the perception of the issues at stake, has changed.

The key issue is: who rules? and for whom? For whom are rights claimed, and against whom? The history of African independence, thus far, is dominated by claims advanced by Westernised, city-based leaders who claimed representativeness on the basis of shared race and their shared exclusion from full humanity and responsibility. With few or marginal exceptions, they then exploited their formal political rule for their own, or their sectional group's profit or security. Power did not pass to the people, but to selected elites. The question in the mid-seventies is whether decolonisation in central-southern Africa will merely repeat this process.

In September 1976 Rhodesia's Ian Smith capitulated, and accepted the principle of majority rule and the right of Africans to at least a share in political power.[27] Here again, the non-authentic nature of African politics emerges. The negotiations toward majority rule in Zimbabwe have depended from the outset on external intervention. The relative strength or role of any particular African leader lies, not on his following within the country, so much as in the support and recognition he receives from outside. South Africa's Prime Minister Vorster and American Secretary of State Kissinger brought Smith to the conference table, but the five front-line Presidents (of Zambia, Tanzania, Botswana, Angola and Mozambique) dictated terms to the Zimbabwe nationalists. The crucial significance of sponsors, and of host countries' facilities, offered to or withheld from national liberation movements or leaders, have constantly distorted internal power relations and decisions. Such manipulations from outside make nonsense of the claim of national self-determination, in the name of which much of the intervention is made.

The explicit attempt, by South Africa and the Western Powers, to foreshorten the armed struggle, to halt the process of radicalisation within the liberation movements, and to install a moderate black government in Zimbabwe,[28] brings us back to the crux of the problem: 'What is basically at issue is not the *whether* or *when* of majority rule, but *what kind* of independent state is to emerge. In particular, is there any prospect for a form of national liberation which provides a democratic alternative to the neo-colonial state?'[29] It has yet to be demonstrated that Africa's options include the possibility of the creation of political and economic structures sufficiently autonomous to justify the description 'national independence'.[30]

The problem of competing moral claims in Africa is brought into sharpest relief in South Africa's struggle to assert its right to exist — even, indeed, to hegemony — in Southern Africa. Here, the issue is not colonialism, with its extracontinental dimension, but racism. The dominant white minority is a settler minority, a group which has staked its existence, as well as its claim to exclusive privilege, within the domestic context of an African country. Like other states in Africa, South Africa relies heavily on external finance, arms, assistance and sponsorship. But South Africa is unique in that it is the only state in Africa with real power, with a developed infrastructure, with organisational and comparative military and economic strength. South Africa produces 22 per cent of the entire African Gross Domestic Product, and 40 per cent of its industrial output, as well as possessing its strongest military forces.

The place of South Africa in Africa is one of the crucial issues facing the continent.[31] The question would remain, although in changed form, even if the white government fell. However, the likelihood of internal revolution is extremely remote,[32] and the chances of external intervention in support of revolution are likewise minimal. The South African government was increasingly isolated in Africa, and the world, after 1960.[33] Then, in the late 1960s, its capacity to survive and the failure of significant intervention against it, led to the new outward-looking foreign policy, seeking dialogue with black African states, and trade and investment through a proposed common market for Southern Africa. Dialogue faltered as the liberation wars of Angola, Mozambique and Zimbabwe accelerated in the early 1970s, and reached crisis point in Angola in 1975. The racial and ideological war, long predicted by Kenneth Kaunda and many others, appeared a belated reality. Angola became 'independent' in the midst of a war whose ramifications included Great Power confrontation on a scale not witnessed in Africa since the Congo.[34] The radical Marxist MPLA was backed by Soviet and Cuban advisers, in opposition to Unita, which had South African

military support, and the FNLA, which was partly financed and armed
by the United States. Henry Kissinger considered Angola the post-
Vietnam testing ground for American will and power, and declared that
'the United States will not accept Soviet intervention in other parts of
the world',[35] especially where it had 'no historical interests' (conveniently overlooking the fact of continued Soviet arms and support to
the MPLA over a period of 15 years, a period during which America
had chosen, first, to support the Portuguese colonial regime which
MPLA had opposed, and then to endorse the anti-Soviet, non-radical,
forces against MPLA).

Angola was indeed a testing-point for South Africa and the West.
Kissinger argued to continue support for the anti-MPLA parties. But the
American Senate, seeing Angola as remote and unimportant to
America's security and national interest, passed an amendment to the
Defence Appropriation Bill in December 1975, and forbade the Ford
administration to grant further aid. South African leaders then faced
the choice to intervene, without massive Western aid, against the forces
of African liberation, or to accept African rule along its borders and
seek a new relationship with independent Africa. They decided that
they could not fight for the West alone,[36] withdrew their military
forces from Angola, pursued partial co-operation with the Mozambique
government, declared themselves in favour of majority rule in Zimbabwe
and of independence in Namibia. Working closely with Zambia's
President Kaunda, Vorster sought to establish a statesman's role,
accommodating even radical governments, and cosmetic changes were
made in apartheid as evidence of South Africa's goodwill and desire for
peaceful change. A number of moderate black leaders responded by
differentiating it from the colonial problem in Zimbabwe and Namibia,
and South Africa was granted status as a fellow African state.[37] Such
recognition is exactly what South Africa currently seeks, reducing the
possibility of hostile intervention against it, depriving its own African
nationalists of nearby bases and support, and securing an external
market that allows it to escape the need to restructure its own domestic economy. The alternative — the stimulation of a local black demand
sufficient to support its expanding industrial output[38] — is politically
inadmissible.

South Africa represents an extreme case of white privilege and white
power, a regularised and tightly structured system of domination.
Domestic African nationalism has reflected the evolution of the movements further north — first claiming rights on the basis of grievance
and deprivation, then asserting claims to self-determination and, after

Sharpeville, claiming the right to rebel.[39] Then began the painful transformation from mass political parties to 'illegal' liberation movements, committed, at least in theory, to armed struggle and social
revolution.

The doctrine of apartheid excludes the possibility of power-sharing
or the granting of formal political rights to the majority of South
Africa's population. In the past, South Africa has justified apartheid
on grounds of white superiority and civilisation, technical competence,
and the concept of guardianship of those racially, or at least culturally,
more backward. This defence was linked with the more general notion
of Western, Christian society, in a battle against Communism and
chaos. South Africa also attempted to insulate itself from outside
pressure or criticism by declaring its racial policies to be matters of
domestic concern, protected by state sovereignty, and the right of the
state against external interference. Lately, however, the position has
changed. The South African government has pursued the logic of
apartheid by deliberately internationalising the issue, and so readjusting
the basis on which apartheid is justified by its proponents.

Apartheid has long been defended in terms of the separate identities
of the peoples involved. Rejecting the pluralist model of different but
basically compatible cultures or interests, or the alternative assimilation-
ist model, South Africa opts for a conflict model, where only strict
separation will both preserve the differences, and ensure that the
different peoples do not destroy each other. These groups of 'peoples'
are defined as separate nations. Thus apartheid's 'basic premise today
is not one of race or colour relations, but one of national relations'.[40]
Black South Africans are denied citizenship or land rights within the
dominant society, but are granted the right of 'national' self-determination and management of their own affairs in their own homelands. The
first homeland to achieve formal independence, the Transkei, did so in
October 1976. What began as a system of internal colonisation, and
became a convenient mechanism of control over a cheap labour pool,
has led to a process of legitimising and institutionalising a lack of black
rights within the Republic, on the grounds that Africans can enjoy these
rights within their own national territories.

These territories are even more fragmented, penetrated, vulnerable
and dependent than are the pseudo-independent states further north.
Many black Africans will continue to live outside them, in white areas.
There may be partial accommodation of any aspiring black elite within
domestic politics which will allow for some movement towards a class
system, but this should coincide on the whole with traditional racial

stratification.[41] Any changes that do occur will be aimed at strengthening white domination, so that the realities of power will change little
by granting 'independence' to the homelands, or by granting Africans
the right to buy houses in Soweto. However, South Africa points to the
homelands as evidence of its contribution to African nationalism, to
national self-determination and political independence, and so justifies
its domestic and foreign policies in rhetoric not unlike that of the
African nationalists of the 1950s and 1960s.

Most African governments, as presently constituted, claim rights
against other states in terms of a perception of international relations
which is basically statist and conservative, despite the ritualistic
rhetoric of liberation against illegitimate, non-African regimes. The
vocabulary, the claims themselves, the very choice of the questions
asked, are, on the whole, alien. The education system which granted
Africa's leaders positions in administration and government was a
Western one.[42] The price of success within that system was approximation to the Western ideal, and through the school Africans exchanged
the village and the land for the city and the office. The personal
rewards have been enormous in terms of wealth, power and status, and
the cost has often been cultural alienation, or cultural schizophrenia.

Ali Mazrui suggests that the most profound impact of colonialism
is cultural.[43] Dependency lies, not only in political and economic
structures, but also in the minds of men. Colonialism represented
ideological aggression, for it established a system of domination and
subordination in which the subordinate became passive, fundamentally
compromised by their own failure to overthrow it. The psychological
effects of implicit collaboration in a system which devalued the
majority — the arbitrary distinctions and the denials of human
equality and full responsibility — cannot be underestimated.[44] It is
more than symbolic that Africans have used the language of the
oppressor to make their claims against that oppressor, and even, often,
to communicate with one another. For the choice has been that of
acquiescence in exclusion, or attempting to overcome exclusion by
accepting the framework of domination, and seeking access to its
rewards through assimilation.

The process of acculturation of Africa's ruling elite, together with
the long colonial heritage of dependence, of powerlessness, is little
altered by formal political independence. Despite some hostility to
Western groupings and values,[45] Africa continues dependent on Western
forms, its governments define development as closer approximation to
Western designs, and seek acceptance into, or better terms within, the

dominant system, rather than the assertion of African rights or roles out-side that system.

There is, for example, within the 'Dar' school in Tanzania,[46] and within MPLA and Frelimo, an alternative world-view, asking different questions and making moral claims of a different kind. This view, too, draws on a radical critique which did not originate in Africa, and is based on a reaction to an analysis of the wider international system in which Africa finds itself enmeshed. It is, however, substantially different from the more conventional 'imitate-integrate' response of most of the older-established African governments. For it advances the possibility of an alternative set of relations, of the destruction – or at least reduction – of those bonds of dependence and exploitation which currently paralyse Africa. In economic terms, it seeks a deve-lopment model on an inward-looking, self-directing and self-generating base; in political terms, it seeks the creation of structures of participa-tion and control which would destroy foreign-sustained intermediary elites.

How authentically African this response is, or whether, given the global power structure, there is any room for Africanicity in any but the most marginal way, is as yet undetermined. But many of those urging a radical alternative look to the achievement of a moral, as well as a functional, autonomy, which would re-establish African initiative, giving Africans the right to create and not simply emulate,[47] to determine their own priorities, and to decide for themselves whether or not the progressive-popular state can preserve indigenous values. Such urgings attempt to give meaning to the claims of national – or racial – self-determination; to demand independence in forms which challenge the on-going system of domination which has kept African states as the weak and manipulated products of forces beyond their shores.

Notes

1. Moral claims are determined by the political interests and ideological perspectives of the claimants, whose moral arguments and principles both reflect their notions of what is justified and good, and also represent an effort to improve their own material, political or psychological position *vis-à-vis* others.

2. A.A. Mazrui, *The Anglo-African Commonwealth* (Pergamon, 1967), p. 81.

3. Ibid., pp. 82-7.

4. See e.g. G. Balandier, *The Sociology of Black Africa* (London, 1970); F. Fanon, *The Wretched of the Earth* (Penguin, 1967), and *Black Skin, White Masks* (Penguin, 1967); A. Memmi, *The Coloniser and the Colonised* (Boston, 1965).

5. W. Zartman, *International Relations in the New Africa* (Prentice Hall, New Jersey, 1966), p. 145; R.O. Matthews, 'Interstate Conflict in Africa: a Review',

International Organization (Spring 1970), p. 360. Shaw points to the growing stratification, the inequality within Africa itself, as middle powers capable of acting as regional centres establish a complex hierarchy in intra-African relations. However, these middle powers remain dependent on external forces and collaborate closely with the great Powers. In global terms, these are weak and ineffective actors. T.M. Shaw, 'Discontinuities and inequalities in African International Politics', *International Journal* (Summer 1975), p. 386.

6. Zartman, *International Relations,* p. 49.

7. 'Arrest the person of the President, and you arrest the state', R. First, *The Barrel of a Gun* (Penguin, 1970), p. 4.

8. See e.g. F.C. Okoye, *International Law and the new African States* (Sweet and Maxwell, London, 1972), pp. 124-73.

9. Tanzania, Zambia, Ivory Coast and Gabon.

10. For a detailed examination of African governments' overall acceptance of international law see Okoye, *International Law,* especially pp. 179-82. Those aspects of international law which African governments have challenged are those most affecting state sovereignty, e.g. a state's rights to control its own natural resources, and questions of foreign investment and 'appropriate' compensation for nationalisation. See also the wider 'Third World' attempts to rework the international economic system, especially in areas of trade and investment. B. Gasovic and J.G. Ruggie, 'On the creation of a new international economic order', *International Organization* (Spring 1976), pp. 309-46.

11. In some circumstances, 'Africanity' becomes a principle overriding state sovereignty – thus the independent African states refused to recognise the white governments of Angola, Mozambique and Rhodesia, and intervention against these becomes a higher African duty in defence of the rightful claimants, the African people. Some African leaders, e.g. Julius Nyerere of Tanzania, extend this principle to South Africa too, while others, e.g. Kenneth Kaunda of Zambia, have always stressed South Africa's 'different' status, as a legitimate sovereign state. See Julius Nyerere, 'Why We Must Fight in Southern Africa', *Objective: Justice* (United Nations Publication, March 1971); Kenneth Kaunda, *Canberra Times,* 21 September 1976; D.C. Anglin, 'Zambia and Southern African "detente" ', *International Journal* (Summer 1975), pp. 497-8.

12. Kwame Nkrumah, *Africa Must Unite* (Heinemann, London, 1964), p. 172; A.A. Mazrui, *Towards a Pax Africana* (Weidenfeld and Nicolson, London, 1967), pp. 74-96.

13. Nkrumah, *Africa Must Unite*, pp. 109-28; A.A. Mazrui, *Violence and Thought* (Longmans, London, 1969), p. 240.

14. Zartman, *International Relations,* p. 145.

15. Arghiri Emmanuel, *Unequal Exchange: A Study in the Imperialism of World Trade* (Monthly Review Press, New York, 1972); Samir Amin, *Neo Colonialism in West Africa* (Penguin, 1973); W. Rodney, *How Europe Underdeveloped Africa* (Bogle L'Ouverture, London, 1972); Colin Leys, *Underdevelopment in Kenya: The Political Economy of Neo Colonialism* (Heinemann, London, 1975).

16. J. Pettman, *Zambia, Security and Conflict* (Friedmann, London, 1974).

17. Kwame Nkrumah, *Neocolonialism: the last stage of Imperialism* (London, Nelson, 1965).

18. For analyses of some sources of African rhetoric see A.A. Mazrui, *Anglo-African Commonwealth*, pp. 11-23; Introduction and K. Grundy, 'The Political Theory of Kwame Nkrumah' in W.A.E. Skurnik (ed.), *African Political Thought* (University of Colorado, Denver, 1967), pp. 67-91; and R. Gibson, *African Liberation Movements* (OUP, London, 1972), p. 10.

19. Tanzania – a partial and contradictory exception. J.S. Saul, 'African

Socialism in One Country', in G. Arrighi and J.S. Saul, *Essays on the Political Economy of Africa* (Monthly Review Press, New York, 1973); J.S. Saul, 'The State in Post-Colonial Societies: Tanzania', *Socialist Register* (London, 1974), pp. 349-73; Tanzanian Studies no. 2, *The Silent Class Struggle* (Tanzanian Publishing House, Dar es Salaam, 1974).
    20. Gibson, *African Liberation Movements*, p. 11; Tanzanian Studies no. 1, *Towards Socialist Planning* (Tanzanian Publishing House, 1974).
    21. F. Fanon, *The Wretched of the Earth* (MacGibbon and Kee, London, 1965), pp. 305-21; Saul, *Socialist Register* 1974, pp. 349-72; I.G. Shivji, 'The Silent Class Struggle', in Tanzanian Studies no. 2, pp. 1-60.
    22. Amilcar Cabral, quoted in *Review of African Political Economy*, 5 (1976), p. 1.
    23. Mazrui, *Anglo-African Commonwealth*, p. 21; R. Blackey, 'Theories of Revolution: Fanon and Cabral', *Journal of Modern African Studies*, 12 (1974), p. 205.
    24. Ideology 'created the conditions for transforming the armed struggle into a people's war, for going over from a liberation struggle to the higher phase of a people's democratic revolution', Samora Michal, 'The Struggle Continues', *Review of African Political Economy*, 4 (1975), p. 18. See also Kwame Nkrumah, *Handbook of Revolutionary Warfare* (Paraf, London, 1968); Grundy in Skurnik, *African Political Thought*, p. 91; Amilcar Cabral, *Revolution in Guinea* (Stage I, London, 1973), pp. 73-90; Henri Oren, 'The Ideological Work of African Liberation Movements', *African Communist*, no. 56 (1974), pp. 82-90.
    25. Competing ideological, ethnic and regional groupings aggravate personality differences, and all are compounded by the 'frustrations of exile'. Propaganda activities and lobbying for outside support and finance become crucial in a situation where there is no means of mobilising or assessing popular support or political effectiveness.
    26. Machel, 'Struggle Continues', p. 19. See also J. Saul, 'Free Mozambique', *Monthly Review* (1975), p. 13.
    27. Nathan Shamuyarira, *Crisis in Rhodesia* (Transatlantic Arts, New York, 1966); Ben Mtshali, *Rhodesia: Background to Conflict* (Hawthorn, New York, 1967); J. Nkomo and J. Nyere, *Rhodesia: the case for majority rule*.
    28. For issues of intervention and Zimbabwe see *Review of African Political Economy*, 5 (1976), Editorial and Briefings. Henry Kissinger told a press conference on his return from central and southern Africa on 13 May 1976, 'The radical elements were gaining the upper hand. The Soviet Union was appearing from the outside as a champion. The moderate regions were coming under increasing pressure, and therefore all the moderate Governments in Africa were in danger and all the Western interests in jeopardy. I think with this trip the [American] Administration started a process which can lead to negotiation of the so-called arms struggle in Southern Africa and permit Black and White populations there to work out a way to live together . . . I think it protected the Western interests in a moderate, constructive evolution of African Affairs.'
    29. Editorial, *Review of African Political Economy*, 5 (1976), p. 4. See also J.S. Saul's question 'smash the post colonial state, or use it?' *Socialist Register*, 1974.
    30. Some African states have achieved a measure of 'autonomy' or at least a lack of efficient external direction, by virtue of their very weakness. Thus Saul describes Amin's Uganda as 'unhinged', an unsteady state which is 'too weak and too internally compromised to stabilise society and economy and thereby effectively guarantee the on-going generation of surplus and accumulation of capital'. 'The Unsteady State', *Review of African Political Economy*, 5 (1976), p. 12.

31. Mazrui, in F.S. Arkhurst (ed.) *Africa in the Seventies and Eighties* (Praeger, New York, 1970), pp. 60-61.

32. Armed struggle in South Africa 'falls little short of suicide', H. Adam, 'Conquest and Conflict in Southern Africa', *Journal of Modern African Studies*, 13 (1975), pp. 627-8. See also Sheridan Johns, 'Obstacles to Guerrilla Warfare – a South African Case Study', *Journal of Modern African Studies*, 11 (1973), pp. 267-304. The consequences of the Soweto riots, leaving 176 Africans dead in June 1976, have yet to be assessed.

33. J.E. Spence, 'South Africa's "new look" Foreign Policy', *World Today*, (April 1968), pp. 137-45; Sam Nolutshungu, *South Africa in Africa: a study in ideology and foreign policy* (Manchester University Press, 1975); Anglin, 'Zambia . . .', pp. 471-503. ·

34. John Marcum, 'Lessons of Angola', *Foreign Affairs*, vol. 54, 1976, pp. 407-22; A. Gupta, 'Collapse of the Portuguese Empire and the Dialectics of Liberation in Southern Africa', *International Studies*, 14 (1975), pp. 1-20; Azinna Nwafor, 'The Liberation of Angola', *Monthly Review*, 27, 9 (1976), pp. 1-12.

35. *New York Times*, 24 December 1975.

36. *The Star* (Johannesburg), 21, 23 December 1975.

37. At the Ninth Extraordinary Meeting of the OAU Council of Ministers in April 1976, Tanzania, Zambia and Mozambique urged separation of the colonial problems of Zimbabwe and Namibia from South Africa's situation, and defended dialogue with South Africa. Opposition to this distinction, and a demand that all African governments shun South Africa's diplomatic 'offensive', was led by Kenya and Nigeria, two 'middle powers' who see their influence threatened by South Africa's increasing role in black Africa.

38. Saul, *Socialist Register*, p. 147.

39. N. Mandela, *No Easy Walk to Freedom* (Heinemann, London, 1965); A. Luthuli, *Let My People Go* (Collins, London, 1966); T. Karis and G. Carter, *From Protest to Challenge: a documentary history of African politics in South Africa 1882-1964* (Hoover, Stanford, 1972); *Sechaba* (African National Congress Newspaper, London).

40. D.P. de Villiers, *The Case for South Africa* (Stacey, London, 1970) p. 45 see also Eric H. Louw, *The Case for South Africa*, ed. by H.H.H. Biermans (MacFadden, New York, 1963).

41. Adam, 'Conquest and Conflict', p. 639.

42. For an analysis of the functions of Western education as role-allocator and social mobility agent, see e.g. P. Foster, *Education and Social Change in Ghana* (London, 1969). But see Mazrui's assessment of Uganda's President Amin, and other East African military men, whose parochial, rural background and minimal acculturation sets them apart from civilian politicians and from West Africa's military elite, and may signal a 'selective retraditionalization' in certain African states. 'Soldiers as Traditionalizers', *World Politics* XXVIII (1976), p. 269.

43. Ibid., p. 267; G. Groks, 'Difficulties of Cultural Emancipation in Africa', *Journal of Modern African Studies* 14 (1976), p. 66.

44. A. Moumouni, *Education in Africa* (Deutsch, London, 1968); A. Memmi, *The Coloniser and the Colonised;* G. Balandier, *The Sociology of Black Africa;* F. Fanon, *The Wretched of the Earth.*

45. Mazrui, 'Racial Self-Reliance and Cultural Dependency: Nyerere and Nkomo', *Journal of International Affairs*, 27 (1973), pp. 105-7.

46. D. Deroon and A. Kuper, 'The "New Historiography" in Dar es Salaam', *African Affairs*, 69 (1970), pp. 329-49; *Tanzanian Studies* papers (Tanzanian Publishing House, Dar es Salaam).

47. Mazrui, 'From Social Darwinism to Current Theories of Modernization', *World Politics* XXI (1968), p. 76.

8 MORAL PRECEPTS IN CHINESE FOREIGN POLICY: THE CONCEPT OF INDEPENDENCE

Michael B. Yahuda

Most students of Chinese affairs who admire and appreciate China's achievements in socialist construction are conscious of the moral qualities of the ideological and indeed practical frameworks which guide decision-making at all levels in Chinese society. All students of contemporary China are highly conscious of the collectivist ideals and the collective morality which pervade Chinese society. Few can be unaware of the moral dimensions of the debates as to how best to narrow urban and rural differences and as to how to reduce the gaps between the elites and the masses, mental and manual labour, etc.

There are very few, however, who are prepared to discern such moral concerns in the conduct of China's foreign policy. Indeed, many of those who most admire China's domestic achievements deliberately eschew careful analysis of Chinese conduct of foreign affairs. Foreign affairs, after all, in China as elsewhere, belongs to the domain of elite politicians. Moreover, it is the arena of contingency accommodations where, to quote Chou En-lai:

> The necessary compromises between revolutionary countries and imperialism must be distinguished from collusion and compromise between Soviet divisionism and US imperialism. Lenin put it well: 'there are compromises and compromises. One must be able to analyse the situation and the concrete conditions of each compromise, or of each variety of compromise. One must learn to distinguish between the man who gave the bandits money and firearms in order to lessen the damage they can do and facilitate their capture and execution, and a man who gives bandits money and firearms in order to share in the loot'.[1]

It is not the intention here to seek to examine such compromises, nor is it the intention to examine the general principles underlying China's foreign policy. Here one should note that the Chinese argue that their principles are constant, but it is their tactics that are flexible and that if there are changes in their foreign policy this has to do with changes in the external environment.

Nevertheless even within the framework of Chinese terms of reference it can be questioned as to whether all their declared principles are wholly compatible with each other. For example, there is the problem of promoting revolution abroad while simultaneously defending China as a socialist country. Put in another way, it is a problem of co-ordinating Party to Party relations, involving revolutionary minded Marxist-Leninist organisations committed to armed struggle, with state to state relations with the country in which these operate. Already a public incident has occurred over Peking's moral support for the Communist Party of Malaya which was regarded officially by the Malaysian Government as interference in Malaysia's internal affairs.[2] Non-interference in the affairs of another country is one of the cardinal constituents of the Five Principles of Peaceful Coexistence — regarded by the Chinese as the best framework for the conduct of international relations and as such it features in the Joint Communiqué establishing diplomatic relations between China and Malaysia in 1974. The Chinese explained that Party to Party relations were conducted on totally different levels from those of the state to state variety so that the Malaysian protests were misplaced. Intellectually and organisationally the Chinese may distinguish between the practice of revolution and the diplomacy of inter-state relations, but the relevant state which is receiving both dimensions of these policies does not. Moreover, there are grounds for believing that the dimension of China's state interests and orientations decisively affects the extent of support given to revolutions in other countries.[3]

Another kind of conflict can be seen in the contrast between the pursuit of revolution at home and the conduct of foreign policy on the basis of compromise and contingency accommodation abroad. For example, this has been graphically illustrated by the pictures showing Chairman Mao happily receiving President Nixon in early 1972 and then the former President four years later in 1976. Although the receptions for Nixon can be defended on the grounds of Maoist principles by reference to the exploitation of contradictions indicated in the earlier quotation from Chou En-lai, these receptions nevertheless contrast sharply with the fierce struggles on revolutionary purity carried on at home.

In this essay, however, we are mainly concerned with general questions of morality, or what have been called in this volume 'moral claims'. Clearly this is not just a question of consistency. It is rather a question of asking whether or not foreign policy statements and actions are based on something larger than the instrumental concerns of

security and utilitarian self interests. For example, are they based more
on general principles deducible or defendable in Marxist-Leninist terms?
We must examine the question as to whether or not there are certain
kinds of moral values genuinely preferred and promoted which underlie
much of China's attitude and conduct in world affairs. In classical
Western philosophical terms we are concerned here with the question of
whether foreign policy in China is dominated in the final analysis by a
view of the good life in societal terms, and as to how this good life may
be achieved.

One of the most dominating moral concepts in China's foreign
policy since 1949 is the concept of independence. As advanced by the
Chinese this is a complex concept imbued with considerable moral
force and passion. The concept may be said to have dominated Chinese
thinking about foreign affairs both in terms of the role of the Chinese
state in the world arena and in terms of the basis on which a new and
more moral world order can be built. The concept, which in Chinese
usage also means self-renewal based on genuine popular support, is one
which arises deep from within China's historical experience over the last
150 years. The careful development and application of the concept of
independence may be seen as one of the main reasons for the success of
the Chinese Revolution under the leadership of the Communist Party
headed by Chairman Mao. It is this concept, too, which sharply demarc-
ates the different approaches of the Soviet Union and the People's
Republic of China to questions of imperialism, proletarian internationalism, national liberation, and so on, as well as their different
approaches to Third World issues and their attempts to establish a new
world economic order.

The Maoist concept of independence is one which goes well beyond
legalistic notions of the trappings of statehood with its formal freedom
from overt external subordination. For Mao in particular, but also for
the Communist Party of China as a whole, the creation of a new China
was always more dependent upon the mobilisation, regeneration and
indeed revolutionisation of the Chinese people themselves than upon
the simple exclusion of imperialist influences from China. Indeed a
comparison between Mao Tse-tung's main writings in the 1930s and
1940s and those of Chiang Kai-shek, as expressed for instance in his
book *China's Destiny*, shows that the latter put far greater emphasis
on the imperialism factor as the primary source of China's ills than did
Mao. In Mao's slogan of the time imperialism was but one of 'the three
mountains' that was addressing the Chinese people. (The other two
were feudalism and bureaucrat-capitalism.)

It is not the intention here to review Mao's strategy in the Chinese revolution. Nevertheless a few points are worth mentioning from our perspective so as to underscore the main aspects of the Maoist and (as they have now become) the Chinese concepts of independence. Much of this may be familiar ground, but the concern here is to show that it is a dominant element in Chinese thinking about international affairs and it is necessary to review certain aspects of China's foreign relations.

Clearly for Mao, the socialist period of the present was one dominated by struggle -- one might almost say dominated by a passionate, moral drama between the two roads of socialism on the one side and the bourgeois road on the other, or public versus self.[4] For his socialism was not, and the move towards communism was not, just a question of abundance. His criticisms of Khrushchev's 'goulash communism' are particularly pertinent here.[5]

Having identified the meaning of communism, the Chinese found Khrushchev's approach wanting in all respects. The comment on raising public consciousness is especially relevant:

> Going forward to communism means moving towards enhancing the communist consciousness of the masses. A communist society with bourgeois ideas running rampant is inconceivable. Yet Khrushchev is zealously reviewing bourgeois technology in the Soviet Union and serving as a missionary for the decadent American culture. By propagating material incentive, he is turning all human relations into money relations and encouraging individualism and selfishness. Because of him, manual labour is again considered sordid and love of pleasure at the expense of other people's labour is again considered honourable. Certainly, the social ethics and atmosphere promoted by Khruschev are far removed from communism, as far as can be.[6]

The clearest disdain for Khrushchev's approach is apparent in the following passage:

> Khrushchev's 'communism' is in essence a variant of bourgeois socialism. He does not regard communism as completely abolishing classes and class differences but describes it as 'a bowl accessible to all and brimming with the product of physical and mental labour'. He does not regard the struggle of the working class for communism as a struggle for the thorough emancipation of all mankind as well as itself but describes it as a struggle for a 'good dish of goulash'. There is not an iota of scientific communism in his head but only

the image of a society of bourgeois philistines.[7]

At the same time, there are very practical instrumental aspects to the Chinese criticisms and the advocation of alternatives. Thus later in the same commentary the Chinese spelt out a programmatic view of the future including a commitment to thoroughgoing modernisation. Nevertheless the moral tone of the objections to Soviet practices are evident. There is also a passionate yearning for tapping the creativity and initiative of the Chinese people.

This in some ways goes back to what has sometimes been called the 'Yenan syndrome'. By this is meant the way in which under conditions of scarcity and isolation the Chinese communists were able to create a new revolutionary society. Here one should note the reports of many foreign journalists and indeed the representatives of the American government who visited Yenan at the time and contrasted the whole demeanour of the people there with that of those they found in the Kuomintang areas.[8] One of the major reasons for the Chinese communists' ultimate success can be seen firstly in their ability to translate the demands of the Chinese Nationalist movement for social revolution into practical concerns. This is something in which the Kuomintang failed utterly after 1927, even though land reform measures were passed by legislatures in Nanking. Because the Kuomintang's power was based ultimately upon landlords, these excellent programmes on paper were not in fact carried out and practised. Chinese communists by contrast were able to create even in their revolutionary bases tremendous social changes along these lines. A second aspect linked to this has been the way in which the Chinese communists, particularly under Mao, were able to provide a new moral framework within which the Chinese people were able to link their own local needs and aspirations to larger universal principles. Fundamental was the complete independence within which the Chinese communists operated.

The nationalist strain had always been a deep one in Mao's thinking. It antedates his embrace of Marxism-Leninism and it stayed with him throughout his life. Indeed the most complete text available of an extensive essay by Mao written in the period between 1917-23 (that is *The Great Union of the Popular Masses* written in 1919), carries the following vivid passage:

Our Chinese people possess great inherent capacities! The more profound the oppression, the greater its resistance: that which has accumulated for a long time will surely burst forth quickly. I venture to make a singular assertion. One day, the reform of the Chinese people will be more profound than that of any other people, the society of the Chinese people will be more radiant than that of any other people. A Great Union of the Chinese people will be achieved earlier than that of any other place or people. Gentlemen! Gentlemen! Our golden age, our age of glory and splendour, lies before us![9]

Against the objection that this was written nearly 60 years ago and that it belongs to a phase of Mao's life long since past, consider this quotation from a piece published at the beginning of the Great Leap Forward in 1958:

Apart from their other characteristics, China's 600 million people have two remarkable peculiarities; they are first of all poor, and secondly, blank. That may seem like a bad thing, but it is really a good thing. Poor people want change, want to do things, want revolution. A clear sheet of paper has no blotches, and so the newest and most beautiful words can be written on it, the newest and most beautiful pictures can be painted on it.[10]

Four months before this was published Mao was telling the other Chinese leaders in confidence:

Whenever we talk about it we say that our country has such an enormous population, it is such a vast territory, abundant resources, so many people, 4,000 years of history and culture . . . we have bragged so much about this, yet we cannot compare with a country like Belgium . . . now our enthusiasm has been aroused. Ours is an ardent nation, now swept by a burning tide. There is a good metaphor for this: our nation is like an atom . . . when this atom's nucleus is smashed the thermal energy released will have tremendous power. We shall be able to do things which we could not do before.[11]

These kinds of considerations are predicated on the fact that such a movement must be independent. Without that there is little that can be achieved. In this sense Mao always linked the necessity of independence with the successful conduct of revolution. In 1936 he told Edgar Snow that the Chinese revolutionaries were not fighting for the emancipation of China in order to turn the country over to Moscow. More than 20 years later Mao recalled Stalin's opposition to the Communists' armed struggle with the Kuomintang after World War II:

The Chinese Revolution won victory by acting contrary to Stalin's will. The fake foreigner (in Lu Hsun's *True Story of Ah Q*) did not allow people to make revolution. But our Seventh Congress advocated going all out to mobilize the masses and to build up all available revolutionary forces in order to establish a new China.[12]

Internationally the Chinese experience has been very different from that of the Soviet Union. Whereas the early Bolshevik leaders began their revolution on the assumption that it could only survive if it sparked off revolutions in the more advanced industrialised countries, a moving away later from the notion of internationalism towards the concept of socialism in one country was in a sense a fall from grace. One only has to note the big debates that preceded the Brest-Litovsk agreement to see how deep this went. The majority of the Bolsheviks at the time argued that as internationalists it was their duty not to sue for peace with the advancing German armies. Rather they should allow the German armies to continue their penetration in the conviction that this would enable the Bolsheviks to instigate a class conflict between the German officers and men which would lead to revolution in Germany. Starting in a minority position, Lenin maintained that the actual hard war revolutionary achievements in Russia should not be lightly given up for the unrealistic hopes of subverting the German armies. Lenin's arguments finally won the day.[13] But it can be argued that it was a costly victory. The passionate internationalism of the Bolsheviks was seen to be at loggerheads with the needs of socialism in Russia and, what is more, it was the interests of the latter which assumed priority. Yet the Bolsheviks had begun their revolution on the basis that if it were to be contained within an isolated backward Russia socialism would hardly survive, let alone develop and prosper.

For China, on the other hand, there has never been any question but that the Chinese people will be able to pursue socialism within the boundaries of the Chinese state. It is well known that their embrace of Marxism-Leninism was in many respect a product of radical nationalist considerations rather than some kind of internationalism. The Chinese insistence that revolution cannot be exported is something that arises fully out of their own experiences. There is no Chinese equivalent to Lenin's march on Poland. Indeed, one may go further and argue that the Chinese concept of proletarian internationalism has always been in many fundamental respects different from that of the Soviet Union. China has had no experience of running the Comintern. On the contrary, the Chinese experience of the Comintern is one in which the Comintern

meddled in Chinese affairs. Indeed in 1948 one Chinese leader, in a
famous piece, argued that in order to be an internationalist one has to
be a nationalist first, and that there was a direct correlation between
the two. China's message to other revolutionaries and to other countries
has always been that it is the internal factors which are primary and the
external ones which are secondary. It is not too farfetched to state
that this has dominated China's approach to foreign relations in so far
as the revolutionary factor is concerned. There is no example of a revolution in another country to which one can point as having been promoted and conducted by the Chinese. Since 1949 they have always seen it
as their internationalist duty to help what they regard as genuine movements of national liberation and genuine Marxist-Leninist organisations.
But never to the point whereby the Chinese, as it were, take over the
conduct of such movements; never to the point at which the Chinese
dictate to the movement concerned what it should do and what it
should not do at any key point in time. To be sure, the Chinese have
tended at various times to argue that there are general principles which
others should follow, but here the Chinese approach seems to be much
more that of a didactic teacher than that of an actual behind-the-stage
general conducting a vast array of forces.

   Interestingly, the one area in foreign relations where Mao is known
to have acknowledged a serious error on his part concerns the question
of judging in the late 1940s and early 1950s the quality of the independence which several Third World countries had gained from their colonial
masters:

> In the initial period after the founding of our state, some people,
> including myself as well as Comrade XX, took the view that the
> parties and trade unions of Asia and the parties of Africa might
> suffer serious damage. It was later proved that this point of view was
> incorrect: it did not turn out as we expected. Since the Second World
> War, thriving national liberation struggles have developed in Asia,
> Africa and Latin America year by year.[14]

This error arose at the time from the conviction that not having arisen
out of the revolutionary armed struggles for genuine independence like
that of China the independence of a country like India could only be a
sham. The Indian government could not but be a puppet of imperialism.
Thus on 19 November 1949 Mao wrote to the Secretary General of the
Indian Communist Party:

> I firmly believe that India, relying on the brave Communist Party of
> India and the unity and struggle of all Indian patriots, will certainly
> not remain long under the yoke of imperialism and its collaborators.
> Like free China, a free India will one day emerge in the socialist and
> peoples' democratic family . . .[15]

By 1953-4 the mood had changed to the extent that Chou En-lai
emphasised the commonalty between China and the newly independent
countries of Asia and Africa in his Bandung diplomacy of 1955.[16] As
John Gittings has pointed out, Mao began to differentiate between
national independence and national liberation. The former could be
won from a colonial power whether the movement had been led by the
proletariat or the national bourgeoisie. Whereas the latter suggested a
more thoroughgoing revolutionary process. Thus while India had
gained its independence China had undergone a process of liberation.[17]

In fact the Chinese continued to have doubts about the fundamental
readiness of national bourgeois governments to stand up to imperialist
pressures in the interests of independence. It was not until 1968 and the
fundamental realignment of world politics as seen by the Chinese
leaders that they began to feel confident that the general trends of
world affairs meant that Third World countries would have to stress the
policies of independence in preference to dependency relationships with
centres of imperialism or neo-colonialism. Thus in October 1959 *Red
Flag,* the Chinese theoretical journal of the Party's Central Committee,
carried an article by a Deputy Foreign Minister which argued that
because of the basic bourgeois character of the national bourgeoisie
'even the national independence they have won is by no means secure'.
By pursuing a capitalist road 'in the final analysis, they can never escape
from the control and bondage of imperialism'.

In the early 1960s, following the break with the Soviet Union, the
Chinese found a further reason to distinguish between the independent
Afro-Asian states. This centred on the issue of genuine opposition to the
United States. Those who were genuinely opposed to US imperialism, in
the Chinese view, necessarily had to exclude the Soviet Union too from
any putative international united front. It was not until the 1970s that
China's confidence in the genuineness of the independence of the Third
World countries has been continually affirmed without question. Never-
theless some issues concerning the point still remain unsettled and we
shall return to them at a later stage.

Regarding the question of imperialism, the Chinese, or rather Mao,
had developed an approach which from the beginning was different

from that of the Soviets.[18] It was in 1946 that Mao painted a scenario
in which he argued that the danger from the United States arose less
from its preparedness to strike out at the Soviet Union than from its
desire to gain control in the first instance of the vast zone between the
Soviet Union and the United States. Only when such areas had come
under US control would the Soviet Union come under direct military
threat. This contrasted very sharply with the view of the struggle
between the two camps as outlined for example by Zhdanov in 1947.
In the Soviet view at that time the main danger was that the United
States might seek to attack the Soviet Union itself. Therefore revolutionaries throughout the world had, in the Soviet view, to avoid
taking unnecessary risks which would provoke the United States into
making such an attack. It was primarily because of considerations such
as these that Stalin, for example, advised the Chinese communists
during their civil war not to engage in armed struggle, but to bury their
weapons and seek to reach an accommodation with Chiang Kai-shek.
Mao, by contrast, argued that since the Americans were in the first
instance trying to build up their strength and gain control of the vast
zone between Russia and the United States, it was resistance in those
countries which could best stop the United States. It was most important that the Chinese revolutionaries carry on the civil war because in
that way they would deny China to the United States and in that sense
they would help to postpone a new world war for a long time. Indeed,
the logic of the position was that by building bases in many foreign
countries the United States, in the Chinese view, was attacking in the
first instance the people of those countries. Therefore if the peoples of
those countries rose in armed resistance against the United States, this
would help the Soviet Union and China and that would also help the
development of revolutionary forces throughout the world. During
the period of the Sino-Soviet alliance this view of the world and the
nature of imperialism was rather superseded by Soviet concepts. In
1958, however, the concept of the intermediate zones lying between
the two camps surfaced once again in Chinese thinking, and it came even
more to the fore once the break with the Soviet Union had become
complete. This is indeed the view that the Chinese advance today in a
more sophisticated form on the basis of the division of the world into
three parts or Three Worlds: The First World consists of the two superpowers; the Third World is made up of those countries with an historical
experience of imperialist exploitation and a current situation of being
less developed economically; and the Second World consists of the
small and medium capitalist countries lying in between these two. In

the Chinese view there is a danger of a new world war arising out of the struggle between the two superpowers, but one of the most effective ways of preventing this is for the countries of the Third World in particular, but those of the Second World too, to resist being dominated economically and otherwise by the two superpowers. Regarding Third World countries the Chinese have gone further. They have identified them as the revolutionary motive force in world history at the present stage.

Since 1968 the Chinese have held that the Soviet Union has become a 'socialist imperialist' country. That is a country which flaunts the banner of socialism while in reality behaving as an imperialist power. Because of this development the Chinese claimed that the socialist camp had ceased to exist.[19] The Chinese nevertheless believe that the general global trends are positive but highly complex. Since the Chinese argue that the principal contradiction in the world today is between imperialism and social-imperialism on the one side and the people of the world on the other, it follows that the main focal point of resistance to the spread of superpower influence and dominance should be regarded as a revolutionary motive force for change. This is reinforced by the fact that many of the governments in the Third World not only resist superpower claims, but they also advance alternative visions of world order and offer practical proposals for changing the present distribution of power and wealth in international society.

The Chinese message to the Third World is quite simply to stress the importance of independence. In the Chinese view if Third World countries struggle for this they will become less and less dependent on exploitative economic relationships and economic dependencies, particularly with the superpowers, and secondly they will begin to become much more self-reliant. In the Chinese view there seems to be a link between pursuing independence of this kind and the growth of more revolutionary developments in the long run. This is expressed in their slogan 'Countries want independence, nations want liberation, and people want revolution'. In fact Chinese commentaries regard this as an objective analysis of the main trend in world affairs.

The Chinese, having identified their country as a socialist member of the Third World, have assumed a rather didactic role with regard to other Third World countries. They do not seek to lead the Third World as a bloc among blocs in world affairs; rather they seek to offer example and instruction. The message is very simply to maintain independence, aim for self reliance and support each other. Consider, for example, the following extract from the speech by the Chinese Minister of Foreign

Trade to the UN General Assembly special session to discuss reform of
the international economic system:

> To be independent and self-reliant, the developing countries must
> first of all smash the heavy fetters imposed on them and free
> themselves from imperialist and particularly superpower exploita-
> tion and control while at the same time eliminating the imperialist,
> colonialist and neo-colonialist forces at home so as to create the
> necessary conditions for the development of national economy.
>   By self-reliance, we mean that a country should mainly rely on the
> strength and wisdom of its own people, control its economic life-
> lines, make full use of its own resources, work hard, increase produc-
> tion, practise economy and develop its national economy step by step
> and in a planned way. Each country should make a distinction be-
> tween different circumstances and determine its own way of practi-
> sing self-reliance in the light of its specific conditions. Many deve-
> loping countries have followed the road of self-reliance in con-
> formity with their own characteristics and conditions and, after
> making sustained efforts and overcoming all sorts of difficulties, they
> have achieved gratifying successes in developing their national industry
> and agriculture, striving for self-sufficiency in foodgrain, developing
> communications and transport and training their own scientific, tech-
> nical and managerial personnel. Facts show that it is entirely feasible
> for the developing countries to develop their national economy inde-
> pendently and self-reliantly.
>   We have learnt from our own experience that in the course of
> developing the national economy independently and self-reliantly
> it is essential to correctly handle the relationship between agricul-
> ture, light industry and heavy industry. In the light of her own
> conditions, China has formulated a general policy of taking agri-
> culture as the foundation and industry as the leading factor in deve-
> loping the national economy and made her national economic plans
> according to this order of priorities: agriculture, light industry and
> heavy industry. Priority is given to the development of agriculture
> to solve the people's food problem, supply industry with raw
> materials and a market and accumulate funds for it. *It must be
> stressed that if a country is not basically sufficient in foodgrain but
> has to rely on imports, it may be taken by the neck at any time
> and find itself in a very passive and dangerous position.* In developing
> industry, we have adopted the policy of putting emphasis on small
> enterprises while combining small, medium and big enterprises, and

based ourselves on domestic needs and capabilities, relied on our own resources, built up our industries from scratch and expanded them step by step.

Self-reliance in no way implies 'self-seclusion' or rejection of external assistance, but means relying mainly on our own efforts while making external assistance subsidiary. Experience has shown that in the development of the national economy it is both beneficial and necessary for countries to carry on economic and technical exchanges on the principles of mutual respect for state sovereignty, equality and mutual benefit and the exchange of needed goods, thus making up for each other's deficiencies and learning from each other.

Mutual assistance and economic co-operation among developing countries are especially important. We are all developing countries, and we understand best each other's difficulties and needs, so we should support and help each other. Such co-operation is based on genuine equality and has broad prospects. (Emphasis added)[20]

The dominant theme is one of independence. A country which is not independent in its economic affairs cannot expect to be so in political terms either. A country which depends on imported foodgrains, as the underlined passage puts it very graphically, 'may be taken by the neck at any time'. The message which the Chinese continually hammer home is that sovereignty and independence extends beyond the trappings of international law. For these to have meaning and substance the people of a country through their leaders must be able to determine their own objectives free of external dependencies. Ultimately this means, to quote Li again, that 'a country should mainly rely on the strength and wisdom of its own people'. It is therefore a moral message and not an instrumental one that the Chinese are passing on. Li is at pains to point out in the extract quoted above that he is not calling for self-sufficiency or autarkic self-seclusion, but rather he is asking fellow Third World countries to rely 'mainly on our own efforts while making external assistance subsidiary'. He then went on to outline how foreign trade and aid could be carried out in such a way as to support and enhance independence. Indeed in a latter part of his speech, Li Chiang went on to assert that the developed countries had a role to play too: 'The developing countries demand that the developed countries should make and honour explicit commitments in such matters as international trade, finance and currency, shipping, the transfer of technology and aid. These demands are entirely justifiable'.

It may be questioned, however, whether most Third World countries are either willing or able to carry out such a programme. Many of them are led by elites who in Chinese parlance would be called 'comprador bourgeoisie' — i.e. the class in developing countries which acts basically as agents for foreign companies and which actively supports dependency economic relationships. Others are led by a variety of strata and class groupings none of whom would find it in their interests to carry out a Chinese type programme.

A further problem concerns the sheer capacity of most of the Third World countries to follow the Chinese programme even if the will were not lacking. Few countries are as richly endowed with natural resources as China. Still fewer have undergone the enormous revolutionary transformations that have characterised China's modern historical experience. It is this experience which enabled the Chinese people to 'stand up' and move forward. China's socialist programmes of self-reliance may be said to be the product of the energising national self regeneration of the people's revolution. It may be doubted whether a people which has not been energised and mobilised in this way can in fact follow the Chinese way. It is certainly highly questionable whether leaders thrown up by a non-revolutionary process and not committed to revolution (like Chinese leaders) would be prepared to embark on the Chinese road of self-reliance. Really to follow that road would be to make fundamental changes in the fabric of the social and political processes which brought most of these leaders to power.

Even though most Third World countries may not be able to implement the full programme as outlined in Li Chiang's speech, it is nevertheless true that China's general message has been highly influential throughout the Third World. This is partly because of the international impact of China's domestic achievements in pursuit of self-reliance, combining both emphasis on production with continued revolution. But it is also partly because of China's international role as a fellow member of the Third World which points out a genuinely independent path of development. That role is sustained also through extensive aid programme which have long been regarded as unique and as models to be emulated by others.

Despite being a relatively underdeveloped economy China has spent several thousand million dollars on aid to the Third World since the late 1950s. The bulk of this aid was spent in the 1970s.[21] The figures are all the more remarkable if it is considered that most of China's aid consists of low capital cost projects emphasising intensive labour and intermediate technology. Since 1964 no interest charges have been applied to loans. No dependency relationships are established. At the earliest possible opportunity the projects concerned become entirely self managed and operated locally. Arrangements are made so that even spare parts can be manufactured locally and where possible local materials only are employed. Chinese workers and technicians on aid projects invariably work at the local rates of remuneration.[22] There is no evidence to suggest that the Chinese use their aid to exercise political leverage. To be sure countries which have special links with China, such as Tanzania or Albania, are especially favoured. Likewise countries which embark on policies particularly liked by China, such as Egypt's severing Russian ties, are frequently offered more extensive aid by the Chinese. The aid is linked to China's foreign policy preferences. But there is no evidence that the Chinese have sought to use their aid as a means of pressurising governments to act in ways they would not do otherwise.

There can be no question but that China's whole approach on these issues arises out of the moral perspectives within which her leaders have operated. Just as the Chinese have been anxious to avoid following a foreign trade pattern which leads to dependency relationships on other countries, so China's pattern of aid distribution is designed to encourage economic independence in others. China does not seek to lead a bloc of Third World countries tied to and dependent upon her. On the contrary, the preferred pattern of development in the Third World as seen from Peking is one in which Third World countries progressively assert their economic independence and establish supportive links with each other. Much as the Chinese support regional associates in the Third World they have taken care not to join such associations themselves. Nor have they suggested that such countries either individually or collectively link themselves to China in a bid to establish alternative economic relations to those which they have with capitalist countries.

This contrasts sharply with the approach advanced by Soviet spokesmen. They still view the world in basically bi-polar terms. Despite the emphasis on détente and on the relaxation of international tensions, the Soviet leadership still maintains that there is a capitalist or imperialist camp headed by the United States which is in conflict with the socialist camp headed by the Soviet Union. To be sure the Soviet view of the capitalist world is much more complex than that of Stalin's day and Soviet foreign policy is tactically much more flexible. Nevertheless at the most fundamental level the Soviet view is still a bi-focal one. The two camps still exist and the socialist one headed by the Soviet Union is still seen as representing the forces of the future. It is still seen as the repository of genuine proletarian virtue. In so far as the Soviet leaders detect positive developments in world affairs these are ascribed to the beneficial consequences of the growing influence and might of the socialist camp headed by themselves. It is this allied to the internal problems and contradictions in the capitalist camp which, in the Soviet view, augurs well for continued détente and for eliciting gradual incremental changes in that camp towards a more socialist future. Those who support or are instrumental in helping such a development, by encouraging closer links with the Soviet Union and its institutions, are regarded as more or less progressive, while those who oppose this are condemned as reactionaries.

With regard to the Third World, variants of this approach are followed. Soviet leaders tend to call upon Third World countries to try to link themselves much more with the socialist bloc. Indeed at times they have identified certain kinds of countries in the Third World as being 'socialist-orientated' countries. Soviet spokesmen have pointed to what they call the road of non-capitalist development, by which they mean state-led industrialisation linked with exclusive trade aid relations with socialist bloc countries. The Soviet leaders see no special virtue in independence *per se* unless this involves an anti-Western posture and a leaning to the Soviet side. Indeed they see positive virtues in newly independent countries establishing dependency economic links with socialist bloc countries. Far from conceiving the Third World as a unified whole, Soviet spokesmen tend to divide the countries concerned (or rather their leaders) into those who are more or less progressive and those who are more or less reactionary. Therefore the Soviet Union has far less compunction than China in actively intervening in the domestic politics of other states. At the same time in the Soviet Union there is profound irritation and anger with the Chinese approach. Consider, for example, the following criticism by the theoretical journal of the Central Committee by the Communist Party of the Soviet Union:

> The Chinese leaders discredit the idea of a socialist orientation and the non-capitalist road of development for the developing countries. Maoist propaganda hushes up the fact that progressive social changes can be effected only in the countries which have embarked upon non-capitalist development, and this road is not only the sole alternative to neo-colonialist subordination but it also ensures radical social transformation. The evolution of the developing countries towards scientific socialism and towards closer co-operation with the socialist community would have been much faster but for Peking's disorientating activities.

The same piece goes on later to decry the 'imposing of the Maoist schemes of economic development upon the Third World' and the discrediting of the policy of developing heavy industry.[23]

To a certain extent it may be argued that both the Soviet Union and China are seeking to transform the Third World after their own image. The Soviets stress heavy industry, the Chinese agriculture. The Soviets emphasise the importance of the industrialised European socialist bloc headed by themselves as the central gravitational point for the future progressive development of the Third World. The Chinese, however, stress the importance of the Third World of which they are a key member, as the current revolutionary motive force propelling world history forward. From a Soviet perspective there are indeed moral claims to their position, yet they clearly run counter to those of the Chinese.

The Chinese passion for independence, as we have seen, arises deep from within their historical experience in general and the revolutionary experience in particular. It was one of the main causes of the Sino-Soviet split and it has dominated China's international outlook since. Firstly, there was the emphasis in 1963-4 and 1965 on the revised concept of the intermediate zones and on the revolutionary content in them. In this phase the Chinese looked for signs of independence and genuine resistance to imperialism amongst Third World countries and also in countries such as France.[24] Secondly, the Cultural Revolution itself may be seen in terms of one notion of Chinese independence, namely that of total isolation. Viewing China as the 'bastion of socialism' China's leaders sought to pursue 'socialism in one country' by insulating that socialism from all external influences. The revolutionary people of China stood alone in their purity with the revolutionary people of the world defying all other states and the two superpowers in particular. Thirdly, in the period since the Cultural Revolution the Chinese have opened much more to the world but on a basis of emphasising state sovereignty and independence above all. The operational framework of analysis was built around Maoist concepts of contradictions. That is of using the contradictions between the two great imperialist powers, the USA and the USSR, on the one hand, and also using the contradictions between them and the rest of the world on the other. The units of analysis were and continue to be states and nations rather than classes. Likewise in the attempt to set up a broad international united front against the two superpowers the units to which the Chinese appeal are independent sovereign states. No other country in the world today stresses the importance of the concepts of sovereignty and sovereign equality of states more than China.

Yet China is still committed to revolution. Proletarian internationalism figures prominently in both the Party and the State constitutions.
China's new leader, Hua Kuo-feng, has gone out of his way to emphasise
the importance of the commitment to revolution and proletarian internationalism. How can this be accommodated with the principled
commitment to the independence and sovereignty of states? The
Chinese Communist Party maintains links with over 70 organisations it
regards as genuinely Marxist-Leninist. By and large these have tiny
memberships and are without influence in the states in which they
operate. They basically take their cue from Chinese publications on
general ideological issues. There is no evidence that the Chinese impose
their views on them or that the Chinese seek to have just one such
organisation as representative of a single country. Thus some West
European countries have several independent organisations recognised
by the Chinese as genuinely Marxist-Leninist.[25] Chinese recognition
gives these organisations a kind of ideological legitimacy, but clearly
the Chinese do not follow here the Leninist practice established in the
Third International of 1919 of recognising only one Communist Party
as the representative of the working class of that country. The orthodox
Leninist view was that the working class can only have one core political
party. Moreover, that party had to be closely linked with and super-
vised by the Communist International. There is no evidence that the
Chinese seek to direct the domestic political activities of such organisations. At another level the Chinese have encountered problems in South
East Asia in particular in seeking to maintain revolutionary party to
party links while also maintaining separate but good state to state relations at the same time. Thus as we have already seen Malaysia formally
protested to the Chinese government regarding the moral support given
by Chinese leaders (wearing their Party hat) in formally congratulating
the Communist Party of Malaya on its 45th Anniversary.[26]

A separate but related problem concerns China's relations with those
countries still considered by China to be socialist. According to Marx's
and particularly Lenin's concepts of proletarian internationalism, fellow
genuine Communists were bound by definition to have a common view
of the principal characteristics of the current world situation. Yet China
has not sought the acceptance of her own views as to the nature of the
balance of world forces at the present time. Fundamental to China's
new international position is the view that the Soviet Union has restored
capitalism at home, and indeed has gone far toward establishing a monopoly capitalist system which is even worse than that of the United

States. It is this which in the Chinese view makes the Soviet Union a more dangerous and expansionist power than the United States. It would have been natural for a leadership so keen to establish its Leninist orthodoxy to have tried to pressurise other socialist countries into accepting its fundamental line. Nevertheless the Chinese have not done so. To take but one example, there is a great contrast between the views of the Vietnamese and their Chinese comrades on this. The Vietnamese still see the Soviet Union as socialist and they argue that the socialist camp continues to exist. China's entire foreign policy is predicated on entirely the opposite view. The Chinese, however, have not demanded that the Vietnamese change their line.

In the Chinese practice of proletarian internationalism it is the principle of respect for the independence of others which predominates. The Chinese leaders must surely consider that their analysis of the Soviet Union and the analysis of the main forces at work in the world today belong to the level of general principles rather than tactics. Their tolerance of the deviance of fellow Marxist-Leninists, therefore, can only be justified in theoretical terms by arguing that the Chinese position is absolutely correct and that it is based on objective facts so that in time the others will *independently* come to recognise its validity too.

It has been argued in this essay that the moral claims of the Chinese leadership regarding international affairs centre on the principle of independence. It permeates their view regarding the relationship between pursuing socialism domestically and conducting foreign affairs with an external world largely made up of non-socialist states. The development of socialism within China may be seen as a variant of socialism in one country. There is quite a conscious refusal to have any kind of dependence on outside forces. Even the case of possible reparations from Japan arising from the 1931-45 conflicts was refused.[27] However much as the Chinese may support the claims of developing countries in their demand for a new international economic order and for the transfer of technology, the moral basis for it does not rest on the argument that the industrialised world profited initially from exploitation and that it must now give back what it has taken. The moral basis for the Chinese support is that the current international economic system is an exploitative one and it is for that reason it must be changed.

The way to change the exploitative international economic system is by stressing sovereign independence and self reliance. For the Chinese, however, that is not simply an instrumental device useful for tactical purposes, but, at a deeper level, it is also a moral and revolutionary principle. For a state to be genuinely independent and for it really to pursue a policy of self-reliance it must, in the Chinese view, 'rely on the strength and wisdom of its own people'. The Chinese adage that the weak can defeat the strong and the small can defeat the big is predicated upon the assumption that the movements or countries concerned must be genuinely independent and therefore able to tap the creative forces and impulses of the people. In the long term, the Chinese argue, such movements or countries will prove indestructible. The moral qualities of the argument here are unmistakable.

The Chinese also maintain at a simple moral level that where there is opposition there will be found also resistance to that oppression. It is this conviction which makes the Chinese leaders believe that the Third World will play the positive role which they assign to it. Explaining this to the United Nations Sixth Special Session on 12 April 1974 Teng Hsiao-ping, representing the view of his government, put it as follows:

> The numerous developing countries have long suffered from colonialist and imperialist oppression and exploitation. They have won political independence, yet all of them still face the historic task of clearing out the remnant forces of colonialism, developing the national economy and consolidating national independence. These countries cover vast territories, encompass a large population and abound in natural resources. Having suffered the heaviest oppression, they have the strongest desire to oppose oppression and seek liberation and development. In the struggle for national liberation and independence, they have demonstrated immense power and continually won splendid victories. They constitute a revolutionary motive force propelling the wheel of history and are the main forces combating colonialism, imperialism and particularly the superpowers.[28]

There is still the problem, however, that while China may be able to follow the policies of independence and self-reliance this may not be possible for most Third World countries. As we have seen China is in a very special position in having undergone probably the greatest revolution of the modern era. That position is based on a long history of a proud people largely independent of the outside world. Other countries lack a similar tradition, nor have they experienced a revolution of such dimensions. Furthermore, China is abundant in resources and is one of the world's great powers. While China may be able to insulate her

economy from the vagaries of the international economic system this is
not necessarily possible for most Third World countries. Even if the
Third World countries have been the most oppressed and the most exploited and even if some of them have been 'awakened' in the Chinese
sense of the word, it is still true that many of them are led by comprador elites whose very existence is dependent upon the maintenance of
special kinds of relations with stronger external forces.

Thus the Chinese stand on independence ultimately has significant
and deep revolutionary qualities. It calls for reliance by the leaders upon
the people. The term 'people' for Mao always had revolutionary
connotations. As he put it on innumerable occasions 'reactionaries
are excluded from the ranks of the people'. The Chinese have maintained for several years that the slogan 'countries want independence,
nations want liberation and people want revolution' is descriptive of an
objective fact describing the general long-term trend in world affairs.

There can be no question, however, that revolution had a higher
claim in Mao Tse-tung's thinking than independence. As a characteristic
quote from Mao puts it:

> I stand for the theory of permanent revolution. Do not mistake this
> for Trotsky's theory of permanent revolution. In making revolution
> one must strike while the iron is hot — one revolution must follow
> another. Revolution must continually advance. The Hunanese often
> say, 'straw sandals have no pattern — they shape themselves in the
> making'. Trotsky believes that the Socialist revolution should be
> launched even before the democratic revolution is complete. We are
> not like that.[29]

The democratic revolution is by no means complete in most of the
countries of the Third World. Since in the Chinese view socialist revolutions are a long way ahead, to be measured in terms of centuries perhaps,
it follows that for the present it is the concept of independence which
is the more dominant in shaping Chinese approaches and attitudes towards international affairs. It is certainly the concept which would be
the more useful in resisting the encroachment of the Soviet Union. As
we have seen, however, in Chinese usage the term independence is
imbued with moral qualities and values which at times exceed established Leninist norms.

Notes

1. Chou En-lai, 'Political Report to the Tenth Congress of the Communist Party of China', *Peking Review,* Joint No. 35 and 36, 7 September 1973.

2. A congratulatory message by the Central Committee of the Communist Party of China signed by Mao and Chou En-lai to the Communist Party of Malaya on its 45th anniversary was printed prominently in the *People's Daily* of 29 April 1975. The text is in *Peking Review,* No. 18, 2 May 1975. The Malaysian government then lodged an official protest with the Chinese government as this was regarded as interference in Malaysia's internal affairs. See *The Annual Register of World Events in 1975* (Longman 1976), p. 268.

3. See Peter Van Ness, *Revolution and Chinese Foreign Policy* (University of California Press, 1970), for a careful analysis which leads to the proposition (p. 190) that 'whether a foreign non Communist Country was seen to be "peace loving" or ruled by "reactionaries", or whether a Communist Party state was viewed in Peking as "socialist" or denounced as "revisionist" largely depended on the extent to which that country's foreign policy coincided with China's own.'

4. This view was first outlined publicly in a systematic way by Mao Tse-tung in 1957. See 'On the Correct Handling of Contradictions Among the People', in *Selected Readings From the Works of Mao Tse-tung* (Foreign Language Press 1967), pp. 350-87.

5. 'Scientific Communism has a precise and definite meaning. According to Marxism-Leninism, Communist society is a society in which classes and class differences are completely eliminated, the entire people have a high level of Communist consciousness and morality as well as boundless enthusiasm for and initiative in labour, there is a great abundance of social products and the principle of "from each according to his ability, to each according to his needs" is applied, and in which the state has withered away'. From 'On Khrushchev's Phoney Communism and Its Historical Lessons for the World – Ninth Comment on the Open Letter of the Central Committee of the CPSU' (14 July 1964). In *The Polemic and the General Issue of the International Communist Movement.* (FLP, Peking 1965), p. 459.

6. Ibid., pp. 461-2.

7. Ibid., p. 464.

8. See, for example, the accounts quoted in Kenneth T. Shewmaker, *Americans and Chinese Communists, 1927-1945* (Cornell University Press, 1971).

9. Translated by Stuart R. Schram in *China Quarterly,* No. 49 (January/ March 1972), pp. 76-87.

10. Translated by S.R. Schram, *The Political Thought of Mao Tse-tung* (Penguin, 1969), p. 352.

11. 'Speech at the Supreme State Conference', 28 January 1958. Translated in Stuart Schram (ed.), *Mao Tse-tung Unrehearsed* (Penguin, 1974), p. 92.

12. Ibid., p. 102.

13. For a brief summary of the debate and for references to the Russian sources see M. Fainsod, *How Russia is Ruled,* (OUP, 1963), p. 90 and 141-2.

14. 'Speech at the Tenth Plenum', 24 September 1962. In Schram, *Mao Tse-tung Unrehearsed,* pp. 191-2.

15. Cited in Schram, *Political Thought,* p. 379.

16. See the study of the Bandung Conference and the reproduction of its main documents in George McT. Kahin. *The Asian-African Conference* (Cornell University Press, 1956).

17. John Gittings, *The World and China 1922-72* (Eyre Methuen, 1974), p. 211.

18. For a clear analysis of this see Gittings, *World and China,* particularly pp. 35-115, for the period up to the end of World War II.

19. See in particular Chou En-lai's speech of 2 September 1968, at the National Day Reception given by the Vietnamese Ambassador in Peking, for the claim that the Soviet Union 'had long since completely destroyed the socialist camp which once existed'. *Peking Review,* No. 36 (6 September 1968), pp. 6-7.

20. Speech by Chairman of the Chinese Delegation, Li Chiang, to the Seventh Special Sesssion of the United Nations in *Peking Review,* No. 37 (12 September 1975).

21. For the figures on the extent of China's aid see Carol H. Fogarty, 'China's Economic Relations with the Third World' in *China: A Reassessment of the Economy,* A Compendium of Papers Presented to the Joint Economic Committee, Congress of the United States of America (July 1975), p. 730.

22. For a Chinese account see *People's Daily,* 22 September 1974, 'Mutual Support and Sincere Cooperation', also available in *China Quarterly,* No. 60 (December 1974), Quarterly Chronicle and Documentation, pp. 836-8.

23. A lengthy editorial entitled 'The Maoist Regime at a New Stage' in *Kommunist,* the theoretical organ of the Central Committee of the CPSU. Translated in two parts in the publication of the Soviet Embassy in London, *Soviet News,* 9 and 16 September 1975. In particular see 16 September, p. 321.

24. It should be noted that as late as 11 May 1964 Mao Tse-tung still had grave misgivings about De Gaulle. A inner Party speech rejected the Soviet Union as a 'dictatorship of the bourgeoisie, a dictatorship of the big bourgeoisie, a dictatorship like German fascism, a Hitler type of dictatorship, they are a pack of ruffians, *even worse than De Gaulle*' (emphasis added). Quoted in Gittings, *World and China,* p. 256. Yet three months earlier in February of that same year Mao contrasted the French favourably with the Russians as still having 'some notion of business ethics'.

25. See, for example, *Peking Review,* No. 3 (16 January 1976), which published condolence messages on the death of Chou En-lai *inter alia* from three separate such organisations in Germany, two in France and two in Japan.

26. See note 2.

27. For an account of the Chinese refusal of Japanese offers to pay reparations for war damage see *China Quarterly,* No. 52 (October-December 1972), Chronicle and Documentation, section on Japan.

28. *Peking Review,* Special Supplement to No. 15 (12 April 1974).

29. 'Speech at the Supreme State Conference', 28 January 1958, translated in Schram, *Mao Tse-tung Unrehearsed*, p. 94.

9 MORAL PRECEPTS OF CONTEMPORARY SOVIET POLITICS[1]

Vendulka Kubálková

The Soviet and East European conception of morality is at the same time related to and distinct from its Western counterparts: related in so far as it has evolved from the same intellectual tradition, distinct because it has gradually developed several characteristics which could seem to separate it from Western conceptions by an increasingly potent intellectual barrier. Thus, to contrast Soviet and Western moral precepts, I would suggest describing the former as an *explicitly ideological-militant paradigm* and I shall try to substantiate in this chapter why I think it merits the introduction of a category of its own.

Moral precepts are central to Marxism-Leninism. The Soviet and East European systems derive their very legitimacy from the moral creed inherited from Marx; in fact the whole of Marxist-Leninist ideology is erected on a set of beliefs and values derived from Marxist classics and interpreted by Party leaders and Party ideologues. Philosophy, including moral philosophy, is sharply distinguished from ideology in the non-Soviet world. In the Marxist-Leninist terms of reference it is closely related to the point of merger, in the sense that philosophy is subordinated to ideology. The task of the Soviet philosophers (if they want to remain in business) is not to strive to understand the totality of social reality on the basis of human experience and reason in a critical and ostensibly value free manner (as their Western counterparts attempt to do), but to make their ideology more intellectually viable, acceptable, believable, consistent, coherent and teachable. Although philosophy in the Soviet and East European societies displays a certain degree of independence, one should bear in mind this close link. The other side of this coin of subservience to ideology is, of course, that the works of the approved philosophers are much better known than those of philosophers in the West, with an audience ready made by decree and waiting. Thus they exercise a considerably greater degree of influence on public affairs than Western philosophers whose views, frustratingly, often do not reach beyond a small academic circle.

In tying moral conceptions to ideology one also pre-empts their fate, given, that is, the esteem in which Western international relations theorists seem to hold 'ideology'. The highly contentious issue of the merits of ideologies in general, and of their place in the understanding of world politics in particular, is obviously beyond the scope and intention of this chapter. Let me, however, by way of introduction draw attention to some rather randomly selected aspects of what is still a minority counter-argument — that the study of ideologies from the point of view of world politics is a worthwhile enterprise, particularly those aspects with a direct bearing on the question of the relevance of studying moral conceptions.

First of all it is probably correct to say that there is nothing in Soviet and East European international behaviour that could not be understood in practical terms and along power political lines. There is no need whatsoever for recourse to Marxist theories, and this applies to moral conceptions in particular. In fact, the argument might run, Marxist ideology is something one can well do without in the theory of world politics. And this is probably correct for any individual international event taken in isolation: one can say that Marxism-Leninism does not prescribe any particular course of action and indeed in any particular instance an indefinite number of actions could be compatible with Soviet ideology. But this would be the case with any other system of beliefs and values, not only the Soviet one. It can be argued, however, that the conduct of international affairs over a period of time can be understood correctly only by keeping ideological motivations in mind: the theory that supplies the *end* to which all communist actions are explicitly directed.

Secondly, as Brzezinski for one has pointed out,[2] dismissing ideologies seems to postulate that Soviet leaders have greater effective (if not supernatural) powers than those they certainly seem to possess. Though they set in motion the machinery for political socialisation (and the existence of this process is not being questioned) in the attempt to inculcate the official ideology, and morality in particular, into people's minds, they themselves are miraculously exempt from the same socialisation process. They themselves, in other words, follow in their decision-making different values from those that they try to inculcate.

Such an argument, and this leads us to point three, postulates the universal validity of a set of moral precepts (obviously Western ones) common to all humankind; Soviet precepts are seen as some devilish aberration, or at least as something completely spurious and alien to human nature, bound to degenerate and 'return back' sooner or later to these universal values. Given this attitude there is very little one can say about the moral virtues of the Soviet political system and of Soviet behaviour, let alone the way the system tries to explain and justify its own rule: in relation to Western values Soviet ones often appear to be their actual negation, and everything to do with that system may be branded as amoral because of its oppressive attitude to the individual and individual values. In the history of human thought such an approach, referred to sometimes as 'external analysis', has frequently been used to reject another philosophical system rather than mount a rebuttal of it: each system as a rule carries its own definitions of truth and criteria of evidence to be used, and 'external analysis', from the standpoint of 'other truth' and evidence, can only lead to conflict and deadlock. In order to be able to refute effectively a system of thought one should therefore use the method of 'internal analysis' or 'imminent critique'[3] which does not *a priori* reject any part of that system. One seeks instead for logical inconsistencies, rather than those that appear in contrast to one's own set of axiomatic postulates.

Fourthly, the dismissal of Soviet ideology might still have been justifiable in the time of Stalin perhaps, but dismissal would be totally out of date now: it would overlook important intellectual developments in the Soviet and East European situation. The practical requirements and the real disappointments associated with a body of Marxist teaching, grown gradually stale in its dogmatic version, have succeeded where the armies of Western critics and revisionists have totally failed.[4] Marxist ideology and its moral component is increasingly perceived as a social instrument for achieving certain internal and external ends, more reliable and less painful than the Stalinist methods of open terror and brutality. To achieve this a perpetual updating and revision of the ideology and its credibility is required, which does not necessarily indicate ideological erosion; perhaps the very opposite. As a side effect of this process, one should add, there is an emerging group of philosophers, in most cases wholly educated in the Marxist-Leninist *Weltanschauung*, who are no longer satisfied with a non-critical apologists role. They are sometimes referred to as 'New Marxists'[5] (in distinction from Western 'Neomarxists'). These 'New Marxists' are not simply Marxologues. They would identify themselves with most of Marx's heritage and, unlike most of the Neomarxists, would still be committed to the construction of communist society and the fundamentals of dialectical and historical materialism, but they represent a new breed of Marxism which is certainly not to be overlooked, particularly from the point of view of its influence on the development of Soviet ideology in the future. From their writings as well as from the writings of dissidents one could reconstruct several moral countercodes, but to discuss them as well will not be possible within the scope of this chapter, where attention will be paid strictly to the official orthodox ideological version of morality.

Fifthly, one of the arguments of the New Marxists against the rejection of Marxism is that, because there is no way to deduce a political system and political action from Marxist thinking, *ergo* Marxism cannot be blamed for the emergence of any particular sort of system and behaviour.[6] Thus, for instance, Stalinism and everything negative that it represents does not follow from Marxism. Marxism is still seen as the most valid methodological approach. If anything the moral crisis that Marx observed in the capitalist system still exists, and what is more has extended to the planet as a whole, with initially intrasocietal inequities now spread on a global scale. Marxism is perceived by New Marxists (and in this respect they and the Western Neomarxists would agree) as still best equipped for this analysis.

Sixthly, there is the well-known argument based on the perceived heuristic sterility of all theories that are likely to come from the Soviet section of the world. Even if it is true to say that there is not yet a Soviet ethics, or if there is, it is either too eclectic[7] or 'pedestrian'[8] to have much to say to Western moral philosophers about the problems of their subject, one should not mix ethics and actual morality. Even if the Soviet and East European regimes totally fail in their attempts to reform their societies through the inculcation of specific values (which they openly declare as their task) these values in one form or another will still be held by a large proportion of the population of a perpetually shrinking world, and they should at least be noted as one of the symptoms of the diseased condition of the world today.

Last, but not least, I believe that, as Richard T. de George has aptly put it, 'to try to understand either Soviet society or Soviet politics without a knowledge of the foundations of Soviet thought is in many respects like trying to understand the Middle Ages without a knowledge of Christianity'.[9] To put it even more bluntly a simile with opera is offered. The refusal to study Soviet ideology could be likened to the refusal of an audience to read a libretto and its claim that the same degree of appreciation and understanding of the plot can be reached on the basis of the music alone. This is partly true — the orchestration and harmony and the acting on the stage are 'universal' and enable one to *follow* and guess the plot, particularly with an occasional word here and there that sounds familiar (detente, peace, freedom, etc.). Needless to say, however, misunderstandings and illusions about the plot could easily arise.

Let us first of all take a brief look at the essential characteristics of Soviet moral conceptions and proceed to a similarly brief outline of how these moral conceptions fit in with Soviet international relations theory.

There is quite a range of definitions of morality[10] to be found in the perpetually growing bulk of Soviet literature on the subject,[11] from a 'functional' definition (as a 'social institution for regulating man's behaviour'[12]) to wider descriptive ones such as 'the totality of principles or norms of men's conduct which regulate their relations to one another, to society, to a certain class, to the state, country, and so on, supported by personal conviction, tradition, education, the force of public opinion of a whole society or of a certain class'.[13] The philosophical theory dealing with morality is referred to as the 'science of morals',[14] in contrast to bourgeois ethics which cannot by definition ever become scientific.[15]

The Marxist pedigree of the 'science of morals' is slightly precarious to say the least. Marxologues still argue whether Marx had a clearly discernible ethical position, explicit or only implicit, and if so where precisely he stood.[16] Thus as in many other cases the view of a Marxologue would not help one very far in understanding Soviet ethics. The Soviet ethical position is in fact more Leninist, or rather Stalinist, than it is Marxist, and from Marx it got a somewhat shaky start. There is a broad moral framework deducible from Marx's whole work, i.e. the moral message of indignation which his works *in toto* convey (although Marx did not devote himself to a separate study of morality), and there is the commitment to the moral goal of communism argued out on the basis of a collectivist understanding of man. The Soviet ethical position, however, did inherit from Marx one serious error. This error consisted in the assumption that morality more or less automatically followed as a part of the social consciousness of the development of social existence (also called social being). The pairs 'social existence/social consciousness' and 'base/superstructure', although they are at the very heart of Soviet thinking, leave a great deal to be desired from the point of view of conceptual clarity and meaning. In the discussion about them their content and relationship has not yet been concluded.[17] Social existence, in standard Marxist understanding, is defined as 'the material life of society, the production of material goods and those relations (in a class society these are class relations) into which men enter in the process of production'. Social consciousness then consists of 'views, notions, ideas, political, legal, aesthetic, ethical and other theories, philosophy, morality, religion, and other forms of consciousness'.[18] Not only have these terms been the subject of controversy amongst Marxists since Marx[19] (because of the conveniently vague and obscure character of

Marx's original formulations), but together with the changing emphasis
on objective and subjective factors and their importance in human
history (i.e. the varying degrees of perceived determinism or volun-
tarism), the mutual relationships of social consciousness and social
existence and base and superstructure have undergone frequent
reinterpretations from one Marxist school to another. In the original
determinist interpretation which one can derive from Engels and less
directly from Marx,[20] it would seem to follow that there is no need to
have a theory about morality: when economic conditions change, the
social reflection of it as a part of both superstructure and social consciousness will follow suit, to the eventual disappearance of morality
together with such other institutions as state and law in communist
society.

Soviet society has painfully discovered, however, that this is not the
case. Morality has not begun to change as dramatically as its ideological
forebears had supposed, and certainly not in the first three decades
of the existence of the Soviet Union. Thus it was Stalin who, paradoxically, became the founding father of Soviet ethics as an independent
theory. Continuing in Leninist footsteps in so far as the subjectivist
emphasis is concerned, he coined the concept of 'relative independence
of certain parts of the superstructure' causing 'lag of superstructure
behind social existence'. Particularly after Stalin's 1950 discourse on
linguistics a considerable amount of chaos was introduced into the twin
notions of base and superstructure and social existence and consciousness. Some social phenomena (e.g. language) were actually declared as
not belonging to either base or superstructure.[21] This was, in a way, the
only way of 'rectifying' Marxism and explaining why morality did not
undergo the changes that classical Marxism had anticipated. At the
same time it opened new fields for theoretical activity that might be
reconciled with the classical legacy. Short of this 'error' the classics
did not leave any recipe for their ideological descendants, and one can
thus (although there are other reasons) explain the body of theoretical
writing on the subject[22] that shares with the classical Marxist non-
formulated ethics only its broad framework, and the conception of man
from which moral goals are derived.

Let us attempt to characterise, within Western terms of reference,
the official Soviet conception of morality in so far as one can generalise
about it from the voluminous Soviet literature. There is a strong similarity to pragmatism, utilitarianism, ethical relativism, Darwinian
evolutionism, natural law ethics and Christian ethics,[23] although Soviet
ethics is an admixture of elements of all these and is not reducible to any

one of them in particular. Soviet ethics is also not without precedent in its self-assuredness, self-containment[24] and highly intolerant attitude to other moral conceptions: it regards itself as not only superior to all 'bourgeois' ethics but also exclusively capable of providing 'true answers'. It thus rejects all other moral conceptions,[25] and refuses to make a distinction between normative and critical ethics (or metaethics) on the basis that the two merge to such a degree that they cannot be meaningfully separated.[26]

In its approach to morality Soviet ethics is historical:[27] morality appears at that moment in history when a split occurs between individual and social interests.[28] Moral diversity is attributable to differing physical and economic conditions. Morality as a part of social consciousness [29] appears and develops with the social consciousness.[30] Thus the existence of morality is bound up with the existence of society and in this respect the Soviet position approaches that of some ethical relativists, with the modification that the morality of any particular society is never relative but always objectively given and necessary for a particular stage of the development of society. In a class society, it would follow, there is always dual if not multiple morality. 'People have always been and will continue to be silly victims of deception and self-deception in politics, as long as they will not learn to search in any moral, religious, political, social phrases, declarations, promises, the interests of one class or another'.[31] Together with Nietzsche the Marxists would postulate that what is good for one is by definition bad for the other. But unlike Nietzsche the Marxists see an end to this highly undesirable state of affairs, since in communist society there will be no classes and the interests of all members of society will coincide. Every morality in history is assumed to have always contained elements of what Marxist-Leninists describe as 'all-human morality',[32] or 'common moments of morality of different human collectivities and classes'[33] representing the 'minimal conditions of moral life'[34] which are negative (do not kill, do not steal, do not fornicate, etc.) and positive (work, respect old people, be brave, etc.).[35] However, the full development of this all-human universally valid morality is to be expected only in communist society. Correcting Marx, the contemporary Marxist-Leninists believe that morality will not 'wither away' with the state but will in fact flourish and replace law (which will 'wither away') and with which morality is seen to be increasingly enmeshed.[36] Thus in communist society there will be for the first time only one morality, the universal one, which will express the interests and feelings of all humankind or most of it. In fact Soviet morality, 'the noblest and most just morality' [37] is already represented as a harbinger of communist morality, and coincides with the morality of all working mankind. It will we are told, 'express the interests and ideals of the whole of working mankind' and will encompass 'the fundamental norms of human morality which the masses evolved in the course of milleniums as they fought against vice and social oppression . . .'[38] The Soviet position is thus basically objectivist: moral norms for each society are the objective norms necessary for its development. Separate moralities are assessed on the basis of their proximity to a moral ideal which is absolute but of a non extra-terrestrial or extrahuman source.

For such an approach it becomes obvious that the *moral ideal* assumes paramount importance. Let us look at the Soviet definitions of their moral ideal. We discover that their position is basically teleological, resembling utilitarian and self-realisation theories. At the root of the Soviet understanding of 'moral' and 'good' (used interchangeably) are still Lenin's formulations, dating from 1920 and 1922.[39] Whatever promotes the revolution is good and moral, and after the successful revolution, it is obviously whatever serves the achievement of communism that serves as a moral criterion. One should not allow oneself to be misled by some roundabout Soviet formulations that say that 'good' is what promotes the interests of society, and that is the construction of communism.[40] The ultimate moral ideal, the absolute moment in the relativity of moral judgements and the criterion by which all actions should be judged, is the ideal of communism.

Apart from setting out unequivocally their main moral criterion, the Soviet treatment of good and moral leaves much to be desired. This applies to the notions of 'right', 'duty', 'happiness', 'justice', etc., too, in so far as they all are derived from the concept of good. Generally speaking, 'good' in non-Soviet formulations is assumed by Soviet writers to be a relative concept, and one that has 'kept changing historically from one epoch to another'.[41] Thus they would not agree with G.E. Moore that good cannot be defined,[42] nor with Mill and Bentham that it is equivalent to pleasure. By defining moral and good the way they do, i.e. as serving the advancement of the construction of communism, they sanctify whatever means that are necessary to that end. All means as long as they lead to this goal are *ipso facto* moral. Thus anything can be justified in the name of necessity, and the meanings of what is 'necessary' and 'expedient' merge. That the means used to achieve the desired end can negate it as a moral ideal becomes obvious; this way of defining 'good' leaves a blank space which can be filled with any action whatsoever.

If the ultimate moral criterion is communism then obviously its precise meaning assumes a crucial importance for the whole of the Soviet conception of morality. This is, however, another stumbling block. The notion of communism is important for every Marxist-Leninist theory, and yet it is not quite clear what precisely it is supposed to mean.

Marx himself defined communism in a very sketchy way[43] and rather negatively, i.e. in terms of what will not exist, rather than what will, and all subsequent definitions have been plagued by a similar problem. Soviet Marxist-Leninists became aware of the need for a less ambiguous formulation of the actual goal of their society, and the most complete outline comes from the 1961 Programme of the CPSU adopted at the 22nd CPSU Congress.[44] This Programme, third in the history of the Soviet Communist Party, was actually designed for the period of the immediate eve of communist society, and outlines the route that is to be taken to ensure the successful entrée of that society into the communist stage of development. According to this Programme

> Communism is a classless social system with one form of public ownership of the means of production and full social equality of all members of society; under it, the all-round development of people will be accompanied by the growth of the productive forces through continuous progress in science and technology; all the springs of co-operative wealth will flow more abundantly, and the great principle 'From each according to his ability, to each according to his needs' will be implemented. Communism is a highly organised society of free, socially conscious working people in which public self-government will be established, a society in which labour for the good of society will become the prime vital requirement of everyone, a necessity recognised by one and all, and the ability of each person will be employed to the greatest benefit of the people.[45]

Again, it would be beyond the scope of this chapter to analyse such a definition; however, the crucial fallacy of Soviet ethics is derived from this definition. Regardless of any attempt to clarify the situation elsewhere in the Programme, it would seem that 'communism' remains extremely loosely defined. Despite its vagueness, the notion of communism is not only given great importance but it is seen to perform a multiple role: on the one hand it is a moral goal as well as a moral criterion, and on the other it is also a political system. What would happen to moral ideals when communism as a political system gets established is not quite clear. Furthermore, by mixing the usage of the term communism, without distinguishing clearly in what sense it is to be used, one creates considerable confusion. The vagueness of the definition, the fact that to a great extent it is still a negative one while it leaves room for positive elements to be added as they evolve, makes for arbitrary usage in practice. Furthermore it is not at all clear who is to decide that the society is a communist one. Perhaps, as in Stalin's time, it will like socialism simply be declared. And on what authority will the communist party, in whose hands the promulgation of communism obviously rests, come to know that it actually is communism? The mixing together of the functions of communism, establishing its content being left to the party, is presented as an advantage however. This is epitomised in the Stalinist notion, reiterated *ad nauseam,* of the 'moral-political unity of the society', and expresses the merger of political aims with moral goals. While striving, at least nominally, toward this still distant political end (although the Programme declares that communism in the USSR should be achieved 'in the main' in the 1980s),[46] whatever the party decides to do automatically becomes by definition 'moral' and 'good'. One should add, however, that at critical junctures like the denunciation of Stalin after the 20th CPSU Congress in 1956, this looseness has posed a serious problem for Marxism-Leninism. Stalin's amoralities (in a Marxist-Leninist sense) still wait for a scholarly explanation.

Many Western critics tend to accuse Soviet moral philosophy of being no more than a secular religion: the facts merge with values (something which Marxism-Leninism presents as a positive achievement). It is argued that such statements as 'communism is the goal of all mankind', or many other frequently repeated slogans, cannot be empirically tested, therefore they are merely values, spuriously presented by the Soviets as fact. However, as we have said at the outset, the Marxist-Leninist system of thought carries its own definitions of truth. When accused of presenting the goal of communism as a fact rather than value, the Soviet answer would be twofold.

Because dialectical and historical materialism assume that society operates according to discoverable laws, the fact that these laws can be identified, leading historically from one type of society to another, prompts them to believe that the coming of communism can, by the same token, be 'scientifically' predicted. In other words they do not seem to distinguish, like some Western theorists do, the elements of

explanation and prediction.[47] The occurrence of certain developments
in the past, and the existence of 'objectively' existing laws that derive
from them, allows Soviet theorists to predict 'scientifically' the occurrence of certain events in the future. Obviously Marxist-Leninists, in
contrast to most Western theorists, answer the question about the possibility of prediction in social theory in the affirmative, adding as a scientific test the capacity of social theory to control future events. Thus
since Marx, one of the characteristics of Marxism (in the Leninist-
Stalinist and contemporary Soviet line of thought) is the belief in the
factual *inevitability* of the advent of communist society. It is a future
for the whole of mankind. A belief in the knowledge of the objective
laws that lead to communism, however, is only the first part of the
answer to *why* the notion of communism plays such an important role
in the whole system of Soviet thought. The second part of the Soviet
defence would be based on an analysis of the human being who, they
believe, can come to fulfilment only in a communist society. Thus the
justification of communism is made in terms of man, the 'most
valuable entity in the world'.[48]

Starting with Marx's sixth thesis on Feuerbach and quotes from the
Economic and Philosophical Manuscripts of 1844,[49] we find that Soviet
theorists understand human nature as a collectivist entity: '. . . the
human essence is no abstraction inherent to each single individual. In its
reality it is the ensemble of the social relations'.[50] In contrast with
most ethical positions in the West (although not all) a man is seen as a
collective being – fully externalised, i.e. with no values of his own
except those which derive from his place in a certain collective. This is
another paradoxical part of the Marxian heritage: it seems beyond any
doubt that the ultimate goal of Marx's theory was to liberate man, and
yet his liberation can only be achieved within and through the collective. Only in a fully fledged communist society can man be free to
develop all of his inherent human characteristics and achieve universal
happiness; only in communist society can there be freedom of expression for everybody, universal justice and material plenty. Only within
or *despite* the collectivity will his interests and those of everybody else
for the first time fully coincide. Until then, however, and in order that
this may be achieved, they have to be tailored to do so. Thus from
Marx onwards Marxism has contained a paradoxical, one may say,
'schizophrenic', value system; for the ultimate achievement of the
desired end, the same values that one strives for and advocates can be
negated. Means are justified by their ends; in Lenin's simile, the chips
fly when the forest is cut down; or in English, the eggs must be broken

for an omelette to be made. Thus Soviet morality is somehow prepared
to prescribe great personal sacrifices in the name of the distant future
of man. This 'postponement' of moral gratification is not without precedent in Western ethical systems either, though Marxism-Leninism, in
contrast to Christianity for instance, brings gratification forward and
does not leave it to another world of existence beyond *this* one.
The recipients will be different, however, from those preparing the
way *now* for their future happiness.

Thus one may characterise the bulk of Soviet ethics, particularly in
the case of the theory of international relations, as an attempt to
devise a system of levers to synchronise conflicting interests and to
transmit them to communist society where all interests will not only
be compatible but will coincide. The ubiquitous dialectic is invaluable
of course in explaining how the incompatible is made compatible,
although as has been frequently pointed out since Stalin's version to say
that something is 'dialectically related' is not an explanation, rather it
restates the problem tautologically.

To restate the point: after the Soviet revolution, which was designed
it was believed according to Marx's recipe, the predictions of the
classics went badly awry and did not occur; new social relations did not
develop with the new economic relations, and if in Stalin's time a doc-
trinal proviso had not been devised it would have been very difficult
to avoid rejecting historical materialism *in toto*. The *deus ex machina*
was once again located in the notion of the relative independence of
certain parts of the superstructure and their active functioning with
respect to the base, i.e. economic conditions.[51] The debate thus started
is still far from concluded and parts of it implicate the very essence of
historical materialism, that is to say the distinction between social
existence and social consciousness. If some parts of the social consciousness, morality in particular, are allowed to play a role as important as parts of social existence, the very distinction between the two
seems to be pointless.

From the notion of the relative independence of the superstructure
(i.e. its lagging behind or 'running ahead of' the substructure), which
was consistent with the subjectivist emphasis introduced by Lenin
generally and caricatured in the extreme by Stalin, there followed
inter alia a very important conclusion which is central to this chapter:
communism is historically inevitable *but* — it will not happen of itself,
its inevitability has to be assisted, communism has to be built. After
the disappointing experience of a Soviet society which 'refused' to behave according to classical expectations, the whole attitude to Marxist

determinism had to be modified. A need was recognised for 'laws of the development of communism' — economic, psychological, sociological — which was an admission by Soviet society that the classical Marxist recipe no longer held, since it had not anticipated a fraction of Soviet social reality and practice.

What is the practical implication of this relatively new emphasis on the active part of the subjective element, almost overwhelming the role of objective economic factors? If a new man is not formed by virtue of a change in economic conditions, then there is obviously a need to form him artificially, to mould him and his ideas and his values; his mind itself must be reached and changed directly by some other means. Thus morality clearly assumes a functional role, reinforcing law and the state. Morality becomes 'one of the basic types of social regulation'.[52] What is required by Soviet law is *ipso facto* required by Soviet morality. In a recent formulation all of this boils down to the perceived need to transform the *ideological into the psychological*,[53] that is to say, 'the knowledge of the moral principles of socialism has to become not only a matter of deep-rooted conviction but one of habit'.[54] But can a functional use of morality not be dismissed as strictly amoral, if not immoral? The Soviet response is, no. In their definitions of morality[55] they openly say that morality is a social institution for regulating human conduct, and this functional role is openly admitted. Soviet writers would argue that bourgeois morality does this just as strongly as the socialist one because, like socialist morality, bourgeois morality is passed from generation to generation, is designed to perpetuate and reinforce the capitalist system, and that its values and beliefs are inculcated just as much as in Soviet society. Morality is always a means, never an end in itself, and its function of strengthening the system is repeated *ad nauseam*.[56]

Awareness of the need to inculcate and educate in order that communism would not be missed by default has led to an unprecedented ideological campaign,[57] particularly after the promulgation of the Soviet *moral code* (!) as part of the 1961 CPSU Programme. The rules enumerated in this code are to be assimilated by every Soviet citizen as a *conditio sine qua non* for the achievement of communist society. The code, we are informed, is supposed not to be an artificial construct but a 'voice of the future'. With such a promulgation the question arises, of course, of the merits of its promulgator — the party, and the paternalistic position which it usurps in Soviet society. The party places itself in the position of moral mentor, which in itself can be described as an amoral act.[58] The party — whose patterns of recruitment and self-perpetuation are more than doubtful — does not provide a guarantee that it consists of the 'most advanced members of the society' who may assume the right to correct every other member of that society, who by definition are never 'mature', possess no independent moral conscience of their own, and remain subject to lifelong supervision and education. With this said we may now be witnessing one gigantic social experiment to prove in practice that, first of all, there is one universal morality which is neither born with man nor received from some external divine agency but is historically evolving, and in this respect objectively given for every stage of societal development, and that secondly, the last stage, before the achievement of universal morality, has to be strongly 'assisted' by social agencies to help human beings to get rid of the 'muck of ages' (to paraphrase Marx) — the surviving remnants, that is, of previous moral conceptions because — last but not least — social consciousness in itself is prone to exhibit considerable staying power and considerable delay in adjusting itself to changing economic conditions.

Let us take a brief look at the moral code,[59] particularly those points of it that are directly relevant to Soviet thinking on international relations. We should emphasise that all that has been said above about moral ideals is explicitly valid for the world as a whole. Advancing the achievement of communism all over the planet serves also as the criterion of morality in international relations. Thus, it would follow that Soviet foreign policy, being a means to this end, is presented to the population as moral by definition and meriting moral support. Perhaps that is why Stalin, despite his supposedly total removal from Soviet history books, seems to have received at least silent approbation for his international successes: it was after all under his command that (via the doctrine of socialism in one country) the Soviet state survived, 'capitalist encirclement' was broken, and the first paragon of communism maintained on the map.

First of all we should once again repeat that the Soviet morality is a collectivist one: thus it seems to be by definition better tailored to collectivities, states, etc., than to individuals. This is the opposite situation to that arising in the West, where individualistic moralities, when stretched to the level of states, seem to crack at the seams and tensions and incompatibilities arise.[60] In Marxist ethics it would seem to be rather the other way around. Soviet morality (although in the name of Man) is obviously designed for groups, classes, states, socio-economic systems, and other such collectivities. Secondly, it is important to bear in mind the closely argued and interconnected nature of the Marxist

Weltanschauung as a whole: thus, for example, its theory of international relations is bound to be closely consistent with its moral
conceptions, at least in formal terms. In fact one cannot begin to understand the Soviet theory of international relations without an understanding of Soviet moral conceptions: it would not make any sense if
taken separately. The Soviet moral code is, one could argue, a 'moral
code of international relations'. Moral conceptions lie at the root of the
main characteristic of Soviet international relations theory, i.e. the
strict differentiation of types of international relations, not according
to their content, but according to the participant in a particular relation.
This is so because in ethical terms Marxism does not distinguish
between the good and a gooddoer and a wrong and a wrongdoer, but
only between gooddoer and wrongdoer. Whatever the former does is
by definition good, whatever the latter does is bad and amoral. In other
words the same action is never judged by the same moral yardstick but
in terms of *who*, i.e. what class, state or socio-economic bloc, under-
takes it. It is an extension and a making absolute of Marx's distinction
of 'just' and 'unjust' in his reference to wars.

A first glance at the moral code reveals, beyond any doubt, that the
world is divided into Greeks and Romans, or in New Testament terms,
into capitalist 'goats' and socialist 'sheep'.[61] Soviet understanding of the
world coincides with this scheme. The world is divided into two main
socio-economic systems (capitalist and socialist), which have been
created as a spillover of the basic two antagonistic classes. The addition
of the 'Third World' makes a triangular model which, however, is still
fully consistent with a basic 'dialectical' dichotomisation because the
'Third World' apex of the triangle is in a state of flux. The triangularity
is obviously regarded as a transitory stage before bipolarity is achieved
(when the tug-of-war of the two main systems over the 'Third World' is
concluded obviously in favour of the Soviet one). This will be in its
turn a transitory stage on the way to achieving a monolithic communist
world.

Identifying sheep and goats does not completely coincide with the
triangular Soviet organisation of the world either, or its present stage
(and indeed class) structure. The 'sheep' are obviously the three groups
of 'progressive forces' which create 'a militant alliance of the main
revolutionary forces of our day'.[62] They are located in the capitalist
world (the international working class plus other progressive anticapita-
list forces), in the Third World (the anti-colonial national liberation
movements), and (as the third progressive force) the totality of the
world socialist system. For the sheep thus defined the moral code

provides a newly found streak of humanism, but because it is exclusive
to this group, it is a very limited humanism. Within these 'revolutionary
forces' norms not so very different from the biblical Ten Command-
ments apply, with the possible modification that work — regarded by
some ethical systems as a necessary if not degrading evil — is 'promoted'
to a moral duty. (This is obviously because of the perceived need to
'build' communism.) Toward the capitalist goat (i.e. the capitalist world
minus the proletariat and other anti-imperialist progressive forces, and
plus some 'Third World' pro-capitalist regimes) the moral code pro-
claims 'an uncompromising attitude'.[63] This amounts to a declaration
of open hatred toward a considerable part of the world, which seems a
sad state of affairs in the second half of the twentieth century. An
'uncompromising attitude', in the self-conscious symbolic jargon of
communism, would sanctify whatever means the progressive forces'
might choose to harm the 'goats'. Wars of national liberation movements
are once again described as 'just' wars; similarly 'just' would be the
encouragement of any subversive action, industrial or otherwise, that
undermines the capitalist system, the 'goodness' and 'morality' of
such actions being once again assessed in terms of the advancement of
the worldwide communist cause (as perceived by the SU).

In comparison with Marx's time the institution of the state, from
the point of view of its moral content, has undergone considerable
change. Whilst morally negative in classical Marxism, since by definition
it was an oppressive instrument of one class against all other classes, it
has since Stalin become a good and worthy institution.[64] In the absence
of antagonistic classes the state in fact allegedly assumes a highly positive
and laudable role; it becomes a surrogate for the traditionally postula-
ted dynamic provided by the antagonistic relationship between the
two main classes. Now that the relations of classes are of a 'nonantagonistic' nature the state may set in motion a revolution 'from above' and
perform highly desirable societal functions. In addition to this 'internal'
function the state performs an important 'external' role (i.e. the 'sheep'
state in the socialist and 'Third World') — it acts as a protective bulwark
against capitalist influence, and Soviet law goes into great detail as to
the respect with which socialist and Third World states should be treated
by capitalist countries. Thus, and this would no doubt cause some sur-
prise to Marx and Engels, the moral code actually makes the love of
one's country (i.e. state) into a moral obligation.[65] The 'class approach
to international relations'[66] results in a concept of state of various
content; likewise sovereignty, and the concept of nation. Patriotism, we
are told, has an economic (social ownership of the means of production

and a socialist system of management), political (the Soviet state system, Soviet democracy) and ideological-theoretical (the teaching of Marxism-Leninism) basis.[67] Thus 'patriotism is totally different from bourgeois cosmopolitanism, which always expresses the interests and the spirit of the ruling classes, and disguises the necessity of class conflict'.[68] In contrast to bourgeois cosmopolitanism, proletarian internationalism is 'that moral quality which expresses itself in the attempts to harmonize national and all-human interests, to consider all nations'.[69] With a class understanding of patriotism and proletarian internationalism it is, of course, possible to conclude that proletarian internationalism 'does not hinder national sovereignty',[70] a sovereignty which is similarly defined in class terms.

Notions such as state, sovereignty, nation and internationalism are treated variously according to whom they are attributed. International relations is also divided into neatly delimited groups according to the same criterion. The inter-state relations amongst countries within the socialist system go under the composite label of 'socialist international-ism' and are presented as the 'prototype of international relations, which will fully and individually prevail in the world when the revolu-tionary transition from capitalism to socialism is completed on a world scale'.[71] The 'passport' into the 'socialist world' is in sharing the same economic foundation and the corresponding political and legal super-structure, and the same moral-political common goal is a commitment to the construction of communism. Thus the socialist state is endowed with *communal morality*. It is assumed that the 'harmonic connection between international and national interests' is achieved not only because once in the socialist system the national interests of all states begin to coincide, but because individual states can flourish only within the bloc. The occasional contradictions are of a 'nonantagonistic nature',[72] or in a less Stalinist way, they are referred to as merely 'partial conflicts' and are easily resolvable. Thus the meaning of socialist internationalism as a kind of international relations is an addition to the standard list of minimal requirements for international relations (respect for sovereignty, independence, the national interests of states, full equality, and non-interference in internal affairs.)[73] The socialist states owe each other 'fraternal and mutual aid'.[74] This 'fraternal mutual aid' not only changes the meaning of the other requirements of international relations but adds a moral (and also legal) right, and duty, for these states to 'protect their unity and mutually assist one another in the struggle against capitalism', as well as to 'co-operate and mutually to assist one another in building socialism and communism in a com-

radely manner'.[75] This merger of the moral and the political is
expressed in the merger of the moral and the legal; the documents and
declarations of communist parties [*sic*] and governments constitute
international agreements *sui generis* and in fact are considered as a
source of international law valid amongst the socialist states.[76] Thus
socialist internationalism places a moral duty upon all socialist states
for the joint protection of socialist achievements.[77] In other words the
'Brezhnev doctrine' is not only not denied by Soviet ideology, but is
morally sanctified by it. In so far as it can be argued that socialist internationalism is arrived at by an extension of the old classical principle of
proletarian internationalism[78] the 'Brezhnev doctrine' is not so much
Brezhnev's as Lenin's and Stalin's, its essence deeply embedded in
Soviet Marxist-Leninist thought.

But obviously the moral goal of communism should not be a privilege open only to socialist states and those countries of the Third World
taking the 'non-capitalist path' of development. Soviet Marxism-Leninism still argues that all humankind 'inevitably' heads in that direction,
well aware of the classical postulate, defeated by Soviet experience in
this century, that communism cannot be achieved in a smaller geographical area than that of the world as a whole, and all at once. Thus
one could argue that if this is the case 'peaceful coexistence' (as applied
to capitalist countries, capitalist oriented Third World countries, and of
late also to China – hence applied to the 'antagonistic enemy') seems
to be by definition immoral, if not an overt *contradito ex adjecto* within Marxist terms of reference. Particularly since, as we have seen, the
emphasis has been placed on the need to *build* communism (domestically) rather than wait for it. The idea of peaceful coexistence at best
would seem to indicate a passive attitude. Would not the idea of peaceful coexistence and détente, therefore, run counter to the moral duty
the socialist states perceive that they possess?

Western audiences are still unaware of what exactly the Soviet leaders mean by peaceful coexistence. As Brzezinski has pointed out some
of the blame for this must be laid on Kissinger's doorstep when he
advised Nixon on his first trip to the USSR to include the phrase
'peaceful coexistence' in the American-Soviet statement as the founda-
tion-stone of the East-West relationship – and this has been the case
ever since. Thus the Russians can dictate the semantic framework of
the relationship in an 'age of instant and universal communications,
[when] words are politics'.[79] But what do the Soviet leaders mean?
It is beyond the scope of this chapter to describe the changing theoretical reasoning behind the idea of peaceful coexistence since Lenin's

times; let us only briefly note that it does not contradict the ultimate goal of communism as much as one would think at first sight. First of all it is not a class principle; it applies exclusively to inter-state relations.[80] And it does not in the slightest hamper the ideological and class conflict, which in fact we are told is to intensify in the period of détente. Intensified ideological hostility does not, however, have to stand in the way of economic co-operation. In fact, as Marshal Shulman has argued, between socialist countries and capitalist ones economic co-operation is a substitute for costly Soviet internal reforms.[81] Thus the tension, often unnoticed in the West, that arises from Soviet statements that they want to co-operate with the West, at the same time informing us that they want to destroy the West.[82] Peaceful coexistence, which in this last form emerged at the time of Khrushchev's 'discovery' that the 'atomic bomb does not observe the class principle' and would destroy more sheep than goats (because in absolute terms there are more of them) has added to the Marxist-Leninist moral treasury chest a *value of peace*. But peace with a very important qualification — *world peace*. Soviet morality therefore does not reject all wars, but only those which cannot be kept to local size. Thus the notion of peaceful coexistence by no means ends the battle between the 'two camps' and does not make the battlefield into a playground. Peaceful coexistence remains as a long-term strategic-tactical shield under the shelter of which the 'sheep' of this world can in fact better proceed in their respective corners to assist 'historical inevitability'. Thus peaceful coexistence did not preclude 'fraternal and mutual aid' to Vietnam, or the Middle East. Indeed, this type of assistance is still regarded as a moral duty.[83] Peaceful coexistence is declared to be an objective necessity in this epoch and for various reasons as extremely advantageous to the communist cause: the general peaceful climate creates more favourable opportunities for the struggle of the working class in capitalist countries, and facilitates the struggle of the peoples of the developing countries for their liberation. The economic co-operation of the socialist and capitalist countries greatly assists the internal 'building of communism' in socialist countries, whilst at the same time capitalism, because of the increasingly sharp conflict between the more and more socialised forces of production and the still private relations of production, has 'no future'.[84] Thus it is naive to expect that détente will mean the relaxation of the ideological grip within the socialist countries or that it will mean the abandonment of the current Soviet ideological campaign, or the avoidance of war. 'War can and must be banned as a means of resolving international disputes. But we must not "ban" civil or national liberation wars. We must not "ban" uprisings, and we by no means "ban" revolutionary mass movements aimed at changing the political and social status quo.'[85] The November 1975 issue of *Communist of the Armed Forces* once again reaffirmed, in fact, Moscow's acceptance of the permissibility of nuclear war, endorsing yet again 'the premise of Marxism-Leninism on war as a continuation of policy by military means'. 'The description of the correlation between war and policy is fully valid for the use of weapons of mass destruction' which makes the value of world peace less than absolute and shows how much some Western writers misunderstand the USSR when they claim that this Clausewitz, Marxist-adopted dictum was abandoned long ago in the SU because of nuclear arms.[86]

There is an end to where the study of a system of thought can take us. Many Sovietologists would hasten to add that Soviet theory and practice are far removed from each other; for instance, that 'neither force, nor tolerance nor synthetic "authority" can put the communist Humpty-Dumpty together again'[87] – if it ever held together – and that the Soviet Union long ago abandoned the revolutionary content of its ambitions, and does not in fact wish a change in the status quo at all. Its moral conceptions, however, remain Manicheanly militant. Therefore their intellectual and heuristic adequacy or inadequacy (some features of which I have tried to demonstrate in this essay) is to a great extent beside the point. Indicating the intellectual blunders of their doctrine will not stop many Soviet citizens from believing that 'happy generations of one communist world will live according to the principles of our [i.e. Soviet] more developed and accomplished communist morality'.[88] Only the next generations will be able to tell. In the meantime one should, at least for their sake, try to follow how the Soviet Union proposes to go about realising its moral goals, not only in practice but also in theory.

Notes

1. I would like to acknowledge the linguistic assistance given to me by Dr Ralph Pettman in connection with the preparation of this chapter.

2. Z. Brzezinski, *Soviet Bloc: Unity and Conflict* (Harvard University Press, 1967), pp. 388ff.

3. See H. Marcuse, *Soviet Marxism: A Critical Analysis* (Penguin, 1971), p. 16.

4. G. Fischer (ed.), *Science and Ideology in Soviet Society* (Atherton Press, New York, 1967), p. 78.

5. See e.g. Richard T. de George, *New Marxism: Soviet and East European Marxism since 1956* (Pegasus, New York, 1968).

6. Ibid., p. 140.

7. E. Kamenka, *Marxism and Ethics* (Macmillan, St Martins Press, 1969), pp. 1-2, 64.

8. E. Kamenka, *The Ethical Foundations of Marxism* (Routledge and Kegan Paul, London, 1972), p. 186.

9. R.T. de George, *Patterns of Soviet Thought: the Origins and Developments of Dialectical and Historical Materialism* (Ann Arbor, The University of Michigan Press, 1970), p. 2.

10. Cf. Soviet selection of definitions in *Moral'i eticheskaia teoria* (Morality and Ethical theory) (Moscow, 'Nauka', 1974), pp. 9ff.

11. Richard T. de George in his *Soviet Ethics and Morality* (Ann Arbor, University of Michigan Press, 1969), p. 177, which is without a doubt the best study in the English language, says that a complete bibliography of Soviet writings on ethics and morality from 1924 to 1968 would include 600 items, and of the 338 Soviet authors on the subject, only 14 have written more than three items. Thus in surveying the field it is difficult to establish the importance of individual writers or make generalisations about the subject.

12. *Kratkii slovar po etike* (Short dictionary of ethics) (Moskva, 1965), p. 226.

13. *Filozofskaia enciklopedia* (Philosophical encyclopedia) (Moskva, 1964), vol. 3., p. 499.

14. A.F. Shishkin: *Osnovy marksistskoi etiki* (Essentials of Marxist Ethics) (Moskva, Izdatel'stvo IMO, 1961), p. 14.

15. A.A. Guseinov, *Social'naia priroda nravstvennosti* (Social nature of morality) (Izdatel.stvo Moskovskogo Universiteta, 1974), pp. 14ff.

16. See for instance Svetozar Stojanović, 'Marx's Theory of Ethics', in N. Lobkowitz (ed.) *Marx and the Western World* (University of Notre Dame Press, Notre Dame, London, 1967), pp. 161-72.

17. For the debate about these categories see e.g. A.E. Furman, 'O predmete istoricheskogo materializma' (About the subject-matter of historical materialism), *Filozofskie nauki* (1965/6), pp. 85-90; M.S. Dzhunusov, 'O vsaimosviazi osnovykh poniatii istroricheskogo materializma' (About the relationship of basic notions of historical materialism), *Voprosy filozofii* (1965/7), pp. 144-6; M. Kammari, 'Nekotorye voprosy teoria bazisa i nadstroiki' (Some questions of theory of basis and superstructure (1956) 10, pp. 42-58; V.P. Tugarinov, 'O kategoriakh' obshchestevennoe bytie 'i' obshchestvennoe soznanie' (About the categories 'social existence' and 'social consciousness'), *Voprosy filozofii* (1958), 1, pp. 15ff.

18. *Filozofskii slovar* (Philosophical dictionary) (Moskva, 1965), p. 318.

19. G. Fischer (ed.), *Science and Ideology*, pp. 61-2.

20. F. Engels, *Anti-Dühring: Herr Eugen Dühring's Revolution in Science* (Lawrence and Wishart, London 1969), Chs. IX, X, XI.

21. J.V. Stalin, *Marxism and Linguistics*, in *The Essential Stalin: Major Theoretical Writings, 1905-1952*, Bruce Franklin (ed.) (Anchor Books, Doubleday & Company Inc., Garden City, N Y, 1972).

22. The Soviet authors themselves acknowledge the differences amongst their views resulting from the 'relative youth of their discipline', cf. Bandzeladze G, *Etika: opit izlozhenia systemy marksistskoi etiki* (Ethics: an attempt to systematise Marxist ethics), 2nd ed., Izdatelstvo, 'Sabchota Sakartvelo' (Tbilisi, 1970), p. 4.

23. Cf. de George, *Soviet Ethics and Morality*, pp. 13 and 27.

24. Bandzeladze, *Etika*, p. 17.

25. Guseinov, *Social'naia*, p. 19; also *Moral'i eticheskaia teoria: nekotorye aktual'nye problemy* (Morality and the ethical theory: some topical problems) (Moskva, 'Nauka', 1974), p. 47.

26. Despite the fact that recently the expression 'metaetika' has been increasingly frequently used, in the sense suggested by a Polish author M. Fritzhand in *Glowne zagadnienia i kierunki metaetyki* (Warsaw, 1970), p. 29, as the 'epistemology and methodology of normative ethics, or more broadly speaking, ethical

discourse', it is obvious that its meaning is confined to the 'methodology of Marxist ethics' with no sharp distinction along Western lines. For the debate on the subject see P.B. Petropavlovskii, 'Metodologicheskie problemy etiki' (Methodological problems of ethics), in Guseinov, *Moral' i eticheskaia teoria*, pp. 228ff.

27. Bandzeladze, *Etika*, pp. 55, 78.
28. Guseinov, *Social'naia*, p. 27.
29. Ibid., p. 19; *Moral' i eticheskaia teoria*, p. 47.
30. Bandzeladze, *Etika*, p. 66.
31. Lenin quoted in Guseinov, *Social'naia*, p. 5; see also ibid, pp. 19ff.
32. Guseinov, *Social'naia*, pp. 133 and 190, *Moral' i eticheskaia teoria*, p. 41.
33. B.C. Shtein, 'Problema prostykh norm nravstvennosti i spravedlivosti v marksistsko-leninskoi etike' (Problems of simple norms of morality and justice in Marxist-Leninist ethics), in *Aktual'nye problemy marksistsko-leninskoi etiki* (Topical problems of Marxist-Leninist ethics) (Tbilisi, 1967), p. 168.
34. Ibid., p. 164.
35. Guseinov, *Social'naia*, p. 133.
36. N.A. Trofimov, 'O perspektivakh razvitia morali i prava v ikh vzaimnom otnoshenii' (On prospects of the development of Morality and Law in their mutual relations), *Voprosy filozofii* (1962) 5, pp. 24-6.
37. *The Road to Communism: Documents of the 22nd Congress of the CPSU*, Moscow, 1961, p. 566.
38. Ibid., p. 566.
39. From 'The Tasks of the Youth Leagues', speech at the 3rd All-Russian Congress of the Russian Communist League (2 October 1920); and 'On the significance of Militant Materialism', a letter written to the periodical *Pod znamenem marksizma* (Under the Banner of Marxism) in 1922.
40. Bandzeladze, *Etika*, p. 5.
41. *Moral' i eticheskaia teoria*, p. 46.
42. G.E. Moore, *Principia Ethica* (Cambridge University Press, 1971), pp. 9ff.
43. K. Marx, *Economic and Philosophical Manuscripts, 1844*, London (Lawrence and Wishart, 1959), p. 103; K. Marx, *Critique of the Gotha Programme* in K. Marx, F.Engels, *Selected Works in One Volume* (Lawrence and Wishart, London, 1970), pp. 327-8, 320.
44. *Programme of the CPSU* (Foreign Languages Publishing House, Moscow, 1961).
45. Ibid., p. 59.
46. Ibid., p. 62.
47. Carl J. Hempel and Paul Oppenheim, 'Pattern of Scientific Explanation', in Herbert Feigl, May Brodbeck, *Reading in the Philosophy of Science* (New York, Appleton-Century, Crofts Inc., 1953), pp. 322ff.
48. A.F. Shishkin, 'Chelovek kak vysshaia tsennost' (Man as the highest value), *Voprosy filozofii* (1965) 1, pp. 3ff.
49. Guseinov, *Social'naia*, p. 10.
50. *Selected Works in One Volume*, p. 29.
51. The functional dependence of social existence and social consciousness is expressed in the philosophy of Marxism in the shape of a *law of reverse influence of social consciousness on social existence*, complemented by the *law of the increasingly active part of consciousness* (italics added), A.S. Molchanova, 'O social'no-reguliatornoi funkcii soznania' (On the social-regulatory function of consciousness), *Problemy social'nykh issledovanii* (Problems of social research) (Tomsk, 1972), p. 34.
52. Guseinov, *Social'naia*, p. 20; see also M.G. Zhuravkov, *Socializm i moral': nekotorye cherty i osobennosti formirovania morali sovetskogo obshchestva*

(Izdatel'stvo 'Nauka', Moskva, 1974), pp. 145ff.

53. Krapivensky, *The Revolution and its Moral Mission* (Novosti Press Agency Publishing House, Moscow, n.d.), p. 85.

54. Ibid., p. 88.

55. See above p.177.

56. M.A. Zhuravkov, 'XII S'ezd KPSS i nekotorye voprosy etiki' (XIInd Congress of the CPSU and some problems of ethics), *Voprosy filozofii* (1962), pp. 3ff. L.F. Il'ichev, 'Current Trends in the Party's Ideological Work', *Pravda*, (19 June 1963), in *Current Digest of the Soviet Press* (3 July 1963), pp. 5-11.

57. *Filozofskie nauki* (1966) 6, p. 123. *Voprosy filozofii* (1966) 9, p. 129.

58. P. Ehlen, *Die philosophische Ethik in der Sovjetunion* (München und Salzburg, 1972), p. 113.

59. The Party holds that the moral code of the builder of communism should comprise the following principles: devotion to the communist cause; love of the Socialist motherland and of the other socialist countries; conscientious labour for the good of society – he who does not work, neither shall he eat; concern on the part of everyone for the preservation and growth of public wealth; a high sense of public duty; intolerance of actions harmful to the public interest; collectivism and comradely mutual assistance: one for all and all for one; humane relations and mutual respect between individuals – man is to man a friend, comrade and brother; honesty and truthfulness, moral purity, modesty, and unpretentiousness in social and private life; mutual respect in the family, and concern for the up-bringing of children; an uncompromising attitude to injustice, parasitism, dishonesty, careerism and money-grubbing; friendship and brotherhood among all peoples of the USSR; intolerance of national and racial hatred; an uncompromising attitude to the enemies of communism, peace and the freedom of nations; fraternal solidarity with the working people of all countries, and with all peoples. *The Road to Communism*, pp. 566-7.

60. I refer here to John Vincent's chapter.

61. Most students of Soviet morality point out this striking similarity. See e.g. de George, *Soviet Ethics and Morality*, p. 103.

62. Brezhnev's speech at the 25th CPSU Congress, *Pravda* (25 February 1976), p. 2.

63. See note 59 above.

64. Stalin, *Report to the Eighteenth CPSU (Bolshevik) on the Work of the Central Committee* (10 March 1939), in *The Essential Stalin*, p. 384.

65. See note 59 above.

66. F.V. Konstantinov (ed.), *Sociologicheski problemy mezhdunarodnykh otnoshenii* (Sociological problems of international relations), (Moskva, 'Nauka', 1970), pp. 5ff.

67. Bandzeladze, *Etika*, p. 358.

68. Ibid., p. 366.

69. Ibid., p. 367.

70. Ibid., p. 368.

71. V. Granov, O. Nakropin 'Socialist Foreign Policy: Its Class Nature and Humanism', *International Affairs* (1965) 11, p. 11.

72. Josef Mrázek, 'A Code of Socialist international Law', *Nová Mysl*, No. 2 (February 1976), translated in RAD Background Report/63 (15 March 1976), p. 9.

73. This is, incidentally, the content of the inter-state relations between socialist and capitalist countries, i.e. 'peaceful coexistence' to which 'mutually advantageous economic, trade, scientific, technological and cultural ties' are sometimes added: e.g. *International Affairs* (1969) 10, p. 45.

74. Quoted from R.H. McNeal (ed.), *International Relations amongst*

Communists (Prentice-Hall, 1967), pp. 99-100.

75. Mrázek, 'A Code . . .' p. 7.

76. Ibid.

77. See also *Documents Adopted by the International Conference of Communist and Workers' Parties* (Moscow, Novosti, 1969).

78. F. Konstantinov, 'Internationalism and the World Socialist System', *International Affairs* (1968) 11, p. 3.

79. Z. Brzezinski, 'From Cold War to cold peace', G.R. Urban (ed.) in *Détente* (Temple Smith, London, 1976), p. 266.

80. Brezhnev's speech (see note 62). p. 4.

81. Brzezinski, 'From Cold War'.

82. Ibid.

83. Brezhnev's speech (see note 62), p. 4.

84. Ibid.

85. *Soviet World Outlook,* vol. 1, no. 2 (12 February 1976), p. 7.

86. W. Zimmermann, 'International Relations in the Soviet Union: the Emergence of a Discipline', *The Journal of Politics*, vol. 31 (1969), no. 1, p. 64.

87. Alexander Dallin, 'The USSR and World Communism', in J.W. Strong (ed.), *The Soviet Union under Brezhnev and Kosygin* (Van Nostrand Reinhold, New York, 1971), p. 223.

88. Bandzeladze, *Etika,* p. 453.

10 CONCLUSION

A little book like this one cannot pretend to have covered the water-front. Though the topic does occur in a number of the chapters the treatment of distributive economic justice in world society, for example, remains too brief. There is nothing said on the concepts of 'just war' and of 'private international violence', and American foreign policy, which post-Vietnam and with President Carter's human rights initiatives became highly conscious of moral issues, is not discussed. This said, however, the study does draw attention to a very important and a relatively neglected subject area as well as introducing the key dilemmas in the field as these appear to political practitioners and to academic analysts alike. There are limits on how many practical questions can be considered in a work of this length, and the choice of essays on China and the Soviet Union was quite deliberate since considerably less is known in the West of the moral dynamics that underpin the foreign policies of these two great powers. What American and European statesmen appear to believe or would have us believe is more readily available to the interested reader, and the fundamental terms of the debates they conduct are more familiar as well.

The racial conflict in Southern Africa is placed in the wider context of claims made by contemporary black African leaders in their pre-colonial and post-colonial predicaments. The issue is a topical one, but it also demonstrates clearly a more general phenomenon — the way morality is contingent upon politics, how claims for 'right' or 'just' consideration depend upon the possession and exercise of socio-economic power; and how possession of such power enables one to co-opt cultural perspectives and define for others what is the 'right', the 'good' and the 'true'.

In many ways, this is the heart of the matter, and it is a perennial problem that readily bears periodic restatement. Professor Miller argues that it is the lesson of experience alone that group or national moral claims are stronger than those based on humankind as a whole. One could extend this case further and argue, as Reinhold Niebuhr has done, that moral conduct is an effective option only for the individual:

> Individual men may be moral in the sense that they are able to consider interests other than their own in determining problems of

conduct; and are capable, on occasion, of preferring the advantages
of others to their own. They are endowed by nature with a measure
of sympathy and consideration for their kind, the breadth of which
may be extended by an astute social pedagogy. Their rational facul-
ty prompts them to a sense of justice which educational discipline
may refine and purge of egoistic elements until they are able to view
a social situation, in which their own interests are involved, with a
fair measure of objectivity. But all these achievements are more
difficult, if not impossible, for human societies and social groups.
In every human group there is less reason to guide and to check
impulse, less capacity for self-transcendence, less ability to compre-
hend the needs of others and therefore more unrestrained egoism
than the individuals, who compose the group, reveal in their personal
relationships.

This phenomenon Niebuhr attributes to 'collective egoism', and to the
'difficulty of establishing a rational social force which is powerful
enough to cope with the natural impulses by which society achieves its
cohesion'.[1]

While the utopian may be 'naive', this 'realist' position, as has been
argued many times, is a distinctly 'unreal' one. The fact remains that
there *are* moral judgements that transcend the national community.
We may all too readily overstate their appeal, and realists argue that any
universalist ethic will remain a minority point of view of limited political efficacy. Here, as E.H. Carr has pointed out, is the 'fundamental
dilemma of international morality. On the one hand, we find the almost
universal recognition of an international morality involving a sense of
obligation to an international community or to humanity as a whole.
On the other hand, we find an almost equally universal reluctance to
admit that, in this international community, the good of the part (i.e.
our own country) can be less important than the good of the whole'.[2]
He concludes himself, however, and it is a good statement of the
position, that:

Just as within the state every government, though it needs power as
a basis of its authority, also needs the moral basis of the consent of
the governed, so an international order cannot be based on power
alone, for the simple reason that mankind will in the long run always
revolt against naked power. Any international order presupposes a
substantial measure of general consent. We shall, indeed, condemn
ourselves to disappointment if we exaggerate the role which morality

is likely to play. The fatal dualism of politics will always keep consideration of morality entangled with consideration of power. We shall never arrive at a political order in which the grievances of the weak and the few receive the same prompt attention as the grievances of the strong and the many. Power goes far to create the morality convenient to itself, and coercion is a fruitful source of consent. But when all these reservations have been made, it remains tr that a new international order and a new international harmony can be built up only on the basis of an ascendancy which is generally accepted as tolerant and unoppressive or, at any rate, as preferable to any practicable alternative.[3]

This last argument becomes even more significant in the light of 'dependency' theory and a world view that complements the fact of nation-states with a consideration of global classes. If we adopt, as neo-Marxists and neo-Leninists urge us to, a picture of humankind in terms of its unequal capacities to produce, distribute and exchange goods and services, a pattern emerges of class inequalities between states and within them and a world heavily loaded in favour of the overdeveloped industrialised sectors of the globe against the rest, that goes far to explain the macro-phenomenon of exploitation. Such a picture is used to endorse claims for radical modifications to the existing world order; for a less oppressive socio-economic regime.

Doomed, as John Herz would argue,[4] to the final frustration of their idealist resolve, those who feel that the present structure of world affairs is hardly the most rational dispensation under which we might labour urge its revision. Hypocrisy, mixed motives and opportunism abound. Any success would be ambiguous at best, probably marginal, and could be brought about only at considerable cost. The feeling is a fact of world affairs, however, and from it flows the desire for change. And so it goes; our competing ideas about what is, and our diverse predilections, where we dare admit them, for what should be. We stand ever, and it is an effective symbol of our enduring plight, with water in the left hand and fire in the right.

Notes

1. Reinhold Niebuhr, *Moral Man and Immoral Society: a study in ethics and politics* (Charles Scribners' Sons, New York, 1934), pp. xi-xii.
2. E.H. Carr, *The Twenty Years' Crisis* (Macmillan, London, 1958), pp. 166-76.
3. Ibid., pp. 236-7.
4. J. Herz, *Political Realism and Political Idealism* (University of Chicago Press, Chicago, 1956), pp. 39-42.

CONTRIBUTORS

H. Bull	Balliol College, Oxford University
A.L. Burns	The Australian National University
V. Kubálková	University of Queensland
J.D.B. Miller	The Australian National University
J. Pettman	The Canberra College of Advanced Education
R. Pettman	The Australian National University
W.H. Smith	The Royal Military College, Duntroon
R.J. Vincent	The University of Keele
M. Yahuda	The London School of Economics and Political Science

INDEX

apartheid, *see* racism

balance of terror 119, 120

capitalism 26, 60, 135, 173, 185, 186, 188; bureaucratic 149
class 26
class war 28
colonialism 26, 73, 87, 110, 131, 132, 134, 139, 141, 142, 166, 194; decolonisation 138
communism 176-82, 186, 187, 188; Chinese 150; Khrushchev 150; morality, view of 53; scientific 150
cosmopolitanism 90, 98, 101, 105, 111; bourgeois 186; partisan 10

dependency 28, 61, 103, 106, 134, 142, 162, 196
determinism 175; Marxist 181, 182
development: global 24
distributive economic justice, *see* justice-distributive
duty 42, 79, 177; Machiavelli 42

elites 11
equality 10, 66, 67, 74, 97, 99, 109; racial 11, 87
ethics: Christian 23, 175; Machiavellian 23, 95; Marxist 183; personal 22; political 22; presumptive 30; Soviet 174, 175, 176, 178, 181; universalist 195
exploitation 11, 28, 135, 165

fact/value dichotomy 17, 18, 115
feudalism 149

globalisation 26

human rights 10, 17, 25, 63, 68, 69, 72, 74, 79, 80, 81, 82, 84, 85, 88, 90, 96, 194
humanism 185
humanitarianism 94

idealism 10, 62, 65, 73, 74, 102
imperialism 26, 60, 147, 149, 154, 155, 163, 166; in Africa 131; social 157

independence: Chinese concept of 11, 149, 150, 157, 159, 163, 165, 167; economic 161
individualism 81
injustice 11, 115, 116, 117; economic 123; racial 123, 135
internationalism 153, 154; proletarian 149, 153, 164, 165, 186, 187; socialist 186, 187
intervention 71, 83; non-intervention 70

justice 11, 17, 39, 48, 49, 52, 53, 60, 63, 70, 92, 95, 97, 99, 108, 115, 125, 177; as compensation 109, 110, 111; as fairness 54; corrective 54, 68; distributive 10, 54, 68, 92, 94, 98, 100, 105, 106, 194; economic 28, 87, 92; global 93, 94, 103, 104, 111; international 97, 98, 105, 109, 111; Marxian concept of 97; national 98, 102, 111; Nozick's theory of 100, 104; Rawls's theory of 29, 61, 99, 100, 104, 105, 106, 107, 108; social 30, 40; universal 180

liberation movements: in Africa 136, 137, 139

materialism: dialectical 179; historical 179, 181
Marxism 135, 173, 180; Marxism-Leninism 170
morality: as science 174; bourgeois 18; Christian 55, 56, 115, 126; Greek concept of 18, 54; group 36; Marxist 172, 174; socialist 182; Soviet 183, 188; universal 36, 47, 48, 50, 52, 53, 65, 74, 176, 183

nation: state 11
national independence 139, 143, 155, 166
national interest 37, 133
national liberation 149, 154, 155, 166; wars of 185, 188
nationalism: African 131, 135, 142; Chinese 151
natural law 23, 24, 25, 39, 41, 46, 53,